LOVING GOD

D0766366

Also by Charles Colson:

BORN AGAIN
EVANGELICALS & CATHOLICS TOGETHER

LOVING GOD

CHARLES COLSON

Hodder & Stoughton

LONDON SYDNEY AUCKLAND

British Library Cataloguing in Publication Data
A record for this book is available from the British Library

ISBN 0 340 70991 X

Printed and bound in Great Britain by
Clays Ltd, St Ives plc

Hodder and Stoughton Ltd
A Division of Hodder Headline PLC
338 Euston Road
London NW1 3BH

*To those who introduced me to the love of God, to those
who demonstrated it in their love for me, and to those who
challenged me to love Him in return
And especially to my co-workers in Prison Fellowship,
who share with me the daily pilgrimage of loving God.*

EDITOR'S NOTE

All the stories in this book are true. In some, names have been changed; in others, editorial liberties have been taken to combine certain events for purposes of clarity or illustration. In one case, the use of allegory proved the most effective literary device to make the point. But in all instances the events underlying the stories are true. Background details have been researched as thoroughly as possible, although at times inferences were drawn from the limited facts available. Where that is the case, it is made evident in the text.

CONTENTS

THE HOLY NATION ·

LOVING GOD

The most pleasurable journey you take is through yourself . . . the only sustaining love involvement is with yourself. . . . When you look back on your life and try to figure out where you've been and where you're going, when you look at your work, your love affairs, your marriages, your children, your pain, your happiness – when you examine all that closely, what you really find out is that the only person you really go to bed with is yourself. . . . The only thing you have is working to the consummation of your own identity. And that's what I've been trying to do all my life.

Shirley MacLaine[1]

It is vain, O men, that you seek within yourselves the cure for your miseries. All your insight only leads you to the knowledge that it is not in yourselves that you will discover the true and the good.

Blaise Pascal

How It All Began:
An Introduction

Two strong forces – one external, one internal – came together to forge my decision and determination to write this book. The external force was the result of what I saw happening in the culture around me over a period of years. The internal force had to do with my own spiritual life. Let me explain.

For a generation, Western society has been obsessed with the search for self. We have turned the age-old philosophical question about the meaning and purpose of life into a modern growth industry. Like Heinz, there are fifty-seven varieties, and then some: biofeedback, Yoga, creative consciousness, EST, awareness workshops, TA – each fad with an avid following until something new comes along.

Popular literature rides the wave with best-selling titles that guarantee success with everything from making money to firming flabby thighs. This not-so-magnificent obsession to 'find ourselves' has spawned a whole set of counterfeit values; we worship fame, success, materialism, and celebrity. We want to 'live for success' as we 'look out for number one', and we don't mind 'winning through intimidation'.

However, this 'self' conscious world is in desperate straits. Each new promise leads only to a frustrating paradox. The 1970s self-fulfilment fads led to self-absorption and isolation, rather than the fuller, liberated lives they predicted. The technology created to lead humanity to this new promised land may instead obliterate us and our planet in a giant mushroom cloud. Three decades of seemingly limitless affluence have succeeded only in sucking our culture dry, leaving it spiritually empty and economically weakened. Our world is filled with self-absorbed, frightened, hollow people.

Amid these debilitating paradoxes of modern life, men and women search for some shred of meaning, some understanding of self. But the obsessive search for self leads only to the narcissistic destruction of what is so avidly sought. Consider the young woman cited in a *Psychology Today* article: her nerves were shot from too many all-night parties and discos, her life an endless round of pot, booze, and sex. When asked, 'Why don't you stop?' by her therapist, her startled reply was, 'You mean I really don't have to do what I want to do?'

And in the midst of all this we have the church – those who follow Christ. For the church, this ought to be an hour of opportunity. The church alone can provide a moral vision to a wandering people; the church alone can step into the vacuum and demonstrate that there is a sovereign, living God who is the source of Truth.

BUT, the church is in almost as much trouble as the culture, for the church has bought into the same value system: fame, success, materialism, and celebrity. We watch the leading churches and the leading Christians for our cues. We want to emulate the best-known preachers with the biggest sanctuaries and the grandest edifices.

Preoccupation with these values has also perverted the church's message. The assistant to one renowned media pastor, when asked the key to his man's success, replied without hesitation, 'We give the people what they want.' This heresy is at the root of the most dangerous message preached today: the what's-in-it-for-me gospel.

The 'victorious Christian life' has become man's victorious life, not God's. A popular daily devotional quotes Psalm 65:9, 'The streams of God are filled with water', and paraphrases it, 'I fill my mind to overflowing with thoughts of prosperity and success. I affirm that God is my source and God is unlimited.'[2] This is not just a religious adaptation of the look-out-for-number-one, winner-take-all, God-helps-those-who-help-themselves gospel of our culture; it is heresy.

Thus, both the world and the church are groping for answers.

As I saw what was happening around me, I also became aware of something happening inside me. This surfaced a few years ago when I was experiencing one of those periods of spiritual dryness we all encounter. When I told a friend, he suggested I watch a videocassette lecture series by Dr R. C. Sproul on the holiness of God.

All I knew about Sproul was that he was a theologian, so I wasn't enthusiastic. After all, I reasoned, theology was for people who had time to study, locked in ivory towers far from the battlefields of human need. However, at my friend's urging I finally agreed to watch Sproul's series.

By the end of the sixth lecture I was on my knees, deep in prayer, in awe of God's absolute holiness. It was a life-changing experience as I gained a completely new understanding of the holy God I believe in and worship.

My spiritual drought ended, but this taste of the majesty of God only made me thirst for more of Him. So I gathered up contemporary books on the subject of discipleship – by the armload. Many were excellent, though they often dealt more with evangelism than discipleship; and most seemed concerned with how to get more out of the Christian life. I wanted to know how to put more into it.

One thing all the books dealt with, of course, was God's love for humanity and how He showed that love by the sacrifice of His Son on the cross. The more I read about this, the more I wanted to know about what I had begun to see as the corollary – how I show my love for Him. Somehow that seemed to be the key to putting more into the Christian life.

The greatest commandment of all, Jesus said, is 'Love the Lord your God with all your heart and with all your soul and with all your mind.'[3] I'd memorised those words but had never really thought about what they meant in practical terms; that is, how to fulfil that command. I wondered if others felt the same way. So I asked a number of more experienced Christians how they loved God.

'Well . . . by loving Him,' one stammered, then added by way of explanation, '. . . with all my heart, soul, and mind.'

'By maintaining a worshipful heart, offering myself as an acceptable sacrifice,' another answered quickly. When I pressed for specifics, he began detailing his devotional reading schedule and prayer life. Halfway through his discourse, he stopped and shrugged. 'Let me think about it some more.'

Faithful church attendance was a frequent response, and tithing ranked high on the list. Several recited favourite sins they no longer pursued while many tried to explain 'loving God' as a feeling in their hearts, as if it were something akin to a romantic encounter. Others looked at me suspiciously, perhaps thinking my query some kind of trick question.

That did it. The cumulative effect of my survey convinced me that most of us, as professing Christians, do not really know how to love God. Not only have we not given thought to what the greatest commandment means in our day-to-day existence, we have not obeyed it. And if this was true for individual believers, what were the ramifications for the church? Perhaps the reason the church was so ineffective in the world was that it had the same needs I did.

Seeing the desperate hunger in the culture, and realising how much we as the people of God need to love God, the message of this book was urgently pressed upon me. To use a rather strange, but perhaps appropriate, analogy, I saw a need to attempt to do for the gospel what Lenin did for Marx.

Though frequently thought of as an arm-waving, fiery revolutionary, Karl Marx was for most of his life a thinker, a theoretician. There was no great workers' revolution during his lifetime, and after his death in 1883, Marxism seemed destined to take its place as just another philosophy spawned by the fertile minds of the nineteenth century. Indeed, it probably would have, were it not for Lenin, a young Russian who voraciously devoured the ideas of Engels and Marx and became a Marxist in 1889.

Three years later, Lenin published *What Is To Be Done?* in which he spelled out the absolute of action, of taking Marx's theories and applying them to life. That book and Lenin's tireless labour inspired a handful of professional revolutionaries who within a few years turned Russia upside down. Lenin's passionate singlemindedness, his absolute commitment and application of Marx's principles changed not only his own country, but today, less than a hundred years later, has enslaved over half the world.

My question then, for individual believers and thus the church, is this: do we view our faith as a magnificent philosophy or a living truth; as an abstract, sometimes academic theory or a living Person for whom we are prepared to lay down our lives? The most destructive and tyrannical movements of the twentieth century, Communism and Nazism, have resulted from fanatics singlemindedly applying fallible philosophies. What would happen if we were actually to apply God's truth for the glory of His kingdom?

The result would be a world turned upside down, revolutionised by the power of God working through individual Christians and the church as a whole.

But we will only be weak and stumbling believers and a crippled church unless and until we truly apply God's Word – that is, until we truly love Him and act on that love.

Thus, forces internal and external have compelled me to write this book. As mentioned, the search leading to the discoveries recounted herein was sparked by the teaching of Dr R. C. Sproul, now my dear friend and tutor. But my decision to begin writing came as the result of a visit to one of the squalid places where I spend so much of my life.

Delaware Prison, Easter morning, 1980 . . . one of the most important mornings of my life . . .

OBEDIENCE

Only he who believes is obedient;
only he who is obedient believes.

Dietrich Bonhoeffer

1

Prologue: Paradox

It was a glorious Easter Sunday, the spring sun sparkling and warm, the air fresh and sweet. Too nice a day to spend in prison, but that's where I was bound.

As I approached the sprawling complex of brick buildings surrounded by barbed wire fences, I remembered my first visit here nine months earlier. As in most states, Delaware's institutions were dangerously overcrowded. The legislature, though unwilling to allocate needed funds, was carping mercilessly at corrections officials. To help make his own assessment of the situation, Governor DuPont had asked me to report on conditions at Delaware State Prison.

On that steamy August day I had visited every corner of the complex. I had walked through dormitories so jammed with sweaty bodies that the air was difficult to breathe. I had seen the psycho ward where a man writhed convulsively against the chains around his bloodied wrists and ankles. Immune to sedation, without restraints he would have destroyed himself. I had continued on to the 'hole', stopping to talk with each man isolated there in solitary lockup.

One, who introduced himself as Sam Casalvera, had been sentenced to life without parole. Sam was tough, his huge, muscled arms testifying to hours of weight lifting. His defiant gaze told me prison – even solitary confinement – had not broken his spirit.

Sam was the exception. By the end of the tour I was overwhelmed, as I am in so many prisons, by the sight and stench of death. It was reflected in the inmates' eyes, in their head-bowed shuffle, in their endless staring at nothing through hand-clutched bars. The suicidal patient chained in the psychiatric unit was perhaps the most rational of all, I thought ironically; he was merely struggling to bring his body and spirit to the same point.

I asked the young chaplain if I could meet with the Christian inmates. We gathered in a small conference room off the warden's office. Of the eight prisoners present, all were lifers, seven were black.* These strong, earnest men were a dramatic contrast with what I had just seen. Joyous about their faith, they had resolute assurance that Jesus was alive and real, even in the midst of the human hopelessness of prison. We prayed together, holding hands around the table, and then I promised I'd be back.

A few months later we sent a Prison Fellowship seminar team into the Delaware prison. With the help of twenty volunteer laypeople from the nearby community, our two staff members (one an ex-con himself) conducted thirty-two hours of teaching. More than one hundred men signed up for that first in-prison seminar, and before the week was over, seventy-five met Christ. That made the week memorable, as did another unusual incident.

One study session was interrupted when two guards burst into the room, clamped handcuffs on a frightened young inmate, and hustled him out of the room to a waiting van. Those in the seminar, who knew only that he was being taken to court, prayed fervently.

Arriving in the courtroom, the inmate stood shaking before a stern-faced judge. 'Young man,' the judge said sombrely, 'I've been examining your records.' He paused, then looked up. 'And I've decided to reduce your sentence to time served. You're a free man.

'Good luck,' he concluded, nodding at the speechless prisoner and rapping his gavel.

'Thank you, your Honour,' the inmate choked; then, more loudly, 'but sir, if it's all the same to you, could I stay in

---

* It was not surprising to find only eight Christians in a prison population of eight hundred. About 1 per cent is the ratio we often find when we begin ministry in an institution.

prison the rest of this week? I'd like to finish the Prison Fellowship seminar.'

The judge, shocked, muttered something about working it out. The man was returned to the seminar's expectant group of believers where there was much celebration.

During the months following I received a series of exciting reports about the Christian fellowship continuing to grow in Delaware. As spring approached, I knew I wanted to spend Easter with these brothers.

Now as I arrived at the front gate on Easter morning, I was met by the corrections commissioner, more than seventy-five Prison Fellowship volunteers, several judges including a justice of the state supreme court, and a bevy of other state officials. We were quickly escorted around the metal detectors and processing rooms – none of the usual search routines this morning.

The Christian inmates, more than one hundred in number at this point, had got permission to host a breakfast for us. As we were served in the mess hall, I took a perverse pleasure in watching the justice turn away from the dried-out porridge and sausages of dubious origin.

One of our enthusiastic hosts rapped his spoon against a cup, and when the group quieted he announced that an inmate, Sam Casalvera, would read a poem composed for the occasion – and dedicated to Chuck Colson.

Sam rose, wearing the broadest grin I'd ever seen; it was obvious he was not the same rebellious convict I'd met in solitary nine months earlier. I didn't need to ask what had happened.

Sam cleared his throat and began reading:

I heard you were coming to worship once more
With souls who were floundering when you came before.

He hesitated, took a deep breath, and continued.

We had direction but needed a push
You made us a promise and also a wish.

Sam paused to take a wrinkled cloth from his pocket and dab his eyes.

> Your promise was kept – Prison Fellowship you sent.
> Whatever I write can't tell you what it meant.
> Some who attended made your wish come true.
> They gave their life to Jesus, as you did too.

Men and women in prison don't cry. It's a sign of weakness, and weakness can be dangerous in prison. But Sam could not control his emotions. Tears flowed down his cheeks and his broad shoulders heaved.

I rose and walked to the front of the hall, put my arm around his shoulders, and took the paper from him. For a moment I thought I would dissolve along with Sam, but somehow I was able to read the remaining lines of his poem. I've loved poetry all my life and treasure many classics, but none have affected me as deeply as Sam Casalvera's earnest stanzas.

After breakfast our inmate hosts escorted us out of the mess hall and on a long procession to the chapel on the other side of the prison. As we began to cross the compound, I squinted through the bright sunlight and stopped short at the scene ahead. A crowd of prisoners surrounded the chapel, some carrying placards. In two hundred prison visits I'd never seen anything like it. Instinctively I reviewed the possibilities: a riot brewing; a demonstration against prison conditions; Muslim inmates protesting our presence?

A few steps further and I could make out, to my amazement and relief, the crude lettering on the signs: COME TO THE CHAPEL, read one. JESUS SETS THE PRISONERS FREE! was another.

Just as people in prison don't cry, neither do they call attention to their faith. To do so invites scorn, ridicule, or worse. But this group of Christians was parading the compound, advertising chapel!

Their daring had broken barriers. Men were gathering from all over the prison. The chapel was packed. And because three hundred prisoners were in solitary lockup, the Christian brothers had mounted four speakers on the chapel roof so the service could be heard throughout the prison. (Judging by the size of the amplifiers, it could also be heard by neighbours for miles around.)

The prison choir began the service. Their task was to warm up the crowd, and they were a roaring success. Even the supreme court justice, sandwiched between two muscular convicts in the front row, loosened up. Struggling at first to maintain his dignity, he gradually began tapping his foot and soon was grinning and clapping with the rest.

As I sat on the platform, waiting my turn at the pulpit, my mind began to drift back in time ... to scholarships and honours earned, cases argued and won, great decisions made from lofty government offices. My life had been the perfect success story, the great American dream fulfilled. But all at once I realised that it was *not* my success God had used to enable me to help those in this prison, or in hundreds of others just like it. My life of success was not what made this morning so glorious – all my achievements meant nothing in God's economy. No, the real legacy of my life was my biggest failure – that I was an ex-convict. My greatest humiliation – being sent to prison – was the beginning of God's greatest use of my life; He chose the one experience in which I could not glory for *His* glory.

Confronted with this staggering truth, I discovered in those few moments in the prison chapel that my world was turned upside down. I understood with a jolt that I had been looking at life backward. But now I could see: only when I lost everything I thought made Chuck Colson a great guy had I found the true self God intended me to be and the true purpose of my life.

It is not what we do that matters, *but what a sovereign God chooses to do through us.* God doesn't want our success; He wants us. He doesn't demand our achievements; He demands our obedience. The kingdom of God is a kingdom of paradox, where through the ugly defeat of a cross, a holy God is utterly glorified. Victory comes through defeat;

healing through brokenness; finding self through losing self.

Of course, our success-mad, egocentric culture cannot grasp that crucial truth. It is understandable only when the false values that obsess us are stripped away, sometimes in the midst of our most abject failures. Surely that was so in my life, and it was so in the life of a man by the name of Boris Kornfeld.

Kornfeld was a Russian doctor. What we know about him can only be pieced together from scanty records and accounts of one who knew him. But what emerges is a classic illustration of the principles of the kingdom of paradox, an example that has been a source of continuing inspiration to me. Let me tell you his remarkable story.

2

A Russian Doctor

No reporters have visited the prison camps of Soviet Russia, unless they have gone as prisoners. So to this day we have little information about the millions who have lived, suffered, and died there, especially during Stalin's reign of terror. Most will remain nameless for all time, remembered only in the hearts of those who knew and loved them. But from time to time, scraps of information have filtered out about a few. One of those few was Boris Nicholayevich Kornfeld.

Kornfeld was a medical doctor. From this we can guess a little about his background, for in post-revolutionary Russia such education never went to families tied in any way to czarist Russia. Probably his parents were socialists who had fastened their hopes on the Revolution. They were also Jews, but almost certainly not Jews still hoping for the Messiah, for the name Boris and the patronymic Nicholayevich indicate they had taken Russian names in some past generation. Probably Kornfeld's forebears were *Haskalah*, so-called 'enlightened Jews', who accepted the philosophy of rationalism, cultivated a knowledge of the natural sciences, and devoted themselves to the arts. In language, dress, and social habits they tried to make themselves as much like their Russian neighbours as possible.

It was natural for such Jews to support Lenin's revolution, for the czars' vicious anti-Semitism had made life almost unendurable for the prior two hundred years. Socialism promised something much better for them than 'Christian' Russia. 'Christian' Russia had slaughtered Jews; perhaps atheistic Russia would save them.

Obviously Kornfeld had followed in his parents' footsteps, believing in Communism as the path of historical necessity, for political prisoners at that time were not citizens opposed to Communism or wanting the Czar's return. Such people were simply shot. Political prisoners were believers in the Revolution, socialists or communists who had, nevertheless, not kept their allegiance to Stalin's leadership pure.

We do not know what crime Dr Kornfeld committed, only that it was a political crime. Perhaps he dared one day to suggest to a friend that their leader, Stalin, was fallible; or maybe he was simply accused of harbouring such thoughts. It took no more than that to become a prisoner in the Russia of the early 1950s; many died for less. At any rate, Kornfeld was imprisoned in a concentration camp for political subversives at Ekibastuz.

Ironically, a few years behind barbed wire was a good cure for Communism. The senseless brutality, the waste of lives, the trivialities called criminal charges made men like Kornfeld doubt the glories of the system. Stripped of all past associations, of all that had kept them busy and secure, behind the wire prisoners had time to think. In such a place, thoughtful men like Boris Kornfeld found themselves reevaluating beliefs they had held since childhood.

So it was that this Russian doctor abandoned all his socialistic ideals. In fact, he went further than that. He did something that would have horrified his forebears.

Boris Kornfeld became a Christian.

While few Jews anywhere in the world find it easy to accept Jesus Christ as the true Messiah, a Russian Jew would find it even more difficult. For two centuries these Jews had known implacable hatred from the people who, they were told, were the most Christian of all. Each move the Jews made to reconcile themselves or accommodate themselves to the Russians was met by new inventions of hatred and persecution, as when the head of the governing body of the Russian Orthodox Church said he hoped that, as a result of the Russian pogroms, 'one-third of the Jews will convert, one-third will die, and one-third will flee the country'.

Yet following the Revolution a strange alignment occurred. Joseph Stalin demanded undivided, unquestioning loyalty to his government; but both Jews and Christians knew their ultimate loyalty was to God. Consequently people of both faiths suffered for their beliefs and frequently in the same camps.

Thus it was that Boris Kornfeld came in contact with a devout Christian, a well-educated and kind fellow prisoner who spoke of a Jewish Messiah who had come to keep the promises the Lord had made to Israel. This Christian – whose name we do not know – pointed out that Jesus had spoken almost solely to Jewish people and proclaimed that He came to the Jews first. That was consistent with God's special concern for the Jews, the chosen ones; and, he explained, the Bible promised that a new kingdom of peace would come. This man often recited aloud the Lord's Prayer, and Kornfeld heard in those simple words a strange ring of truth.

The camp had stripped Kornfeld of everything, including his belief in salvation through socialism. Now this man offered him hope – but in what a form!

To accept Jesus Christ – to become one of those who had always persecuted his people – seemed a betrayal of his family, of all who had been before him. Kornfeld knew the Jews had suffered innocently. Jews were innocent in the days of the Cossacks! Innocent in the days of the czars! And he himself was innocent of betraying Stalin; he had been imprisoned unjustly.

But Kornfeld pondered what the Christian prisoner had told him. In one commodity, time, the doctor was rich.

Unexpectedly, he began to see the powerful parallels between the Jews and this Jesus. It had always been a scandal that God should entrust Himself in a unique way to one people, the Jews. Despite centuries of persecution, their very existence in the midst of those who sought to destroy them was a sign of a Power greater than that of their oppressors. It was the same with Jesus – that God would present Himself in the form of a man had always confounded the wisdom of the world. To the proud and powerful, Jesus stood as a Sign, exposing their own limitations and sin. So they had to kill Him, just as those in power had to kill the Jews, in order to maintain their delusions of omnipotence. Thus, Stalin, the new god-head of the brave new world of the Revolution, had to persecute both Jew and Christian. Each stood as living proof of his blasphemous pretensions to power.

Only in the gulag could Boris Kornfeld begin to see such a truth. And the more he reflected upon it, the more it began to change him within.

Though a prisoner, Kornfeld lived in better conditions than most behind the wire. Other prisoners were expendable, but doctors were scarce in the remote, isolated camps. The authorities could not afford to lose a physician, for guards as well as prisoners needed medical attention. And no prison officer wanted to end up in the hands of a doctor he had cruelly abused.

Kornfeld's resistance to the Christian message might have begun to weaken while he was in surgery, perhaps while working on one of those guards he had learned to loathe. The man had been knifed and an artery cut. While suturing the blood vessel, the doctor thought of tying the thread in such a way that it would reopen shortly after surgery. The guard would die quickly and no one would be the wiser.

The process of taking this particular form of vengeance gave rein to the burning hatred Kornfeld had for the guard and all like him. How he despised his persecutors! He could gladly slaughter them all!

And at that point, Boris Kornfeld became appalled by the hatred and violence he saw in his own heart. Yes, he was a victim of hatred as his ancestors had been. But that hatred had spawned an insatiable hatred of his own. What a deadly predicament! He was trapped by the very evil he despised. What freedom could he ever know with his soul imprisoned

by this murderous hate? It made the whole world a concentration camp.

As Kornfeld began to retie the sutures properly, he found
himself, almost unconsciously, repeating the words he had
heard from his fellow prisoner. 'Forgive us our trespasses, as
we forgive those who trespass against us.' Strange words in
the mouth of a Jew. Yet he could not help praying them.
Having seen his own evil heart, he had to pray for cleansing.
And he had to pray to a God who had suffered, as he had:
Jesus.

For some time, Boris Kornfeld simply continued praying
the Lord's Prayer while he carried out his backbreaking,
hopeless tasks as a camp doctor. Backbreaking because there
were always far too many patients. Hopeless because the
camp was designed to kill men. He stood ineffectively against
the tide of death gaining on each prisoner: disease, cold,
overwork, beatings, malnutrition.

Doctors in the camp's medical section were also asked to
sign decrees for imprisonment in the punishment block. Any
prisoner whom the authorities did not like or wanted out of
the way was sent to this block – solitary confinement in a tiny,
dark, cold, torture chamber of a cell. A doctor's signature on
the forms certified that a prisoner was strong and healthy
enough to withstand the punishment. This was, of course, a
lie. Few emerged alive.

Like all the other doctors, Kornfeld had signed his share of
forms. What was the difference? The authorities did not need
the signatures anyway; they had many other ways of 'legalis-
ing' punishment. And a doctor who did not cooperate would
not last long, even though doctors were scarce. But shortly
after he began to pray for forgiveness, Dr Kornfeld stopped
authorising the punishment; he refused to sign the forms.
Though he had signed hundreds of them, now he couldn't.
Whatever had happened inside him would not permit him to
do it.

This rebellion was bad enough, but Kornfeld did not stop
there. He turned in an orderly.

The orderlies were drawn from a group of prisoners who

cooperated with the authorities. As a reward for their cooperation, they were given jobs within the camp which were less
than a death sentence. They became the cooks, bakers,
clerks, and hospital orderlies. The other prisoners hated
them almost more than they hated the guards, for these
prisoners were traitors; they could never be trusted. They
stole food from the other prisoners and would gladly kill
anyone who tried to report them or give them trouble.
Besides, the guards turned a blind eye to their abuses of
power. People died in the camps every day; the authorities
needed these quislings to keep the system running smoothly.

While making his rounds one day, Kornfeld came to one of
his many patients suffering from pellagra, an all-too-
common disease in the camps. Malnutrition induced pellagra which, perversely, made digestion nearly impossible.
Victims literally starved to death.

This man's body showed the ravages of the disease. His
face had become dark, one deep bruise. The skin was peeling
off his hands; they had to be bandaged to staunch the
incessant bleeding. Kornfeld had been giving the patient
chalk, good white bread, and herring to stop the diarrhoea
and get nutrients into his blood, but the man was too far
gone. When the doctor asked the dying patient his name, the
man could not even remember it.

Just after leaving this patient, Kornfeld came upon a
hulking orderly bent over the remains of a loaf of white bread
meant for the pellagra patients. The man looked up
shamelessly, his cheeks stuffed with food. Kornfeld had
known about the stealing, had known it was one reason his
patients did not recover, but his vivid memory of the dying
man pierced him now. He could not shrug his shoulders and
go on.

Of course he could not blame the deaths simply on the
theft of food. There were countless other reasons why his
patients did not recover. The hospital stank of excrement and
lacked proper facilities and supplies. He had to perform
surgery under conditions so primitive that often operations
were little more than mercy killings. It was preposterous to

stand on principle in the situation, particularly when he knew what the orderly might do to him in return. But the doctor had to be obedient to what he now believed. Once again the change in his life was making a difference.

When Kornfeld reported the orderly to the commandant, the officer found his complaint very curious. There had been a recent rash of murders in the camp; each victim had been a 'stoolie'. It was foolish – dangerously so at this time – to complain about anyone. But the commandant put the orderly in the punishment block for three days, taking the complaint with a perverse satisfaction. Kornfeld's refusal to sign the punishment forms was becoming a nuisance; this would save the commandant some trouble. The doctor had arranged his own execution.

Boris Kornfeld was not an especially brave man. He knew his life would be in danger as soon as the orderly was released from the cell block. Sleeping in the barracks, controlled at night by the camp-chosen prisoners, would mean certain death. So the doctor began staying in the hospital, catching sleep when and where he could, living in a strange twilight world where any moment might be his last.

But, paradoxically, along with this anxiety came tremendous freedom. Having accepted the possibility of death, Boris Kornfeld was now free to live. He signed no more papers or documents sending men to their deaths. He no longer turned his eyes from cruelty or shrugged his shoulders when he saw injustice. He said what he wanted and did what he could. And soon he realised that the anger and hatred and violence in his own soul had vanished. He wondered whether there lived another man in Russia who knew such freedom!

Now Boris Kornfeld wanted to tell someone about his discovery, about this new life of obedience and freedom. The Christian who had talked to him about Jesus had been transferred to another camp, so the doctor waited for the right person and the right moment.

One grey afternoon he examined a patient who had just

been operated on for cancer of the intestines. This young man with a melon-shaped head and a hurt, little-boy expression touched the soul of the doctor. The man's eyes were sorrowful and suspicious and his face deeply etched by the years he had already spent in the camps, reflecting a depth of spiritual misery and emptiness Kornfeld had rarely seen.

So the doctor began to talk to the patient, describing what had happened to him. Once the tale began to spill out, Kornfeld could not stop.

The patient missed the first part of the story, for he was drifting in and out of the anaesthesia's influence, but the doctor's ardour caught his concentration and held it, though he was shaking with fever. All through the afternoon and late into the night, the doctor talked, describing his conversion to Christ and his new-found freedom.

Very late, with the perimeter lights in the camp glazing the window-panes, Kornfeld confessed to the patient: 'On the whole, you know, I have become convinced that there is no punishment that comes to us in this life on earth which is undeserved. Superficially, it can have nothing to do with what we are guilty of in actual fact, but if you go over your life with a fine-tooth comb and ponder it deeply, you will always be able to hunt down that transgression of yours for which you have now received this blow.'

Imagine! The persecuted Jew who once believed himself totally innocent now saying that every man deserved his suffering, whatever it was.

The patient knew he was listening to an incredible confession. Though the pain from his operation was severe, his stomach a heavy, expansive agony of molten lead, he hung on the doctor's words until he fell asleep.

The young patient awoke early the next morning to the sound of running feet and a commotion in the area of the operating room. His first thought was of the doctor, but his new friend did not come. Then the whispers of a fellow patient told him of Kornfeld's fate.

During the night, while the doctor slept, someone had

crept up beside him and dealt him eight blows on the head with a plasterer's mallet. and though his fellow doctors worked valiantly to save him, in the morning the orderlies carried him out, a still, broken form.

But Kornfeld's testimony did not die.

The patient pondered the doctor's last, impassioned words. As a result, he, too, became a Christian. He survived the prison camp and went on to tell the world what he had learned there.

The patient's name was Alexander Solzhenitsyn.

3
Faith and Obedience

Boris Kornfeld is the great paradox personified. A Jew who betrayed the faith of his fathers. A doctor whose years of training were senselessly wasted. A political idealist whose utopian vision led only to a barren Siberian prison. A prisoner who gave up his life for nothing more than a loaf of stolen bread. In every one of these areas, Boris Kornfeld was a failure – at least in the world's system of values. Yet God took that failure of a man and through his singleminded obedience used him to lead to Christ another who would go on to become a prophetic voice and one of the world's most influential writers.

For Kornfeld's words did their convincing, convicting work, touching what Solzhenitsyn later called 'a sensitive chord'. That was his moment of spiritual awakening; 'God of the universe, I believe You again! Though I renounced You, You will be with me,' he cried out.[1] It was a spiritual transfusion – life taken from one man and pumped into another for God's sovereign purpose.

And in his conversion Solzhenitsyn saw clearly the kingdom paradox. For in the emptiness of that Russian gulag, he perceived what pleasure-seeking millions in the abundance of Western life cannot. He wrote later, 'the meaning of earthly existence lies, not as we have grown used to thinking, in prospering, but in the development of the soul.'[2]

Kornfeld's brief Christian life was lived in circumscribed circumstances, almost in isolation. In many ways it would seem that his decision not to sign the medical forms, his reporting of the corrupt guard, even his few hours of testimony to a perhaps terminally ill patient were futile, would gain him nothing but that which came in the end – a brutal death at the hands of his captors. Yet Kornfeld's faith was strong, sure, and sincere. And somehow his fellow Christian and the Holy Spirit had communicated one fact to him: what God demanded of him was obedience, no matter what. Singleminded obedience in faith.

And that lesson of the Russian doctor's life was my lesson at Delaware: what God wants from His people is obedience, no matter what the circumstances, no matter how unknown the outcome.

It has always been this way. God calling His people to obedience and giving them at best a glimpse of the outcome of their effort.

Most of the great figures of the Old Testament died without ever seeing the fulfilment of the promises they relied upon.[3] Paul expended himself building the early church, but as his life drew to a close he could see only a string of tiny outposts along the Mediterranean, many weakened by fleshly indulgence or divided over doctrinal disputes.

In more recent times, the great colonial pastor Cotton Mather prayed for revival several hours each day for twenty years; the Great Awakening began the year he died. The British Empire finally abolished slavery as the Christian parliamentarian and abolitionist leader William Wilberforce lay on his deathbed, exhausted from his nearly fifty-year campaign against the practice of human bondage. Few were the converts during Hudson Taylor's lifelong mission work in the Orient; but today millions of Chinese embrace the faith he so patiently planted and tended.

Some might think this divine pattern cruel, but I am convinced there is a sovereign wisdom to it. Knowing how susceptible we are to success's siren call, God does not allow us to see, and therefore glory in, what is done through us. The very nature of the obedience He demands is that it be given without regard to circumstances or results.

A scriptural analogy of the unquestioning obedience God expects is found in Jesus' healing of the centurion's servant.[4]

Matthew and Luke tell how the officer came to Christ on behalf of his paralysed servant; when Jesus offered to go home with him, the centurion quickly replied that he knew Christ need only give the command and the man would be healed. The centurion understood about such things because when he ordered his troops to go, they went; in the same way he perceived Jesus' authority as that of a military commander to whom one gives unquestioning allegiance. Joyful to discover such faith, Jesus not only healed the servant, but used the centurion as an example of faith in His comments to the crowd.

The Bible makes clear, and experiences such as Kornfeld's confirm, that unquestioning acceptance of and obedience to Jesus' authority is the foundation of the Christian life. Everything else rests upon this. It also provides the key to understanding what is for many the great mystery of Christianity: faith.

Saving faith – that by which we are justified, made right with God – is a gift of God; and, yes, it involves a rational process as well since it comes from hearing the Word of God (more on that in later chapters). 'All right,' the struggling Christian may say, 'but practically speaking, how does my faith become real? How do I get that vibrant, strong faith of Christian maturity?'

That's where obedience comes in. For maturing faith – faith which deepens and grows as we live our Christian life – is not just knowledge, but knowledge acted upon. It is not just belief, but belief lived out – practised. James said we are to be doers of the Word, not just hearers. Dietrich Bonhoeffer, the German pastor martyred in a Nazi concentration camp, succinctly stated this crucial interrelationship: 'Only he who believes is obedient; only he who is obedient believes.'

This may sound like a circular proposition, but many things are – in truth and in practice. Think of learning how to swim. We are told what to do. We gingerly enter the water, launch out, and promptly forget everything we've been told. We flail about, splashing frantically, gasping and sinking. Finally, usually at the point of utter despair, we capture for a

moment the sensation of staying afloat. Realising it is possible, we remember our instructions and begin to follow them.
They work. Like learning to balance a bicycle or mastering a
foreign language, faith is a state of mind that grows out of our
actions, just as it also governs them.

So obedience is the key to real faith – the unshakeable kind
of faith so powerfully illustrated by Job's life. Job lost his
home, his family (except for a nagging wife), his health, even
his hope. The advice of friends was no help. No matter where
he turned, he could find no answers to his plight. Eventually
he stood alone. But though it appeared God had abandoned
him, Job clung to the assurance that *God is who He is*. Job
confirmed his obedience with those classic words of faith:
'Though he slay me, yet will I trust in him.'[5]

This is real faith: believing and acting obediently regardless of circumstances or contrary evidence. After all, if faith
depended on visible evidence, it wouldn't be faith. 'We walk
by faith, not by sight,' the apostle Paul wrote.

It is absurd for Christians to constantly seek new demon-
strations of God's power, to expect a miraculous answer to
every need, from curing ingrown toenails to finding parking
spaces; this only leads to faith in miracles rather than the
Maker.

True faith depends not upon mysterious signs, celestial
fireworks, or grandiose dispensations from a God who is seen
as a rich, benevolent uncle; true faith, as Job understood,
rests on the assurance that *God is who He is*. Indeed, on that
we must be willing to stake our very lives.

There was a time when eleven men did just that. They
staked their lives on obedience to their leader, even when
doing so was contrary to all human wisdom. The act of
obedience produced a faith that emboldened them to stand
against the world and, in their lifetimes, change it forever.

Forty days after His resurrection, Jesus summoned His
disciples to meet Him on the Mount of Olives. Imagine their
excitement, believing as they apparently did that this very
day their Master would establish His kingdom on earth and

fulfil the great promise the Jews had clung to through centuries of suffering and exile. Christ would be king, not just of Israel but of the whole world. And they would be at His side, judging the nations, reckoning accounts, rewarding the righteous. Centuries of injustice would be set straight. These eleven men, most of them uneducated fishermen, had gambled their lives on Jesus; had lost everything at the Crucifixion; had seen their hope revived in the Resurrection; and this day would see the Jesus they had trusted ruling the earth. How their hearts must have raced in anticipation as they scampered through the streets of Jerusalem and up the gentle slope of the mountain.

Then the breathless majesty of the moment was upon them; their beloved Jesus was waiting for them, looking searchingly into each of their eyes. His mere presence produced such awe that one by one they dropped to their knees. This was the Coronation.

Finally one of them burst out with the question they all wanted to ask: 'Lord, are you at this time going to restore the kingdom to Israel?'[6]

Jesus was sharp, rebuking in His reply. 'It is not for you to know the times or dates the Father has set by his own authority.' He had already commanded them to wait in Jerusalem; now He told them that a power would come to them there. 'And you will be my witnesses in Jerusalem, and in all Judea and Samaria, and to the ends of the earth.'[7]

Then it was as if the universe breathed, putting a sea of space between Him and them. Before they could protest, He was gone, ascended into a cloud.

It is difficult to even imagine the wild emotions those eleven men must have experienced at that moment. Holy awe? Terrifying fear? And what initial disappointment! They were left alone, outcasts in their own land. They had few human resources. And on top of all that, they had been commanded to go back and wait – the hardest thing of all for strong-willed men to do.

Knowing how very human they were and where each had come from, we can surmise the options they must have considered: Philip, the timid one, would want to hide in the hills; James and John would want to quickly spread the word; Simon the Zealot would want to organise a guerrilla campaign; others would see their hope in moves such as seizing control of government – the same options so many believers today find so appealing.

But Jesus had ordered them to go to Jerusalem and *wait*. Wait for what? Contrary as it must have been to their every instinct, 'wait' is precisely what they did. They obeyed and, hard though it is to understand, did so with 'great joy'.

For ten days they waited – 120 of them in all, gathered together, of one mind and continually in prayer. They waited. And then it came.

With the force of a thousand tornadoes the power promised rested on them and the Holy Spirit empowered these ordinary men to do the work of God. Each of the eleven became a giant of faith. As a result, within a century half the then-known world came to Christ.

The disciples' decision to obey Jesus after the Ascension proved a pivot point of history. The world was never the same again.

The disciples' realisation that Christ is who He says He is compelled them to obedience. That is the historic reality of Christianity.

Understanding this is crucial, for it distinguishes Christianity from all other religions. The Christian faith rests not merely upon great teachings or philosophies, not upon the charisma of a leader, not upon the success in raising moral values, not upon the skill or eloquence or good works of its advocates. If it did, it would have no more claim to authority than the sayings of Confucius or Mao or Buddha or Mohammed or any of a thousand cults. Christianity rests on historic truth. Jesus lived, died, and rose from the dead to be Lord of all – not just in theory or fable, but in fact.

With that understood, Christianity must evoke from the believer the same response it drew from the first disciples: a passionate desire to obey and please God – a willingly entered-into discipline. That is the beginning of true discipleship. *That is the beginning of loving God.*

For the disciples it was clear-cut; Jesus audibly instructed them to return to Jerusalem and wait. But how do we know what we are to do? Such clear instructions do not usually come with our conversion; no voice from heaven gives us marching orders. So where do we turn to find them?

A lawyer, a Pharisee attempting to trick Jesus, put a similar question to the Master centuries ago. 'Teacher,' he said, 'which is the greatest commandment in the Law?'[8] Christ's response has been engraved in the memories of believers ever since: 'Love the Lord your God with all your heart and with all your soul and with all your mind. This is the first and greatest commandment.'

'But how do we love the Lord?' we ask. Jesus answered this in a discussion with His disciples: 'If you love me, you will obey what I command.'[9] Or, as the apostle John wrote later 'This is the love of God, that we keep his commandments.'[10]

And that leads us to just one place: the Holy Bible. To obey His commandments, we must know His commandments. That means we must know and obey the Scriptures, the key to loving God and the starting point for life's most exciting journey.

But be warned: Unless you are prepared to have your comfortable notions uprooted, you may want to stop reading right now.

A few years ago a magazine article about my prison ministry concluded that 'prison radicalised the life of Chuck Colson.' It is understandable that the reporter might have thought that, but it is simply not so. I could have left prison and forgotten it; I wanted to in fact. But while every human instinct said, 'Put it out of your mind forever,' the Bible kept revealing to me God's compassion for the hurting and suffering and oppressed; His insistent Word demanded that I care as He does.

What 'radicalised' me was not prison, but taking to heart the truths revealed in Scripture. For it was the Bible that confronted me with a new awareness of my sin and need for repentance; it was the Bible that caused me to hunger for righteousness and seek holiness; and it was the Bible that called me into fellowship with the suffering. It is the Bible that continues to challenge my life today.

That is radical stuff. It is irresistibly convicting. It is the power of God's Word and it is, all by itself, life-changing. Certainly this was the case for a young man whose experience and life have taught me so much – perhaps because I can identify with him so clearly.

Wise in the ways of the world, powerful, steeped in the good life, he was to all appearances successful and satisfied with himself and his life – at thirty-one a young man on the move. Yet his life, too, was changed – radically – by the Word of God.

THE WORD OF GOD

We owe to Scripture the same reverence which we owe to God.

John Calvin

Divine inspiration not only is essentially incompatible with error but excludes and rejects it as absolutely and necessarily as it is impossible that God Himself, the supreme Truth, can utter that which is not true.

Pope Leo XIII

4

Take Up and Read

The Mediterranean sky curved hot and clear over the terrace of the home of Aurelius Augustinus outside Milan, Italy. Beyond the garden wall, acres of fruit trees carpeted the valley, rising to meet the soft green vineyard-covered hillsides. Within the wall, Augustine and his best friend, his student Alypius, sat with the visitor Ponticianus. Though his chest ached, his busy schedule pulled at him, and his mind was thoroughly unsettled, Augustine was taking time to speak with this important government official.

Brilliant, learned, and handsome, Augustine held one of the most enviable professorships in the city. When he spoke, the words of this professor of rhetoric crashed like thunder. When he argued, he was overwhelmingly persuasive. Few felt themselves his equal.

As the three men exchanged polite conversation, Augustine's mother appeared frequently, ostensibly offering refreshments and other hospitable overtures; in reality she was hovering, keeping a close eye on her son.

Monica was a protective mother, strong-minded, practical, utterly determined that her beloved son become a Christian. She prayed for him daily and had since he was a small boy. But while Augustine loved his mother, he paid no attention to her.

Monica had hardly let her son out of her sight since she was widowed in North Africa while Augustine was a teenager. He had had to trick her to come to Italy alone, lying about his departure so he and his mistress and their illegitimate child could sail off without her. But before long Monica had followed him to Milan. She had even succeeded in getting him engaged to a good Christian girl and in sending away his mistress of fifteen years. But his fiancée was very young and his marriage two years off; so Augustine was again sleeping with a woman. Sex was necessary to him, he said, for he had no power to resist his natural desires.

Monica could not understand her son's strange ideas about right and wrong. He indulged in such licentiousness without, apparently, a pang of conscience, but lamented the time when he had stolen fruit from a neighbour's pear tree with a gang of youthful rowdies. Augustine dwelt on this mere childish prank as though it were the great evil of his life while practising habits much more sinful in his mother's eyes.

Yet she had never stopped hoping for his conversion, and lately her hope had been stronger than ever. Augustine had recently broken with his religion, a strange cult following the teachings of a Persian named Mani who claimed that powers of darkness controlled every physical being. Augustine had quit astrology, too, and had been going to church. Perhaps the bishop was right, Monica thought.

She had visited an African bishop many years later, pleading with him to talk with her son. But the church-man refused, telling her that Augustine was not ready to talk.

'Let him be,' the bishop had advised. 'Only pray to the Lord on his behalf.' The bishop knew Manicheanism well; he believed someone as bright as Augustine would see its nonsense eventually.

Monica was not put off so easily, however. She had wept uncontrollably, begging the bishop to speak to her son. Finally, losing patience, he told her to leave. But she had taken his parting words, 'It is impossible for the son of such tears to perish,' as a promise from heaven and had often reminded Augustine of them, triumphantly.

But Augustine could not become a Christian just to please his mother.

In the garden, Augustine's visitor, idly looking about him as he contemplated his departure, picked up a book lying on a small table nearby. A puzzled smile crossed his face.

'The apostle Paul,' he said. 'Are you reading this, Augustine?'

His host nodded. 'Not only am I reading it. I have been wearing it out. And wearing myself out trying to grasp the meaning of the Christian faith.' He looked around, making sure his mother was not lurking within earshot.

'Did you know I am a Christian?' Ponticianus smiled hesitantly.

Augustine and Alypius nodded. They had heard this rumour.

'But I thought this would be one of your philosophical books,' Ponticianus said. 'I never dreamed I would find *you* reading the Bible.'

'The philosophers have helped me understand the Bible,' Augustine admitted. He explained that until recently he had believed that only what he could see, measure, rationally and systematically prove could be real. The idea of an invisible, spiritual God seemed just talk. But studying Plato and his followers had convinced him that the real things were invisible, spiritual.

'This has helped me a great deal.' Augustine was candid to a fault. Yet he watched Ponticianus carefully, his posture tense. 'But there is a major difference. To follow Plato, one merely thinks like Plato. To follow Christ is something much more. You must put your whole life into it and leave behind whatever hinders you from following Him. I don't know what it is exactly that enables a man to give himself to God – to commit himself to a life of sacrifice and faith. That's more than adopting a particular point of view, isn't it?'

Ponticianus nodded, as did Alypius. Alypius, younger than Augustine, practically worshipped the scholar.

Wrapped in his own thoughts, Augustine went on speaking, almost as though working out a problem for himself. 'Plato takes you up on a high mountain peak where you can see the land of peace. But you do not know how to get there.

There must be a highway leading straight to that land, but you can't find it.' He shook his head wearily.

Augustine had few illusions about himself. He knew how easily his mind fell into habits and was chained by them. His women. His pride. *I am utterly depraved*, he thought, *and the mind alone is no match for the seduction of evil pleasure.*[1]

As Augustine spoke, Ponticianus had grown excited. Now he jumped up, paced briskly in front of his host for a moment, then whirled to point a finger at him.

'Have you heard of Antony?'

'Well,' Augustine drew back a bit, startled at his visitor's abruptness, 'I do know several Antonys, but none worth mentioning in the context of this discussion.'

'No – no – Antony the monastic – the one Athanasius wrote the biography of. Many Christians have been greatly influenced by it.' To Ponticianus's astonishment, neither of his listeners had heard of this Antony.

'I must tell you then . . . Antony was a rich young fellow, born into a Christian family in Egypt. His parents died when he was just entering his teens; their large estate fell to him. He grew up fast, carrying that responsibility. He had all the money in the world and all the cares, too.

'In church one Sunday the Scripture reading came from Christ's reply to the rich young ruler: "If you want to be perfect, go, sell your possessions and give to the poor, and you will have treasure in heaven. Then come, follow me."

'Something in that familiar passage hit Antony. It was as though Jesus had given those words directly to him, personally, that very moment. Antony didn't even wait for the service to end. He rushed out of the church and set about preparing his records so that his property could be sold and the profit distributed to the poor.

'From that day, Antony devoted his life to prayer. He went to live in a hut on the edge of town, farming to keep himself alive. Fifteen years later he moved into the desert. He wanted to show that the power of God would supply living water in an arid land, that from little or nothing He could bring forth the fruits of the Spirit.'

Ponticianus then dramatically described the miracles of Antony's life, telling how though he sought complete obscurity, he became famous, even living in the desert. People travelled great distances to meet with him. And as a result of his example, small groups of men and women began to form communes devoted to prayer.

'To me, Antony is a sign that God will meet us wherever we are,' Ponticianus concluded, looking directly into Augustine's eyes, 'even in the wasteland of our lives.'

Augustine now rose to stand beside his guest, placing his hand briefly on his forearm. He was clearly moved. 'I can hardly believe I've never heard of him,' he said. 'Nor any of his followers. Are there any in Italy?'

'In Italy?' Ponticianus was astonished. 'Why, right here in Milan there is a small community of such men. They live outside the city walls. Ambrose has charge of them.'

'Ambrose!' He was the pastor whose preaching Augustine had been hearing, originally out of curiosity about the man's style, for Augustine had a professional interest in any good speaker. But Ambrose's substance had made a deeper impact than his style. *Because of him*, Augustine mused, *I have grown interested in the Scriptures again.*

Augustine had first tried reading the Scriptures while a teenager, but was not impressed. At the time he had been in love with beautiful language, and the language of Scripture had seemed dull and plain, far inferior to that of the great Roman writers. But years had passed since then. Great rhetorical flourishes seemed less important than they once did. *Under Ambrose's influence, the simplicity of Scripture has begun to sound like the simplicity of profundity.*

Already Augustine was ready to concede that what the sacred writings said was true. But he could not do anything halfway. He knew the truth of Scripture demanded a commitment to Christ; and commitment to Christ meant total change. He would have to give up misusing sex. More, he would have to give up all his dreams of success and glory. He would have to please God and not the world around him. *Part of me wants to*, he said to himself; *part is unable to.*

Ponticianus interrupted Augustine's thoughts. 'When I think of Antony, of his immediate obedience to the Word of God that morning, of what he left without looking back, I am moved to tears.' He reached out to grasp his host strongly by both shoulders. 'When God calls someone, Augustine, nothing on earth can stop him.'

Outwardly Augustine carried on politely, thanking Ponticianus for coming, saying his farewells. Inwardly his disturbed thoughts travelled elsewhere. After his guest left, he paced across the terrace, lashing himself mentally.

As Ponticianus spoke, you turned me back upon myself, O Lord. You took me from behind my own back, where I had placed myself because I did not wish to look upon myself. You stood me face to face with myself so that I might see how foul I am, how deformed and defiled, how covered with stains and sores. I looked and was filled with horror, but there was no place for me to flee to get away from myself.

He thought back bitterly to the day twelve years before when, after reading Cicero, he had decided to dedicate his life to search for wisdom – to prefer to know the truth over any other pleasure in life. But he only talked about it; he never did it. He drifted along in life, living for success and anything that made him happy for a few hours.

You know, O Lord, how during my university days at Carthage I found myself in the midst of a hissing cauldron of lust. I was in love with the idea of love. Although my real need was for you, I placed my hopes in what was merely human and often enough in the bestial as well.

Still, I thought of myself as a fine fellow. You know, O Lord, how I grew proud in the imagination of my heart . . .

When I thought of my Christian upbringing and determined to read the Scriptures, inflamed with self-esteem I judged them but a hash of outmoded Jewish superstition and historical inaccuracies.

Augustine had been frustrated with himself before, but never to this point.

I remember how one day you made me realise how utterly wretched I was. I was preparing a speech in praise of the emperor, intending that it should include a great many lies, which would certainly be applauded by an audience that knew well enough how far from the truth they were. I was greatly preoccupied by this task. As I walked along one of the streets in Milan, I noticed a beggar who must, I suppose, somehow have had his fill of food and drink since he was laughing and joking. Sadly I turned to my companions and spoke to them of all the pain and trouble which is caused by our own folly. My ambitions had placed a load of misery on my shoulders, and the further I carried it the heavier it became, but the only purpose of all the efforts we made was to reach the goal of purposeful happiness. This beggar had already reached it ahead of us.

Perhaps I shall never reach it.

Alypius looked in astonishment at his friend. He had heard Augustine talk about his misery, of course, but now he seemed to be in true anguish. His face was flushed, his eyes darting frantically.

'What is the trouble with us?' Augustine asked aloud in a strangled voice. 'What is this? What did *you* hear? The uneducated rise and take heaven by storm and we, with all our erudition but empty of heart, see how we wallow in flesh and blood. Are we ashamed to follow them? Isn't it shameful for us not to follow them?' He could not continue, but turned and ran into the garden beyond the wall.

Really alarmed now, Alypius followed his mentor closely, afraid of what Augustine might do to himself. He also had to know how this struggle would end, for whatever Augustine became, he wanted to become also.

Getting as far from the house as he could in the little garden, Augustine slumped onto a bench, his body showing the struggle within. Scarcely conscious of what he was doing, he tore at his hair, slapped his forehead, locked his fingers together and clasped his knees.

I know I have a will, as surely as I know there is life in me. When I choose to do something or not to do it, I am certain that it is my own self making this act of will. But I see now that evil comes from the perversion of the will when it turns aside from you, O God. I can say with your apostle, the good I would I do not.

You have raised me up so that I can now see you must be there to be

perceived, but I confess that my eyes are still too weak. The thought of
you fills me with love, yes, but also with dread. I realise that I am far
from you.

Augustine continued to think of his life – his hopes for a
good position, a comfortable home, for admiration and fame
as a thinker and writer. He thought of the women in his life
and something whispered, 'From the moment you decide,
this thing and that will never be allowed to you, forever and
ever.' His habits spoke up insistently, 'Do you think you can
live without us?'

So he sat in the garden, his friend nearby, utterly silent in
the stillness of the summer heat. Only inside did the storm
rage. Misery heaped up, until finally it seemed his chest
would burst. He threw himself under a fig tree, sobbing,
unable to stop.

O Lord, how long? Will I never cease setting my heart on shadows
and following a lie? How long, O Lord? Will you be angry forever?
How long? How long? Tomorrow and tomorrow? Why not now? Why
not in this very hour an end to my uncleanness?

Then . . . a voice.

He heard a voice . . .

A childish, piping voice so high-pitched he could not tell
whether it was male or female.

The voice seemed to come from a nearby house.

It changed tunelessly, over and over . . . 'Take up and
read. Take up and read. Take up and read.'

What did the words mean? Were they part of some
children's game?

'Take up and read. Take up and read.'

Were the words for him?

'Alypius, do you hear that?' he called. His friend stared
back in silence.

'Read what?' Augustine shouted into the sky.

The letters of the apostle Paul were nearby. They had, in
fact, started the conversation about Antony. Like Antony,
was he hearing God's words to him? Was he to take up the
Scriptures and read?

Augustine ran and snatched up the book Ponticianus had

noticed and began reading the page at which the book was open – Romans 13. The words burned into his mind: 'Not in orgies and drunkenness, not in sexual immorality and debauchery, not in dissension and jealousy. Rather clothe yourselves with the Lord Jesus Christ, and do not think about how to gratify the desires of the sinful nature.'

Instantly, as if before a peaceful light streaming into his heart, dark shadows of doubt fled. The man of unconquerable will was conquered by words from a book he had once dismissed as a mere fable lacking in clarity and grace of expression. Those words suddenly revealed that which he had so long vainly sought. Now he knew with assurance he had confronted truth. Those very words, 'clothe yourself with the Lord Jesus Christ,' had settled it; whatever it cost, he would give his life to Christ.

Putting his finger in the book to mark the spot, Augustine told Alypius what had happened inside him. Thrilled at his friend's joy, Alypius said he would join him. He, too, would follow Christ. The two then called Augustine's mother.

Monica's joy was even greater: 'Praise God,' she said, 'who is able to do above that which we ask or think.' Shortly thereafter, she and Augustine enjoyed together a great mystical vision. Nine days later, Monica, her lifelong prayers answered, passed peacefully from this world.

'Take up and read.' For the next forty-four years Augustine did just that. He read the Scriptures to work out his own salvation and then read and interpreted them to settle complex theological disputes within the early church. His classic defence of the authority of Scripture laid the foundation for Christians of every age thereafter. No serious Bible student has been able to ignore Augustine's monumental contribution to the church's understanding of the Old and New Testaments. His life and thought drew on the revered pen of God's Spirit.'

Prior to his conversion Augustine thought the Scriptures a collection of texts that must be interpreted and revised in comparison to the 'advanced wisdom' of the philosophers.

But in the garden he saw that the Scriptures were not just words to be interpreted; they were words that interpreted their reader. Through Scripture, God spoke personally and inerrantly to him. And as God's voice, Scripture knew infinitely more about Augustine than Augustine knew about Scripture.

Immediately after his conversion, Augustine began to write freely, quickly completing several books. His autobiographical *Confessions*, replete with quotes and paraphrases from Scripture, has provided intellectual challenge and spiritual illumination to Christians for centuries.

Augustine went on to become the Bishop of Hippo, one of the most influential men in his world, while the seemingly eternal Roman Empire fell apart. In response he wrote his masterpiece, *The City of God*, which gave Christians new hope and direction in the midst of turmoil and despair. Some say he almost singlehandedly rescued the gospel from the ruins of the Empire.

All this began when God, through a child's voice, said to him, 'Take up and read.' Obedient, Augustine found words that exposed his dilemma with a brilliant light and told him plainly what he had to do.

5

Just Another Book?

Augustine's story captures my imagination. Here was a great scholar who had studied and understood the Greek philosophers and read widely in the classics, a genius teaching at a leading university; yet this man of great intellect and compelling personality was utterly transformed by the Word of God. What power those Scriptures hold!

The Bible – banned, burned, beloved. More widely read, more frequently attacked than any other book in history. Generations of intellectuals have attempted to discredit it; dictators of every age have outlawed it and executed those who read it. Yet soldiers carry it into battle believing it more powerful than their weapons. Fragments of it smuggled into solitary prison cells have transformed ruthless killers into gentle saints.[1] Pieced-together scraps of Scripture have converted whole villages of pagan Indians.[2]

Yearly, the Bible outsells every best-seller. Five hundred million copies were published last year alone.[3] Portions have been translated into more than 1800 languages and even carried to the moon.

Literary classics endure the centuries. Philosophers mould the thoughts of generations unborn. Modern media shapes current culture. Yet nothing has affected the rise and fall of civilisation, the character of cultures, the structure of governments, and the lives of the inhabitants of this planet as profoundly as the words of the Bible.

'My word that goes out from my mouth . . . will not return to me empty, but will accomplish what I desire and achieve the purpose for which I sent it,' said the Lord through the

prophet Isaiah. Even those who are hostile to the Word sense
its inherent power, as I discovered during a fascinating
encounter with one of today's most renowned atheists.

In 1978 British interviewer David Frost invited me to a
televised debate with Madelyn Murray O'Hair. The show
was to be taped before a live New York audience and then
broadcast nationwide on NBC.

Before the taping I studied transcripts of Mrs O'Hair's
past encounters with believers to familiarise myself with her
methods and material. I learned that during her debates she
would appear to quote the Bible at length to support her
militant anti-Christian views. But, in fact, she craftily used
passages out of context and subtly rearranged words to
change their meaning. In light of this, though I knew it would
arouse her ire, I decided to take my Bible to the debate.

From the opening round Mrs O'Hair was true to form,
angrily spitting invectives at Christians in general and me in
particular. When I was speaking and she was off-camera, she
contorted her face and made obnoxious gestures in a coarse
effort to distract me. Aggressively interrupting, glibly mis-
quoting Scripture, she scored her blows early, to the crowd's
delight.

I kept my Bible unobtrusively at my side, but when she
shouted, 'The Bible teaches you to kill,' I leaned across a
startled David Frost and thrust it at her. 'Wait a minute!' I
demanded. 'You know this book, Mrs O'Hair. Find where it
says that. Read it to me.'

She blanched, for a moment groped for words, then drew
back in her chair shaking her head furiously. I thrust the
leather-covered book toward her once more. She recoiled
again. Even in the heat of the moment I was struck by her
absolute refusal to touch the Bible.

With that, the tide of the confrontation was turned, and
she seemed subdued and on the defensive thereafter.*

After the taping I once more asked Mrs O'Hair to find the
passages she had referred to, but she still refused to take the

---

* For reasons unknown to me, this debate was never aired by NBC.

Bible in her hands. Of course, if she was determined to remain an atheist, Mrs O'Hair was correct not to draw too close, for the holy Sword might pierce her heart.

Just another book? Hardly. The Bible's power rests upon the fact that it is the reliable, errorless, and infallible Word of God. And if that is true – as the Scriptures claim it is – then it has authority over the life of every believer. On this assertion the Christian faith stands or falls, for if the Bible is faulty, so is our faith.

I confess that for a long time I struggled with this central proposition of the faith, that the Bible is the infallible Word of God simply because it says it is. My lawyer's mind demanded evidence, something more than just this bold self-definition, which seemed at best a tautology.

So if the Christian faith – my faith – depended on the truth or falsehood of this argument, it was imperative that I examine it more closely.

The first thing I realised was that the Bible's claims about itself really only raise the questions. Without such prompting, it would never occur to us that a book written thousands of years ago might be absolutely authoritative for our lives. We would treat it like any other book of philosophy or religion. Take it or leave it. Or take part of it, discard the rest. But a book presenting itself as the Word of God, without error? That bold claim forces the question: is it or isn't it?

The next step was to find an authority to answer the question. As a believer, I had to turn to the One in whom I believe, Jesus Himself. Christ plainly asserted the authority and infallibility of Scripture. Consider just a few examples:

When He began His ministry, Christ used Scripture to announce His commission. 'The Spirit of the Lord is on me, because he has anointed me to preach good news to the poor. He has sent me to proclaim freedom for the prisoners and recovery of sight for the blind, to release the oppressed, to proclaim the year of the Lord's favour,' He read from the scroll of Isaiah.[4] Indeed He repeatedly cited the Old Testa-

ment Scriptures as the authority for His work and the
verification of His person.[5] He used the Word as His sole
defence against Satan and He asked His Father to sanctify
His disciples in the truth ('Thy Word is truth').[6]

Jesus rested His entire ministry and His authority upon
His delegation from God and the revelation of God in
Scripture: 'All authority in heaven and on earth has been
given to me.'[7] So if we claim faith in Jesus, we must take His
word for the authority of Scripture; it was His authority for
His authority.

As I considered that fact, I realised it solved one problem
and led to another. We depend on Scripture for the fact that
Jesus said these things; but how do we know He really said
them? How do we know His words and the events of His life
are accurately recorded in the Bible?

Because this is so crucial, no question has been more
exhaustively and critically examined through the centuries.
My own study brought me to these basic conclusions.

The men who penned the New Testament were Hebrews,
and scholars agree that the Hebrews were meticulous in
precise and literal transcriptions. What was said or done had
to be recorded in painstaking and faithful detail; if there
was any doubt on a particular event or detail, it was not
included.

Moreover, the gospel accounts were written by contemporaries of Jesus who had firsthand knowledge of His life and
the events of the early church (unlike, for example, Buddhist
literature which was developed two centuries after Buddha's
death). 'We proclaim to you *what we have seen and heard*,' said
the apostles.[8]

And external evidence continues to add historical verification. New archaeological discoveries in the field of biblical
studies have added weight to the evidence that the Gospels
were written by contemporaries of Jesus. For example, at one
point critics attributed the Gospel of John to the late second
century and considered it possibly a romanticised fable
about a simple Galilean peasant 'deified' long after his death.
However, a recently discovered early papyrus on which John

18 was written was scientifically determined to have been written *no later than* 125 A.D.*

Critical historical issues are not all neatly resolved, of course, and probably never will be. Yet it is an underreported fact that the more evidence is uncovered, the more scholars agree (even those who don't consider Jesus deity) that the New Testament is a reliable accounting of what the writers saw and heard.

This led me to the final challenge of the proposition: *granted*, Jesus used Scripture as His authority and said it was to be ours; *granted*, what He said was accurately recorded; but how do we know He was right? In short, how do we know that Christ's view of the Scriptures is true?

Well, if Jesus is God and perfect man, as He claims, He cannot be mistaken in what He teaches and He cannot lie. An infallible God cannot err; a holy God cannot deceive; a perfect teacher cannot be mistaken. So He is either telling the truth, or He is *not* who He says He is.

Therefore, if Christ's divinity and perfect humanity are established, we know that His view of the Scriptures as infallible and authoritative is true. The real proof of the Scriptures' authenticity, then, turns on the proof of Christ's authenticity. And resolving Christ's authenticity is the key to breaking the otherwise circular argument that the Bible says Jesus is the Son of God and Jesus says the Bible is true. But what proves Christ's authenticity?

It is the fact that He was bodily raised from the grave. The historical truth of His victory over death and His consequent eternal kingship over the world affirms Jesus' claim to be God. The Resurrection establishes Christ's authority and thus validates His teachings about the Bible and Himself. Paul minces no words about this: 'If Christ has not been raised, your faith is futile.'[9]

Some might think Paul rash for staking the case for

---

* Since this fragment is a copy, the original must have been earlier and indeed contemporaneous with the rise of the early church.

Christianity on the bodily resurrection, but the apostle made his bold assertion for two reasons.

First, Paul was absolutely certain about Christ's resurrection. He had encountered Jesus face to face on the road to Damascus and had talked both with the apostles who were with Jesus and with many of the five hundred eyewitnesses who saw the resurrected Lord.

Second, Paul was simply being honest. For if Christ was not bodily raised from the dead – if He had remained dead – then He was not God and could not have the authority He claimed. And if that were true, Christianity was a cruel hoax.

In the final analysis the question is simply this: if we believe the Scripture narrative was faithfully recorded, *how can we know the Scripture writers were telling the truth when they asserted that Jesus rose from the dead?*

My answer came from an unlikely source: the Watergate cover-up.

6

Watergate and the Resurrection

Saturday, June 17, 1972, was warm and oppressively humid, typical of summer in Washington DC. As Special Counsel to the President of the United States I was on call day and night, leaving little time for myself or my family. But this Saturday we were enjoying a rare, uninterrupted family day at our suburban McLean home. The President had just returned from the triumph of his presidency, the Moscow summit, and was resting in his Florida hide-away.

Patty and the kids were stretched out by the pool, and I was starting up the grille for a cookout, when the phone with the direct line to the White House switchboard rang. It was John Ehrlichman, one of the President's senior assistants; without explanation he brusquely asked what seemed like a ridiculous question: 'Where is your friend Howard Hunt?'

Hunt was a shadowy ex-CIA agent I'd known casually and had recommended for a minor White House job investigating leaks of government documents. But it had been months since I'd seen him or heard from him. So I pressed Ehrlichman: what in the world was so important about Howard Hunt's whereabouts to interrupt my quiet Saturday afternoon?

It was then I learned for the first time that a group of ex-Cuban freedom fighters had been arrested while breaking into the Democratic National Committee offices. One of the men had had a piece of paper in his pocket with Hunt's name on it. I can still remember my distracted thoughts as I hung up the phone. *Hunt's no amateur. He wouldn't get involved in a common burglary. Yet if he had been . . . I know him . . . my name could be dragged in.* Then I shrugged and dismissed these foreboding thoughts, went back to the pool and steamy sunshine and grilled some hamburgers.

That was how Watergate began for me.

During the following weeks I was comforted by my belief that no one in the White House or the Nixon campaign would be so stupid as to think they could find anything of value at the headquarters of a bankrupt party being ignored by its own candidates. This was no moral judgment, just practical politics. Even as the burglars' connection to Howard Hunt and his compatriot G. Gordon Liddy was uncovered, that was dismissed; both men had been part-time White House consultants but had been removed from the rolls months earlier.

Though a burglary under DC law, the break-in was really nothing more than campaign spying, I thought – like stealing the signals out of the other team's huddle. Certainly it was nothing much more than things I had done or others had done to me in my twenty years of political campaigns. (It was not until two years later, the summer of 1974, when the infamous 'smoking gun' tape was released, that the world as well as some of us on the inside learned that in the early days after the break-in the President was involved in attempting to sidetrack the FBI's investigation; that would later become *the* cover-up.)

In light of what happened later it sounds naïve, but at the time I believed nothing more was at stake than surviving the political brickthrowing through the November elections. The whole affair would then be neatly buried beneath the electoral landslide and we would get on with the more important business of governing the country. Or so I thought.

In the post-election euphoria that November no one paid much attention to Watergate. I recall only occasional discussions about it with the President, who was consumed with the frustrating negotiations to end the war in Vietnam. Henry Kissinger was shuttling back and forth to the Paris peace talks. Bob Haldeman, Chief of Staff, and John Ehrlichman were busy reorganising the bureaucracy for the second term. John Mitchell, former Attorney General and campaign manager, had moved back to his lucrative law firm in New York. And I was packing up my office, preparing to return to my own Washington law practice.

Then in January, 1973, Watergate, at least from my perspective, began to take on new implications. Howard Hunt, fearing imprisonment, sent his lawyer to see me. As the attorney demanded assurance of clemency for Hunt (which I refused to give him), I learned for the first time that the Watergate burglars were being given funds for support and legal fees. This was dangerous business, and I told Haldeman so later.

'Come on, Chuck,' he laughed, looking unusually mellow as the winter sunlight flooded through the tall office windows behind him. 'There's nothing wrong with raising a defence fund. Angela Davis* did it. Why not us?'

I stared at Bob, wondering whether he was putting on an act for my benefit or whether he really believed that. I concluded that he was sincere, and looking back, I now realise that as a practising Christian Scientist, Haldeman would not allow himself to think or see anything wrong. Ehrlichman, also a devout Christian Scientist, likewise seemed to ignore or deny the problems associated with Watergate.

But Haldeman and Ehrlichman were not the only ones doing this. Judging from the memoirs of the others, written over the succeeding decade, only the President's young counsel John Dean acknowledged that he had any real apprehension before January, 1973. He also said he shared his concerns with no one.

How could so many lawyers – Ehrlichman, Mitchell, Krogh, Dean, Nixon, and Colson, to mention only a few –

* A celebrated Communist activist accused of murder.

have been so oblivious to what later became so obvious? What deadly blindness it proved to be.*

Following the visit of Hunt's lawyer, I consulted my law partner, Dave Shapiro, a two-fisted trial veteran who had scrapped his way up from the streets of Brooklyn. Together we broke out the law books. It was then, late January, 1973, as we reviewed the tight columns of fine print in the criminal statutes, that I began for the first time to understand the possible criminal implications for the White House.

So in mid-February, with the Vietnam War finally over, I summoned up the courage to confront the President. It was during our last meeting in the Oval Office before I returned to my private law practice that, at an opportune moment, I gave President Nixon the painful advice, 'Whoever did order Watergate, let it out . . . let's get rid of it now. Take our losses.'†

The President had been leaning back in his chair, legs crossed and feet propped up on his massive mahogany desk. The words were barely out of my mouth when he dropped his feet and came straight up in his chair. 'Well, who do you think did this? . . . Mitchell? Magruder?'‡ He was angry, righteously so I supposed, that I would suggest putting the finger on a loyal aide. He was also, I still believe today, oblivious of the possible criminal implications, even as the net was being drawn increasingly tighter around us all.

According to the exhaustive records compiled from tape recordings, mountains of documents, endless Congressional

* I think there are two reasons for this. First, by definition a conspiracy is the sum total of a lot of bits and pieces; the individuals involved often see only their own particular bits and pieces, rarely the entire mosaic. Second, the only exposure criminal law that 98 per cent of all attorneys have is one course in law school and occasional court-assigned criminal cases, usually quickly settled by out-of-court plea bargains – a remarkable commentary on the American judicial system. The closest most lawyers come to the drama of courtroom confrontation is watching Perry Mason with the rest of the populace on late-night television. My first experience with the obstruction of justice statutes was when I was prosecuted – and sent to prison – under one.

† From official White House transcripts of February 13, 1973, released by Watergate Special Prosecutor.

‡ Same source as above.

WATERGATE AND THE RESURRECTION

hearings, and massive volumes of testimony, the first serious Oval Office discussion of likely criminal involvement took place the morning of March 21; that was the fateful meeting when John Dean warned the President of the 'cancer on his presidency.'

Later on March 21 (the specific dates are important) Haldeman called Mitchell in New York and Mitchell, in turn, told Jeb Magruder, his campaign assistant, he would 'assist' him if he went to jail. That was also the day $75,000 in additional money was dispatched to Hunt for 'lawyer's fees.' The President conferred again with Haldeman and Ehrlichman and Dean. And that same evening the President, without disclosing anything that had gone on that busy day, called me at home for a thirty-one minute conversation.

Though I had officially left his staff, it was not surprising to receive a call from the President; he had told me he wanted to continue to call on me for advice. What was surprising was the President's impatient, almost distracted voice. I had spent countless hours across a desk from him or on the phone and could almost always read his mood. When big issues were on his mind, like Vietnam bombings or dealings with China, the President was remarkably cool. When little things came to his attention, like sniping in the press, he seemed the most unnerved.

The evening of March 21 he quickly dispensed with small talk and plunged into Watergate.

'What's your judgment as to what . . . what ought to be done now . . . whether, uh, there should be, uh, a uh, report made or something, you know, or just hunker down and take it or what?'

The official transcripts show my reply. 'The problem I foresee in this is not what has happened so far – that is, the mystery of the Watergate. I don't know whether somebody else higher up in the Committee for the Re-election is gonna get named or not but, uh, to me that isn't of very great consequence to the country if it happens. The thing that worries me is that, is the possibility of somebody, uh, charging an obstruction of justice problem – in other words that

the subsequent actions would worry me more than anything.'

I then went on to suggest that the President remove Dean
and appoint an independent Special Counsel to handle
Watergate for him. Though I wasn't aware then of earlier
meetings with Dean and the others, it was, as hindsight
confirms, good advice. But those chilling words 'obstruction
of justice' must have made the President's day. No wonder he
didn't call me again for two weeks!*

After March 21 everything changed – it was all downhill,
and fast. Conversations grew thick and heavy the next week:
talk of perjury, 'stone-walling', obstruction of justice, the
kind of stuff that gives grown men weak knees and sweaty
palms.

On March 23 Judge Sirica released a letter from one of the
Watergate burglars who had made a deal; he would tell all in
exchange for a lighter sentence. That afternoon Haldeman
called me with a series of questions: Had I promised clemency to Howard Hunt? Had I urged the campaign people to
get intelligence on the Democrats? Bob's voice was cool, as
always, but from the way he repeated my answers, I was
certain someone else was in the room with him – the President. His questions also revealed what was happening behind the massive iron gates of 1600 Pennsylvania Avenue.
The occupants were stocking the bunkers for what they now
realised would be a bloody siege. Increasingly distrustful of
my colleagues and sensing that all was not well, I dictated a
memorandum of our conversation as soon as I hung up the
phone.

Thinly disguised panic began to sweep the plush offices of
the stately old building that houses the most influential and
powerful men in the world. Events escalated so fast there was
no way to keep track of them. As the press bannered alle-
gations that campaign officials had ordered the break-in,
Dean rushed off to Camp David to write a 'report'.

* Transcript of recorded conversation not introduced in Watergate trial
and not made public until 1981.

On March 26 the grand jury reconvened to hear new charges from one of the original burglars. That same day Dean called Magruder and taped his conversation.

On March 27 Haldeman and Ehrlichman discussed the crisis for two and a half hours with the President. Also, Mitchell met with Magruder to discuss clemency, while Mitchell's wife, Martha, made one of her legendary calls to the *New York Times*, charging that someone was trying to make a 'goat' out of her husband.

While at Camp David on March 25, John Dean had secretly contacted an old law school classmate for advice on the best criminal lawyer he could hire. Five days later he retained a tough ex-Kennedy administration prosecutor, Charles Schaeffer. Then on April 8, 1973, Dean met with Watergate prosecutors to bargain his testimony for immunity and save his own hide, as he acknowledged with refreshing candour in his memoirs.[1]

Within hours the cover-up collapsed. Magruder, already in contact with the prosecutors, began negotiations in earnest. Dave Shapiro, sensing it was now 'every man for himself,' coaxed me into taking a lie detector test to establish my innocence, then gave the results to the *New York Times*. The prosecutors called me; I offered to testify.

The White House was like a front-line command post under heavy shelling. Though men like Ehrlichman and Haldeman put on a brave front, they trusted no one and were taping every phone conversation.

Daily headlines fed the public fresh tidbits, mostly from stories leaked by aides or their lawyers seeking to clear their skirts or entice the prosecutors into a better deal. Meanwhile, the prosecutors were so busy with White House officials offering testimony that they couldn't handle the traffic in and out of their offices. Suddenly Watergate was a three-ring circus.

History reveals that after the criminal investigation of the White House began – as it did with Dean's April 8 meeting with the prosecutors – the end of Mr Nixon's presidency was only a matter of time. The cover-up was discovered – and doomed – and this is why the dates are so important. For though the cover-up technically dated back to the June, 1972 break-in, the serious cover-up – the part everyone knew or should have known was criminal – really began March 21, 1973. And it ended April 8, 1973.

With the most powerful office in the world at stake, a small band of hand-picked loyalists, no more than ten of us, could not hold a conspiracy together for more than two weeks.

Think of what was at stake: Each of us involved – Ehrlichman, Haldeman, Mitchell, and the rest – believed passionately in President Nixon. To enter government service for him we had sacrificed very lucrative private law practices and other endeavours; we had sacrified our family lives and privacy; we had invested our whole lives in the work, twenty-four hours a day if necessary. Only a few months earlier the President had been re-elected in an historic landslide victory; the ugly Asian war was finally over; we were riding the crest in every way.

Think of the power at our fingertips: a mere command from one of us could mobilise generals and cabinet officers, even armies; we could hire or fire personnel and manage billions in agency budgets.

Think of the privileges: a call to the military aide's office would produce a limousine or jet airplane; the National Gallery delivered classic paintings to adorn our office walls; red-jacketed stewards stood in waiting to serve food and drink twenty-four hours a day; private phones appeared wherever we travelled; secret service men were always within sight – as many as we wanted.

Yet even the prospect of jeopardising the President we'd worked so hard to elect, of losing the prestige, power, and personal luxury of our offices was not enough incentive to make this group of men contain a lie. Nor, as I reflect today, was the pressure really all that great; at that point there had certainly been moral failures, criminal violations, even perjury by some. There was certain to be keen embarrassment; at the worst, some might go to prison, though that possibility was by no means certain. But no one was in grave danger; *no one's life was at stake.*

Yet after just a few weeks the natural human instinct for self-preservation was so overwhelming that the conspirators, one by one, deserted their leader, walked away from their cause, turned their backs on the power, prestige, and privileges.

So what does all this have to do with the resurrection of Jesus Christ? Simply this:

Modern criticism of the historic truth of Christianity boils down to three propositions: first, that the disciples were mistaken; or second, that the disciples knowingly perpetrated a myth, intended as a symbol; or third, the eleven disciples conceived a 'Passover plot' – spirited the body of Christ out of the tomb and disposed of it neatly – and to their dying breaths maintained conspiratorial silence.

Let's consider each.

The first is the shakiest. After all, a man being raised from the dead is a rather mind-boggling event – not the kind of thing people are likely to be vague or indecisive about. The Scriptures state very honestly that the disciples were so staggered by Jesus' reappearance that at least one demanded the tangible proof of fingering the wounds in His hands and side. Jesus knew human nature, knew they needed physical evidence. Luke says, 'He showed himself to these men and gave many convincing proofs that he was alive. He appeared to them over a period of forty days . . .'[2] The records of the event, written independently by various eyewitness reporters, belie the possibility that the disciples were mistaken.

But could it have been a myth? This second theory seems plausible at first since it was customary in the first century to convey religious truths through symbols. But this assumes that all the disciples understood that they were using a symbolic device. Even a cursory reading of the Gospels reveals not allegory or fable, but a straightforward, narrative account. Moreover, Paul, an intimate associate of the original disciples, shatters the myth theory altogether when he argues that if Jesus was not *actually* resurrected, Christianity is a hoax, a sham.[3] Nothing in Paul's writing remotely suggests mythology.

The myth theory is even more untenable than the mistake theory. So if one is to assail the historicity of the Resurrection and therefore the deity of Christ, one must conclude that there was a conspiracy – a cover-up if you will – by eleven men with the complicity of up to five hundred others. To subscribe to this argument, one must also be ready to believe that each disciple was willing to be ostracised by friends and family, live in daily fear of death, endure prisons, live penniless and hungry, sacrifice family, be tortured without mercy, and ultimately die – all without ever once renouncing that Jesus had risen from the dead!

This is why the Watergate experience is so instructive for me. If John Dean and the rest of us were so panic-stricken, not by the prospect of beatings and execution, but by political disgrace and a possible prison term, one can only speculate about the emotions of the disciples. Unlike the men in the White House, the disciples were powerless people, abandoned by their leader, homeless in a conquered land. Yet they clung tenaciously to their enormously offensive story that their leader had risen from His ignoble death and was alive – and was *the* Lord.

The Watergate cover-up reveals, I think, the true nature of humanity. None of the memoirs suggest that anyone went to the prosecutor's office out of such noble notions as putting the Constitution above the President, or bringing rascals to justice, or even moral indignation. Instead, the writings of those involved are consistent recitations of the frailty of man. Even political zealots at the pinnacle of power will save their own necks in the crunch, though it may be at the expense of the one they profess to serve so zealously.

Is it really likely, then, that a deliberate cover-up, a plot to perpetuate a lie about the Resurrection, could have survived the violent persecution of the apostles, the scrutiny of early church councils, the horrendous purge of the first-century believers who were cast by the thousands to the lions for refusing to renounce the Lordship of Christ? Is it not probable that at least one of the apostles would have renounced Christ before being beheaded or stoned? Is it not likely that some 'smoking gun' document might have been produced exposing the 'Passover plot'? Surely one of the conspirators would have made a deal with the authorities (government and Sanhedrin probably would have welcomed such a soul with open arms and pocketbooks!).

Blaise Pascal, the extraordinary mathematician, scientist, inventor, and logician of the seventeenth century, was convinced of the truth of Christ by examination of the historical record. In his classic *Pensées*, Pascal wrote: 'The hypothesis that the apostles were knaves is quite absurd. Follow it out to the end and imagine these twelve [sic] men meeting after Jesus' death and conspiring to say that he had risen from the dead. This means attacking all the powers that be. *The human heart is singularly susceptible to fickleness, to change, to promises, to bribery.* One of them had only to deny his story under these inducements, or still more because of possible imprisonment, torture and death, and they would all have been lost.'[4]

As Pascal correctly observes, man in his normal state will renounce his beliefs just as readily as Peter renounced Jesus *before* the Resurrection. But as the same Peter discovered *after* the Resurrection, there is a power beyond man that causes him to forsake all. It is the power of the God who revealed Himself in the person of Jesus Christ.

Take it from one who was inside the Watergate web looking out, who saw firsthand how vulnerable a cover-up is: Nothing less than a witness as awesome as the resurrected Christ could have caused those men to maintain to their dying whispers that Jesus is alive and Lord.

This weight of evidence tells me the apostles were indeed telling the truth: Jesus did rise bodily from the grave; He is who He says He is. Thus, He speaks with the absolute authority of the all-powerful God. And that fact breaks what might otherwise be considered a circular argument.

Thus we can arrive at some crucial conclusions about Holy Scripture:

(1) The Bible is the Word of God. For the Son of God who speaks with absolute authority did not use the Scriptures as pious sayings or as a guide for the fulfilling Christian life. He regarded Scripture as the *revelation* of God Himself.

(2) Jesus entrusted His own life to the Scriptures, relying on them totally. He submitted to the *authority* of Scripture.

(3) Examining Jesus' stand on Scripture throughout His ministry, it is clear that He believed the Word infallible and *inerrant* – that is, reliable and without error.[5]

How can we who purport to follow Him do any differently?

7
Believing God

As an attorney, I have always believed strongly in the importance of precedents; that's how lawsuits are decided – on the basis of what courts have decided in the past, the body of common law developed over the years through careful deliberation. So naturally as I examined the case for the authority of Scripture, I looked to the evidence of the centuries. There I found a consistent flow subscribing to the authority and infallibility of the Word from Jesus Himself down through the early church and throughout church history.

St Paul, the first church theologian, resoundingly affirmed the truth of Scripture.[1] Irenaeus, brilliant second century apologist whose writings stemmed the early tides of heresy, argued that the Scriptures were 'perfect since they were spoken by the Word of God.'[2] Augustine wrote, 'I have learned to hold the Scriptures alone inerrant.'[3]

In the sixteenth century, Luther spoke movingly of the Word of God as 'greater than Heaven and earth, yea, greater than death and Hell, for it forms part of the Power of God and endures everlastingly.'[4] His fellow reformer John Calvin argued that that which distinguishes Christianity is the knowledge that God has spoken to us and so 'we owe to the Scriptures the same reverence which we owe to God.'[5]

Jonathan Edwards, second president of Princeton University, ardently defended these views, as did John Wesley, Thomas Aquinas, Charles Haddon Spurgeon, and the other great names of the church too numerous to recount. The Roman Catholic position has been unwavering; a 1943 encyclical sums up its classical view: 'Divine inspiration "not only is essentially incompatible with error but excludes and rejects it as absolutely and necessarily as it is impossible that God Himself, the supreme Truth, can utter that which is not true. This is the ancient and constant faith of the Church." '[6] In this encyclical on promoting biblical studies, Pope Pius XII began by calling Scripture 'heaven-sent treasure'.[7]

If Jesus, the Head of our church, and the weight of precedents point so clearly to a wholehearted acceptance of and subscription to the Scriptures, why does twentieth century culture manifest a steady decline in biblical belief? Gallup reports that in 1963, 65 percent of all Americans believed the Bible to be infallible; that number dropped to 37 percent in 1982.[8] Why?

I believe it is because the prevailing attitudes of the culture have thoroughly infiltrated the ranks of faith and belief. The relativism of the modern mind-set is loath to subscribe to the absolute authority of anything, and that attitude has seeped into *our* perspective, resulting in a barrage of questions, attacks, and rewrites of the Scriptures.

So, though evangelicals say they hold fast to their orthodoxy, in truth they are succumbing to relativism and modern cynicism. It is no wonder really, for millions sit in church pews Sunday after Sunday never bothering to think about what they believe or why; thus they are easy prey for the trendy clichés that dismiss Scripture as the 'legends' of *unenlightened* ancients. (How semantics influence our values! Words like 'progressive' can reverse the rules of logic. That is, the longer historical evidence persists, the less reliable it becomes; the newer the conclusion, the less proven by history, the more 'progressive' and, presumably, more appealing it is.)

In such a climate, commonly voiced objections insidiously become accepted as facts that no one bothers to challenge. And if many were honest they would have to admit that these objections also provide a convenient rationalisation for not picking up a Bible and wrestling with its hard and convicting truths.

What are some of these objections?

One we often hear is *'The Bible is unbelievable'*. The parting of the Red Sea, the raising of Lazarus, the visitation of
angels, and the like confound our natural senses and reason.
Of course they do. They are *supernatural*. But that is the
essence of what God is – super-natural. Beyond the natural
senses.

If there is no supernatural, there is no God.

Second: *'The Scriptures don't really matter.'* Going to services,
being faithful to family, and operating ethically in one's
dealings – these are the 'Christian' standards, reason many
churchgoers. After all, God knows we are doing our best.

This is an echo of a widespread belief in America – a
form of civil religion – that says it doesn't matter what
you believe so long as you believe in something. This
kind of thinking, by doing away with individual responsibility, ignores a central truth of our Judaeo-Christian
foundation.

Third: *'It's out of date.'* The events in Scripture took place
thousands of years ago when shepherds tended flocks and
primitive tribal customs prevailed. Times change, says this
modern relativist; ancient ritual is irrelevant to today's
morality.

Yes, the biblical account deals with ancient times, for
ancient Israel was the particular place God chose to covenant with His people and some 1,200 years later to enter
time and space through Jesus Christ. But God's truth is
eternal.

Time passes. Customs change. Truth remains. Absolute
objective truth can never depend on custom, common
perceptions, or changing trends, and it remains true whether
believed or not.

Though it is sometimes difficult to understand the cultural
backdrop of the biblical drama, the play remains unchanged.

Fourth: *'We lived under the new covenant so we needn't bother to
read the archaic, outdated laws of the Old Testament.'*

It is impossible to appreciate Jesus apart from the historical context in which He lived. Without understanding the

Old Testament covenants between God and His chosen people and humanity's consistent failure to adhere to them, God's grace and the supreme atonement of the cross lose their significance. The Old Testament, as well, is indispensable in teaching us about the character of God and the promises fulfilled in Christ.

Fifth: '*The red letters count more than the black.*' An astonishing number of Christians accept Jesus' teachings as the Word of God but reject the writings of 'Paul and all the others' as human opinions.

But where do we find Christ's words? He didn't write them down Himself. His words are reported by the Gospel writers. So is Luke more believable than Paul? We have no indication that Luke met Jesus face to face, but we know Paul did. In a court of law, therefore, Luke's red letters would be hearsay; Paul's black letters direct evidence.

Ultimately, if we believe all Scripture is inspired by God,[9] all must be given equal weight.

Sixth: '*There are so many contradictions and different interpretations that I can't accept the Bible as literally true.*'

Confusion over how to read, interpret, and understand the Bible is the single greatest cause of biblical illiteracy and scepticism.

Though it is unique, in a structural sense the Bible must be read like any other book: metaphor is metaphor, poetry is poetry, parables are parables. Scripture must be read in context and according to its literary genre (the technique of communication the author selected).

Remember, too, that any author writes so his readers can understand. When critics attack the literal truthfulness of Scripture by citing language like 'the sun rose', they are ignoring basic rules of literary communication. Of course, the sun does not rise; the writer is simply communicating in terms he and his contemporaries understand. (Even in our enlightened age, of course, TV weather forecasters still give the times each day for *sunrise* and *sunset*.)

By applying the basic rules of logical interpretation, examining historical narratives in the light of didactic teaching, taking the explicit over the implicit, we can clear up much of the ruckus over the Bible's seeming contradictions.*

And seventh: '*I just don't get anything out of the Bible.*'

These critics expect the Bible to be the ultimate quick-fix, self-fulfilment manual, in the same category as all the how-to books crowding our bookstore shelves, intended to fulfil our every need and desire. Of course, we find spiritual fulfilment in reading the Scriptures, but the holy Word of God is intended to do much more than that: it is to satisfy the believer's deepest hunger for knowledge about acceptable living and service for his sovereign King.

Objections like the above reveal why the family Bible is more often used to adorn coffee tables or press flowers than it is to feed souls and discipline lives. They also reveal why Christians do not know how to love God. For we should read God's Word not for what we can get out of it, not for what it will do for us, but for what it will teach us to do for our God.

'Your word is truth,' Jesus said.[10] Nothing less than knowledge of that truth is demanded of Christ's disciples. That knowledge comes only from fervent study of truth, that is, study of His Word. This is indispensable to genuine discipleship. *It is indispensable to loving God.*

But perhaps the real reason we do not pursue that radical discipleship rooted in the Word of God is that we have not recognised the clear choice before us. Perhaps we believe *in* God – as 98 percent of all Americans say they do – but we do not *believe God*, that is, obey His Word. That choice is most clearly illustrated for us in the sharp contrasts of two biblical accounts: first Eve in the Garden of Eden and then Christ in the wilderness of Judaea. Consider the responses of each when confronted with Satan's challenge regarding the Word of God.

Satan came to Eve as a serpent, asking with beguiling

---

* It is not my purpose to examine the issues of interpretation and study of Scripture in depth. But because of the importance of this issue, I strongly recommend further reading on the subject in such highly readable and instructive sources as *Knowing Scripture* by R. C. Sproul (Inter-Varsity Press, 1977).

innocence, 'Did God really say, "You must not eat from any tree in the garden?"'*

If Eve answered yes, she would be lying; God hadn't forbidden *all* the trees. But a straight no wouldn't be truthful either. So, unaware of the trap being set, Eve replied, 'We may eat fruit from the trees in the garden, but God did say, you must not eat fruit from the tree that is in the middle of the garden, and *you must not touch it* or you will die.'[11] (In her answer Eve demonstrated that she knew God's Word, though she elaborated by adding the words, 'You must not touch it.' Adding to Scripture is as dangerous as taking away from it – and this perhaps was part of Eve's undoing.)

'You will not surely die,' the serpent reassured her. Surely a loving God would not mean anything so cruel as that. No, the beguiler continued, 'God knows that when you eat of it your eyes will be opened, and you will be *like* God, knowing good and evil.'

What an irresistible proposition – as it is today. After all, Eve was made in God's image; shouldn't she know what He knew? And be *like* Him? The serpent was simply helping her interpret what God had meant to say in the first place.

So Eve succumbed, probably believing she was doing the right thing. Adam immediately joined her. And this temptation has plagued humanity every since: the desire *to be like God*. Simply put, it is humanism, man's ultimate arrogance – his pretension that he can be his own Lord. And it began in the Garden.

Satan continued enticing humanity with that same lure, as the history of the Old Testament bears witness. And seventy-five generations later the beguiler appeared to Jesus Christ with the same temptation.

The Devil's first challenge was simple: 'If you are the Son of God, tell this stone to become bread.' (A minor thing for One who would later multiply a few loaves and fish to feed five thousand.) But Jesus understood this was not only a

---

* Before the Fall, the serpent was a crafty but engaging creature, not the slithering reptile he became after God's curse was put on him.

challenge to His authority, but a temptation to choose the material over the spiritual. So He relied solely on the Word of God, answering: 'It is written: "Man does not live on bread alone."'[12]

A pause . . . and then a second attack: the tempter offered Christ the kingdoms of this world. (This temptation has caused power-hungry men from Alexander to Hitler to cut a bloody swath through history.) But again Jesus answered from the Word of God: 'It is written: "Worship the Lord your God and serve him only."'[13]

Finally, the Devil played his trump. 'If you are the Son of God,' prove it. 'Throw yourself down from here.' Then Satan quoted from Psalm 91: 'He will command his angels concerning you to guard you carefully.' But once again Christ stood on the firm foundation of the Word. Unlike Eve, He quoted Scripture precisely: 'It says: "Do not put the Lord your God to the test."'[14]

These two great confrontations with Satan present us with the clear contrast. Eve knew what God said, but when put to the test, she disobeyed His Word. Her disobedience caused the fall of humanity.

Jesus also knew what God said. Put to the test, He obeyed and trusted His whole life to the Word. His obedience – even unto the death of the cross – is the way of our redemption from the Fall.

If presented with the choice, to be like Eve or be like Jesus, most of us would hasten to line up with Christ. We Christians are usually quick to say we want to 'be like Jesus'. But if we are honest about what those familiar Sunday school words really mean, we'll see they compel us to adopt His attitudes; and that means belief *in*, and submission to, the Scriptures. Instead, we find a thousand ways to resist their truth, to rationalise their calling on our lives. For deep inside we know that obedience to the Scriptures without concern for consequences is penetrating and painful. It requires us to die to self and follow Christ. It demands that we recognise the sin in our lives and that we acknowledge and repent of that sin.

This is the first major intersection on the spiritual pilgrimage. Many prefer to turn off at this point, or think they can live the Christian life on their own terms – that is, without the conversion in attitude and action that must follow the conversion of heart.

I do not think anyone illustrates this better than the man in the next chapter, an infamous character of a generation ago.

I first heard about Mickey Cohen from the chairman of Prison Fellowship, George Wilson. George, for years the manager of Billy Graham's business operations, had got to know Cohen in the 1950s when the man attended some of Billy Graham's first crusade meetings.

After George had told me about a hilarious episode involving himself and Cohen, I was prompted to read more about the man in old newspaper accounts, in Cohen's autobiography, and in the accounts of another person you'll meet in the story, Jim Vaus. As I did this minor investigation into the life of a rather flamboyant character, and later as I began gathering material for this book, it struck me that Mickey Cohen's story pathetically but perfectly illustrates what genuine repentance means and how impossible it is to love God without it.

SIN AND REPENTANCE

We are not sinners because we sin;
we sin because we are sinners.

R. C. Sproul

8

A Christian Gangster?

Most of the nightclubbers turned to look when the troupe entered the Starlight Room of the Ambassador Hotel. Comedian Buddy Lester paused in his act as tough-looking bodyguards and extravagantly dressed women swirled about a short, pudgy man whose thick, inverted-v eyebrows accented big brown eyes.

As the party snaked its way through the round tables, jewelled hands reached out from all sides to welcome the newcomer. Though attired in a pearl grey, custom-made suit and exuding expensive cologne, the figure was not imposing. Apparently his presence was, for the maître d' seated the patron with reverence, bowed, and personally brought hot towels with which the man wiped his face and hands thoroughly, meticulously, as though trying to erase the oily handshakes he had just endured.

Later, oblivious to the sycophants smoking and drinking around him, the abstemious figure held court for stars and would-be stars. As he sipped his ginger ale and scanned the room for friends he might have missed on his way in, Jimmy Durante, Sammy Davis, Jr., and Humphrey Bogart made their way over to share a few laughs. Others, their faces not so readily recognisable, approached the table with a whispered question or pressed a folded note into a bodyguard's hand.

The Hollywood of the late 1940s was a tinsel town at the height of its glamour. Movies like '12 O'Clock High', 'Sunset Boulevard', and 'All About Eve' were rolling out of its mammoth production studios. Film stars were larger than life, their furs, jewels, and limousines the props for roles they played to the hilt – even when they left the set. Gossip columns linked starlets and mobsters, movie moguls and politicians' daughters. Celebrities measured their status by the number of morning headlines devoted to their exploits the night before.

And within this gilded world ruled a short figure with a receding hairline and an abrupt New York accent. An unlikely king, he could cause a sensation even at the celebrity-packed Starlight Room.

Myer Harris Cohen, known to friends and enemies alike as Mickey, mobster and 'number-one bad boy' of Los Angeles, had invented his own role in life and written the script to please himself. Born poor in New York City, he had once been a New Jersey punk and strong-arm man. Later he moved to the West Coast and became a self-styled gangster in the tradition of Al Capone, whose work he greatly admired. Cohen was tough to the core, with an immense ego and an innate sense of self-preservation. Contracts were repeatedly put out on his life; his home was bombed; his car machine-gunned.

By 1949, Cohen was top man in the Los Angeles underworld, handling half a million dollars every day from his gambling casinos, floating crap games, private gambling clubs, legalised poker games, and the biggest nonsyndicate bookie business west of Chicago. He had a luxurious home, a glamorous wife, and entertained lavishly for his friends. Nothing happened in that glittering town without his say-so, for Cohen's charisma was power not glamour. Yet he had the charm of a kid brother who wanted nothing so much as to be liked.

People first drawn to Cohen because of his power were surprised when they became his friends; ruthless as he was at running the rackets, Mickey was equally generous and kind to those he cared for.

But Cohen had won his power with muscle – physical and financial – and he retained it with those same forces. Anyone behind the scenes knew this all too well . . .

The director in the control booth adjusted his headset as he told his assistant to switch to camera two. Pressing the microphone closer to his lips, he spoke to one of the cameramen out on the floor of the television studio. 'Now, Jim. Close in. There. That's great. Hold that tight head shot.'

Beyond the window of the monitoring booth a heavy grey-haired man in sheriff's uniform sat at the polished desk on the cramped set. Red and blue bunting draped a screen behind him; an American flag stood on a platform to his left. The desk hid the ample paunch straining the buttons of his stiff grey shirt, but the glaring lights reflected off the sweat beading his high, balding forehead. He was obviously concentrating on keeping his gaze direct and obeying the director's orders to 'pretend you're talking to your neighbour over the back fence'.

'Most of you folks feel the same way I do about Los Angeles,' he was saying. 'It's the nearest thing to paradise on God's earth. But a great big ol' snake has got hisself coiled around this city. And that snake's name is Organised Crime. In my first term I went after him, like I said I would. Today we're right to the place where we can almost lop that varmit's head right off. We just need to get rid of its number one man. So if you elect me next Tuesday, the first thing I'll do is rid us forever of the chief of the underworld out here – Mickey Cohen.'

In the booth the director smirked and the sound engineer chuckled, looking down at the two men lingering at the edge of the set beyond the bright circle of light trained on the sheriff. The director's assistant, clipboard in hand, ventured toward the figures in the shadows and spoke to the shorter of the two.

'You planning on going on the lam, Mickey?'

'Sure. Getting Tumbleweed elected ain't been no joyride. I deserve a vacation.'

The sweating sheriff Mickey Cohen had in his pocket had denounced him convincingly, just as he had been instructed. The broadcast would be worth the price Cohen had paid for it.

This kind of drama was all in a day's work for Mickey Cohen. Unfortunately, many of his other scenarios were more sinister. One of these, a 'piece of work' he undertook in 1949, would cause the first crack in his power base.

It revolved around Alfred Pearson, owner of an LA radio repair shop. Pearson was a skinflint who enjoyed nothing more than a good lawsuit followed by a foreclosure. He had filed several nuisance suits against the city of Los Angeles, and in one case had succeeded in attaching the $4,000 home of a widow named Elsie Philips over a $9.00 repair bill she owed him. As time went on, the mayor of LA decided the well-publicised case reflected badly on his city and that he had had quite enough of Alfred Pearson. So Mayor Fletcher Brown instructed the chief executive for the police commission and another of his political lieutenants to contact Mickey Cohen about the matter.*

Mickey, who hated Pearson's cruelty to the poor, graciously offered to have him 'knocked in', but the mayor didn't want Pearson dead, just beaten within an inch of his life. Mickey thought this an inefficient way to do business, but the police commissioner promised him that there wouldn't be a cop within miles of Pearson's store on a certain Saturday between noon and one o'clock; Mickey and his boys could 'run down this deal' on Pearson in good style. Since he enjoyed playing Robin Hood, Mickey agreed. (He later bought Philips' home back for her when it was suggested this would look good for his image.)

Mickey and his associates arrived at the radio shop at the appointed day and hour. Mickey went in alone first. The shopkeeper was working in the back of the store behind a locked iron screen that separated the repair shop from the showroom where new television sets and radios were displayed. Mickey politely asked the man to come talk with him, but Pearson refused to come out from behind the screen.

Cohen left, waited fifteen minutes, and sent in an associate – a small man with a pencil behind his ear, posing as a

* This version of the Pearson incident is taken from Cohen's autobiography.

reporter. When the little guy succeeded in enticing Pearson out of his stronghold, the others moved in.

With baseball bats and tyre irons, Cohen's boys methodically broke Pearson's arms and legs and cracked open his skull. Taking their time about it, they delivered blow after blow with a calm recital of the man's lawsuits. Pearson screamed for help, cursed, and practically tore his store apart trying to get away.

The noise attracted the neighbours; soon some three hundred bystanders were assembled in front of the store, but no one intervened on the shopkeeper's behalf. Instead, they cheered Cohen and his boys on as if they were a liberating army.

However, someone unacquainted with Pearson's business practices came along at the end of the beating, saw the bleeding man crawling out of the store, and raced off to get the police. Cohen, of course, had left the scene by this time.

Two rookie cops apprehended Mickey's boys a few blocks from the store, ordered them out of the car, and lined them up on the sidewalk. Finding the bloodied irons and bats and learning from the licence plate that the car had been stolen, the cops thought they had made the biggest bust since Dillinger. Cruiser sirens wailing, they hustled the men off to the Wilshire police station.

While the cops had been frisking the men on the sidewalk, an amateur photographer happened by, clicked the shutter, and took the photos to the LA *Times*. A seasoned police reporter took one look at the pictures and jubilantly recognised the men as hoods in the upper echelon of Cohen's organisation.

Meanwhile, Mickey was at Slapsie Maxie's, a club he was using as his floating office. When he heard of the arrest, he called the captain of the Wilshire station and got his men released. It wasn't much of a problem since the captain was on his payroll, but the professional in Mickey disapproved of any job done badly.

To his detriment Mickey found out just how bad it was. The *Times* printed the photo and the story broke, implicating him and the police and forcing the authorities to arrest and indict him.

At the trial, the jury brought in a verdict of 'not guilty', but the Pearson incident had given Mickey the kind of publicity he didn't want – and it would return to haunt him.*

Late one night in that same year, 1949, Cohen received a phone call from one of his employees, a man named Jim Vaus. Vaus was an electronics wizard, one of the original wire-tappers. He had first worked for the police in criminal investigations, then for Hollywood stars seeking evidence in divorce proceedings, and finally for Cohen and other under-world figures. Even so valued an employee as Vaus wouldn't have dared call Cohen that late at night unless what he had on his mind was urgent. The gangster invited Jim and his wife, Alice, to come to his home in Brentwood immediately.

In Cohen's living room, Jim Vaus explained that he had attended something called a Billy Graham Crusade in down-town LA and had become a Christian. Mickey was Jewish and considered all Gentiles Christians. He said he didn't understand what Vaus was talking about. Jim explained that becoming a Christian involved a personal commitment to Jesus Christ as Saviour and Lord.

Mickey paused, then smiled indulgently. 'That's good to hear, Jim. As far as I'm concerned, this little Jew's in your corner 100 per cent. All I'd like ya to promise me is that I don't want to ever hear ya turned back.'

'Well, I'm giving up everything,' Vaus said.

Mickey didn't know what 'everything' meant. Jim Vaus's renunciation of his criminal life forced him to come up against – or, as they would say, double-cross – other under-world figures not as understanding as Mickey. For example, Vaus was due to fly to St Louis that week for a piece of work that was to expand a horse-race betting scam that had already netted bushels of gambling money for Jim and

---

* Tried a number of times for murder, armed robbery, and assault, Mickey Cohen was never convicted of a violent crime.

several underworld partners. When Jim called his St Louis associates, told them about his conversion and that he wasn't coming, they assured him they would be . . . coming for him.

One day, as expected, the musclemen came. They told Vaus it was time to settle the score and that they expected him to come quietly. Jim knew they had been ordered either to cripple him for life or kill him. He stood on his porch steps and for forty-five minutes told them what had happened to him, how Jesus Christ had transformed his life. At the end of his account, the hoods turned and walked away. They never came back.

Mickey's strange 'good boy' streak was revealed as he backed Vaus's decision for Christ by releasing him from his 'employment'. Of course, his motives were mixed as usual. Cohen loved nothing more than associating with famous people, and the young evangelist Billy Graham was becoming a hot item in the local papers. Radio star Stuart Hamblen, a cowboy with a reputation as a rounder and hard drinker, had made a decision for Christ at the crusade and immediately broadcast the news of his reformation to his huge radio following. As a result of this and other celebrity conversions, the young Graham was on his way to becoming a celebrity himself. Mickey asked Vaus if he would introduce him to 'that guy who's converting all those famous folks.'

Through a series of circumstances, Mickey did meet Graham. Intrigued, the gangster agreed to hear the evangelist preach at a private meeting of a group of Hollywood people that included Stuart and Suzy Hamblen as well as western stars Roy Rogers and Dale Evans. Unsure of what to expect, Mickey didn't want his attendance publicised – an unusual desire on his part. So elaborate arrangements were made to get him to the meeting without an accompanying bevy of reporters.

First, the Hamblens drove Graham and his associate George Wilson to a designated street corner in the lower reaches of Hollywood. Billy remained in the car; George Wilson stepped out and waited on the sidewalk. A dark green

Cadillac, of the vintage when Cadillacs resembled the swan boats in an amusement park Tunnel of Love, rolled up to the kerb. The door opened and Wilson got in the back seat. There Mickey Cohen greeted him cordially.

Next, Cohen leaned forward and whispered in the driver's ear. The man got out, walked up to Hamblen's car and spoke with him. George could see them both gesturing, their voices low. Then Mickey's driver returned and repositioned himself behind the wheel. Suddenly both cars exploded into action, screeching away from the kerb and swinging on two wheels around the first hairpin turn. A group of reporters had got wind of Cohen's plans and the little man was determined to shake them.

Stuart Hamblen more than obliged, relishing the high-speed chase, deliberately choosing a route that sent both cars charging up and flying over steep hills and roaring down to bottom out on stomach-churning flats.

George Wilson, a man of determinedly even temperament, tried to keep his gaze on the road as the car careened through the Hollywood hills, but his eye was caught by a giant pastel Kleenex box on the back seat between himself and Cohen. Surely no gangster used pink tissues, he thought. He had seen machine guns in violin cases in the movies; perhaps underworld types in real life used Kleenex boxes for smaller weapons . . . like handguns. Inching away from the box, Wilson fixed his eyes on the dubious comfort of the flying landscape.

After fifteen minutes of creative aerial driving, the two cars finally lost the pack of reporters and arrived at the home of Holmy Hills, a producer. Mickey, who had noticed that the ride hadn't worried Graham's man – though Wilson did seem to have an aversion to Kleenex – determined to stick next to such a cool guy during the course of the meeting.

Fifty or sixty people crowded together on chairs and the floor to hear Billy Graham. After the tall young preacher finished his gospel message, J. Edwin Orr, another evangel-ist, got up to give an invitation. He also invited people who were simply interested in learning more about Christianity to raise their hands; he wanted to give them copies of the Gospel of John.

Mickey whispered to his new friend, George Wilson, that he would like a copy. George insisted that if Mickey wanted one he would have to raise his own hand. Impressed by what he had learned about Christianity that night, the gangster did so.

Jim Vaus's conversion led him to make restitution for the crimes he had committed. He had stolen $15,000 worth of electronic equipment from the telephone company and a local radio station. He sold his house and automobile in order to pay back the money. When a notice of his actions appeared in the paper, he received a call from Cohen.

'How you going to get around with no car, Jim?' Mickey asked.

'Well, the buses and streetcars are still running.'

'Sure, but lookit, let me loan you a car.'

'Thanks, Mickey, but no.'

'Why not?' his former boss asked.

'I'm working for a new boss now, Mickey. There are new rules. I can't take something that somebody got through crime.'

'But watcha gonna do? You're in a spot. I'm just trying to help you out as a friend.'

Vaus told Mickey not to worry about him, that God could supply all his needs. Then he went on to tell what had happened when the St Louis boys came to call. 'If the Lord can do that for me, Mickey, why should I worry about a little thing like money?'

'That's a fabulous come-off, I'll admit,' Cohen said slowly. 'But if you need me, you don't be stupid . . . you call.'

As it turned out, Mickey was the one needing help. The Alfred Pearson incident had piqued the federal government's interest in Mickey Cohen, and eventually he was indicted for tax evasion. While the criminal authorities couldn't put Mickey away, the IRS did a thorough job of proving he had spent far more than he had reported as income. In

1951 Cohen was convicted and sentenced to five years in jail.

While in prison, however, Mickey continued to operate, making sure through underworld connections that his obsession with cleanliness was taken into account. Mickey used tissues constantly as a buffer against dirt, dust, and almost the sensation of touch itself. He could not open a door until he had placed a tissue around the knob, nor answer the phone until he had wrapped the receiver in a tissue. In prison Mickey was allowed to shower three or four times a day and was given six rolls of toilet paper daily to use in place of his Kleenex.

When Mickey came out of prison in October of 1955, he no longer had his power in LA, nor the muscle to regain it. Yet he still yearned for the high life. He glumly concluded, 'If I couldn't live my life style, I might as well have been back in the joint.' But from then on the IRS kept track of every penny he spent.

Jim Vaus called Mickey shortly after his release and offered his help, including the loan of a car. Recalling Vaus's reply to the same offer a few years earlier, Mickey shot back, 'The buses and the streetcars are still running, aren't they?' But Mickey accepted the loan. Vaus also stocked Mickey's apartment with groceries and let him have the run of the office where Vaus now carried on a ministry to young people.

Before Mickey went to prison, Vaus had introduced him to a leading Christian layman in Los Angeles, W. C. Jones. Bill Jones was a small, impeccably groomed man with a high forehead, a straight nose, and eyes set to gaze into the distance. Rescued by Christ from addiction to alcohol and gambling, in the past Jones had placed innumerable bets with Mickey's operatives. He was well-qualified to talk with the gangster about Christ's ability to transform lives. Bill Jones took Mickey on as a special project after he came out of prison, devoting hours to cultivating their friendship.

Mickey seemed to be changing. At least he paid more attention to those who truly had his welfare at heart. Also, he had always been oddly charitable, raising money for the

Irgun Freedom Fighters in Israel, donating funds to hospitals, sending out Thanksgiving baskets. Now he appeared to see that personal acts of charity could not compensate for a life of crime. He went with his probation officer to speak at camps of delinquent boys about the tragic course they were pursuing.

Seeing this new current within Mickey, and after spending hours with him, Bill Jones urged him to commit his life to Christ. He explained God's plan of salvation, beginning by telling Mickey that God loved him and had a wonderful plan for his life.

Mickey thought that was great.

Then Jones told him that he was sinful, like all mankind, and separated from God.

Mickey had trouble with that one. For one thing, he was a Jew, and a Jew was one of God's chosen people. How could he be separated from the God of the Jews? Besides, he wasn't such a bad guy. 'I always strive for the best. Even with my limited education ... I always strive to do things in a professional way ... I mean I have my own principles about things. Like when I pulled off a heist, it was a bad reflection upon my own self if anybody just standing around got hurt. I worked clean, see ... Especially after my Cleveland and Chicago days, I was never a person who would take the life of anybody unless it was absolutely a must ... No one who knew ever said Mickey Cohen wasn't one of the finest.'

Jones said that wasn't quite the point. He moved on to explain about God's provision for man's sin in Jesus Christ and that Mickey had to individually receive Christ as his Saviour and Lord so that he might know and experience God's love and plan for his life. Bill quoted Revelation 3:20: 'Behold, I stand at the door and knock: if any man hear my voice, and open the door, I will come in to him.'

'That means you, too, Mickey,' Bill Jones said. 'You said that you're not the kind of people that Billy Graham or church folk generally like. But it's not up to them; it's up to Christ, and he says *anyone*.'

'So fine,' Mickey said. 'I'm glad to hear it.'

'But you've got to act on it, Mickey,' Jones said. 'This is called the penitent's prayer. If you'll repeat it after me, you can know right here and now that you will be reborn as a son of God. You will live in heaven forever. You've seen the high life, Mickey, but none of us have seen anything like heaven. So will you pray with me?'

To Bill's surprise and delight, Mickey repeated the prayer.

Had Mickey Cohen, famous Hollywood gangster, really become a Christian?

Bill Jones was convinced Mickey's decision was genuine. What a testimony! As the word spread through the Christian community, there was jubilant response. What a trophy! In a day when the evangelical church was seldom in the news, this was headline stuff.

But Jones also knew that Mickey was badly in need of further instruction about the Christian life. He called Jim Vaus and discussed the possibility of flying Mickey to New York to meet with Billy Graham, who was soon to begin a crusade in Madison Square Garden. Vaus agreed to help pay for Mickey's expenses in New York.

Within a few days Cohen had flown east and moved into the Waldorf-Astoria. Graham met with him and in a marathon session tried to explain the significance of what Mickey had done in his prayer with Bill Jones. Though Mickey was amiable, Graham sensed a wall of inner resistance that could not be scaled.

Nevertheless, Mickey showed up two days later at the Graham Crusade in the Garden, along with several bodyguards and a flock of reporters. Speculation was rife: Would Cohen go forward, making public his commitment?

Mickey tried to get backstage to be photographed with Graham. The evangelist, who spent the time just prior to preaching in prayer and meditation, wisely refused to allow the photographers near him. Mickey was then escorted to an area reserved for special guests.

No matter what Cohen's motives were for attending, he stayed, though obviously displeased with the lack of royal treatment. And he was thoroughly uncomfortable, for the

Spirit of God was at work; Graham's message seemed particularly appropriate for the disgruntled gangster with the giant box of Kleenex by his side.

'You and I deserve hell,' thundered Graham. 'You and I deserve to spend eternity separated from God . . . Oh, yes, the Scriptures teach that you're a sinner. And so am I . . .

'You may think you are a good and upright person and that you have done nothing worthy of damnation. You may say, I am honest in my business dealings; I love my kids; I give to the United Way. But there's no middle ground between heaven and hell. You are either on the road to one or the other . . .

'The Bible shows us the perfect example of a man who wanted to escape his responsibility for his own sinfulness before god – the Roman ruler, Pilate. After Jesus had been tried by the Sanhedrin, he was taken before Pilate. But Pilate was just like you and me; he wanted to remain neutral. He declared Christ innocent, then took a bowl of water and washed his hands in front of the whole multitude. "I am washing my hands of this just man," he said. Then he allowed Christ to be led away and crucified.

'Tradition tells us that Pilate spent the last years of his life up in the mountains of Switzerland, washing his hands constantly. When anyone asked him, "What are you doing?" he said, "I am trying to wash the blood stain of Jesus Christ off my hands." Through all eternity Pilate will try to wash the blood stain off, but he will never be able to do it.

'Tonight you have to make your choice. Every man, every woman, every boy and every girl, you will have to make your choice between pleasure and Christ, amusement and Christ, popularity and Christ, money and Christ. Whatever is keeping you from the kingdom of God, you will have to make a choice tonight, and if you refuse to make the choice, that very act means you have already made it.'

For one wild, impetuous, holy moment, Mickey Cohen wanted to take his giant box of Kleenex and fling it away forever. But in the next moment he found himself ripping several tissues out and dabbing at his forehead, his neck, his hands, and wanting to take it on the lam out of there. He endured the rest of the service for the vainglory of leading the reporters outside and having his picture taken under the marquee bearing Billy Graham's name.

After he returned to Los Angeles, Mickey dropped Bill Jones and contacted Jim Vaus less frequently. He began hanging around with his underworld cronies again. This perplexed and upset Jones, who went to Mickey and told him that as a new Christian he ought to be putting as much mileage between himself and his mob connections as possible.

'Jones,' Mickey replied, 'you never told me that I had to give up my career. You never told me that I had to give up my friends. There are Christian movie stars, Christian athletes, Christian businessmen. So what's the matter with being a Christian gangster?

'If I have to give up all that – if that's Christianity – count me out.'

9

Whatever Became of Sin?

Mickey Cohen quietly lived out his last years at his suburban Los Angeles home, dying of cancer on July 29, 1976. Mickey was alone when he stepped from this world. His wife had divorced him years earlier, there were no clamouring crowds of reporters, no dancing girls, no bodyguards. The overpublicised accounts of Mickey's exploits had faded from memory; even his public flirtation with Christianity became a minor story, buried in old newspaper microfilm.

Why Mickey was first drawn to Christianity we will probably never know. Maybe he saw it as a way to gain respectability he could never earn on his own. Maybe he saw a glint of hope – and real power. Whatever it was, the image of Jesus knocking at the door was as compelling to him as it has been to millions through the centuries; and he began to open that door, only to discover that doing so involved a choice. He must surrender himself or close the door. When he finally understood what was demanded of him, what repentance meant, he closed the door. Mickey Cohen could not repent.

Though Cohen's life reads like a movie script, the crucial point of this dramatic story is that, at heart, each one of us is exactly like Mickey Cohen – sinful and struggling with repentance.

Granted, he was flamboyant and neurotic, a gangland figure guilty of every crime in the book. Granted, his guilt made the headlines, his sins were public knowledge (some of us have experienced that, too, though).

But in voicing his comical, outrageous, poignant question 'What's the matter with being a Christian gangster?' Cohen was echoing the millions of professing Christians who, though unwilling to admit it, through their very lives pose the same question. Not about being Christian gangsters, but about being Christianised versions of whatever they already are – and are determined to remain. C. S. Lewis called these hybrids 'hyphenated Christians.'

And, like Mickey, we cannot love God – cannot obey Him – and remain what we are. We must repent.

For most of us, the word 'repentance' conjures up images of medieval monks in sackcloth and ashes or Old Testament prophets rending their garments in anguish. Or we see repentance as something someone 'really wicked' – like Mickey Cohen – must do to sanitise his corrupt life.

But repentance is much more than self-flagellation, more than regret, more than deep sorrow for past sins; and it applies to everyone. The Biblical word for repentance is 'metanoia' in the original Greek. *Meta* means 'change' and *noia* means 'mind', so literally it means 'a change of mind'. One church scholar describes it as 'that mighty change in mind, heart, and life, wrought by the spirit of God'.[1]

Thus, repentance is replete with radical implications, for a fundamental change of mind not only turns us from the sinful past, but transforms our life plan, values, ethics, and actions as we begin to see the world through God's eyes rather than ours. That kind of transformation requires the ultimate surrender of self.

The call to repentance – individual and corporate – is one of the most consistent themes of Scripture. The Old Testament contains vivid accounts of kings and prophets, priests and people falling before God to plead for mercy and promising to change. The demand for repentance is clear in God's commands to Moses,[2] and its broken-hearted reality and passion flows through David's eloquent prayer of contrition.[3] It is the consistent refrain of the prophets.[4]

Repentance is the keynote of the New Testament as well. It

is John the Baptist's single message: 'Repent, for the kingdom of heaven is near.'[5] And according to Mark's Gospel, 'Repent and believe the good news', were among Jesus' first public words.[6] And His last instructions to His disciples before the Ascension included the directive that 'repentance and forgiveness of sins will be preached in his name to all nations.'[7] All told, the words 'repent' or 'repentance' appear more than fifty times in the New Testament.

Repentance is an inescapable consequence of regeneration, an indispensable part of the conversion process that takes place under the convicting power of the Holy Spirit. But repentance is also a continuing state of mind. We are warned, for example, to repent before partaking of communion.[8] Also, believers 'prove their repentance by their deeds.'[9] Without a continuing repentant attitude – a persistent desire to turn away from our own nature and seek God's nature – Christian growth is impossible. Loving God is impossible.

If all this is true, then, some may ask, why is repentance so seldom preached and so little understood? I believe there are three reasons.

Noted church historian J. Edwin Orr sums up the first: *the appeal of modern evangelism is 'not for repentance but for enlistment.'*[10] To put it even more bluntly, some evangelists see converts as trophies in a big game hunt and measure their success by numbers; thus, they do not want to frighten off their prey.

One Christian leader, asked why he never mentioned repentance, smiled and replied, 'Get 'em first, let them see what Christianity is, and then they'll see their need to repent.' Tragically, this attitude pervades the church not only because we're afraid the truth will scare newcomers, but because it might also drive a number of the nodding regulars right out of their comfortable pews.

Repentance can be a threatening message – and rightly so. The Gospel must be the bad news of the conviction of sin before it can be the good news of redemption. Because that message is unpalatable for many middle-class congregations preoccupied with protecting their affluent lifestyles, many pastors endowed with a normal sense of self-preservation tiptoe warily round the subject. And the phenomenal growth of the electronic church has only aggravated this trend, for while the Sunday morning pew-dweller is trapped, unable to escape gracefully when a tough subject like repentance comes up, the TV viewer has only to flip a switch or go out to the refrigerator.

The result of all this is a watered-down message that, in large part, accounts for today's epidemic spread of easy believism, Christianity without cost, or 'cheap grace' as German martyr, Dietrich Bonhoeffer, so aptly labelled it a generation ago – grace in which 'no contrition is required, still less any real desire to be delivered from sin . . . a denial of the living word of God, in fact, a denial of the incarnation.'[11]

The second reason repentance is so ignored or misunderstood comes much closer to home, as I have discovered: *often we are simply unwilling or unable to accept the reality of personal sin and therefore to accept our need for repentance.*

We have no difficulty seeing Mickey Cohen's sin, but we would certainly never put ourselves in the same category with this old-style gangster. He probably broke most of the Ten Commandments (and we haven't?). Well, even if we aren't perfect, we're a lot better than Mickey Cohen. After all, nobody's perfect, and God understands we're only human. Most good professors grade on a curve; God probably does, too.

Why is it so hard for us to see our own sin? That it has always been this way is eloquently illustrated by King David.

Soon after he was enthroned, David committed not only the sin of adultery with Bathsheba, but also the sin of murder by having her husband sent to certain death in battle. Though he was described as a man after God's own heart and administered justice and righteousness, David was blind to his own sin. He could not see what he had done until the prophet Nathan, sent by God, described the sin in parable form, attributing it to someone else. Nathan asked David to judge the man, which David did: *death*. Only then did Nathan tell David that it was his own sin.[12] What he was quick to judge in others, David was unable to see in himself.

We are all like David, for in our fallen state we have an infinite capacity for justifying whatever acts we commit. Psychologists call this the 'self-serving bias' and confirm the truth of William Saroyan's comment, 'every man is a good man in a bad world – as he himself knows.'[13]

And this leads us to the third reason for our shallow understanding of repentance: *our culture has written sin out of existence*. Even Christians who should understand the basic truth that *all* are heirs of Adam's fall and thus *all* are sinners are influenced, often blinded, by humanist values.

Humanism began in the Garden when the tempter invited Eve to be 'like God'. Ever since it has encouraged us to believe what our sinful nature wants us to believe – that we are good, getting better through science and education, and can through our own efforts become perfect, masters of our own fate. We can be our own god.

In recent decades popular political and social beliefs have all but erased the reality of personal sin from our national consciousness. Take, for example, the passionately advanced argument that society, not the individual, is responsible for the evil in our midst: individuals commit crimes because they are forced to, not because they choose to. Poverty, racial oppression, slums, hunger – these are the real culprits; the wrong-doer is in reality the victim. President Lyndon Johnson's attorney general, Ramsey Clark, summed up that viewpoint, asserting that poverty *is* the cause of crime.[14] And President Jimmy Carter, after the power blackout and resulting widespread looting in New York, echoed, 'Obviously the number one contributing factor to crime . . . is high unemployment among young people, particularly those who are black or Spanish speaking.[15]*

---

* A study conducted a month later by New York City's Criminal Justice Agency, Inc. revealed that 45 per cent who were arrested looting had jobs and only 10 per cent were on welfare rolls. In most cases people stole things they did not need.

This desire to treat their fellow-man with compassion is commendable. But if carried to the extreme, this attitude destroys individual accountability and encourages the very behaviour that is so offensive.

No one political camp has a monopoly on perpetuating this myth. Ronald Reagan, accepting an award from the National Conference of Christians and Jews, repeatedly asserted his belief in the 'basic goodness' of man, winding up with a quote from Anne Frank's diary dated July 5, 1944: 'In spite of everything, I still believe that people are really good at heart.'[16] (What tragic irony!)

Richard Nixon was fond of quoting DeTocqueville: 'America is great because she is good and if America ever ceases to be good, America will cease to be great.'* (I confess that I, along with millions of others, got goose bumps whenever he used that quote.)

Politicians tell people what they want to hear, and people like to be told they are really 'good'. So speech lines like these are sure-fire applause-getters. But good politics can make bad theology; and when we begin to believe our own press releases, we become victims of our own delusions.

Whatever became of sin? Karl Menninger's startling book title and theme is the most timely question anyone could ask of the church today.

The answer lies within each of us, but to find it we must come face to face with who we really are. This is a difficult process. That hidden self is buried deep inside our hearts, and, as Jeremiah warned, the human heart is deceitful above all things.[17] Confronting that true self is an excruciating discovery, as I learned in prison after my conversion.

---

* This quote is often attributed to Alexis DeTocqueville even though the Library of Congress can find no record of it among his works.

10

It Is in Us

Most people make it through life without seeing their sins plastered across banner headlines. Their trangressions remain their own private property. At the most they are shared with a priest or minister, a close friend, or perhaps a prayer group. I have not had that luxury.

Having been at the centre of the biggest political upheaval of this century, I've had my sins – real and imagined – spread mercilessly across the front pages around the world, re-enacted in living colour on movie and TV screens, and dissected in hundreds of books. As a result, I am often asked which of my Watergate perfidies causes me the greatest remorse.

My invariable reply, 'None. My deepest remorse is for the hidden sins of my heart which are far worse,' either puzzles or infuriates the media.

But it is an honest answer. My Watergate wrongs could be explained (though not justified) as political zealotry or expedience, misplaced idealism, blind obedience to higher authority, or even capitulation to the natural temptation of the human will, which Nietzsche said seeks power over others above all else. The sins for which I feel the greatest contrition are those sins so perfectly illustrated by an episode from my life thirty years ago, etched in my consciousness as clearly as though it happened yesterday . . .

I was a brand-new Marine lieutenant, as proud and tough as basic training could make a man. My spit-shined shoes reflected the sun like two mirrors, matched in brilliance only by my polished gold bars.

In the midst of Caribbean manoeuvres, our battalion was landed on Vieques Island, a tiny satellite of Puerto Rico. Most of the mountainous little land was a Navy protectorate used for landing and target practice, but on one end a clan of poverty-stricken souls endured the ear-splitting shellings just to eke out a living selling beer and cold drinks to invading Marines.

Before landing, we officers were instructed to buy nothing from these pedlars who, though strictly forbidden to enter the military reservation, invariably did so. The order was given with a sly smile and wink because no one obeyed it.

The second day in the field, I was leading my platoon of forty grimy, sweating riflemen up and over a craggy ridge when just across the next ridge I spotted an old man leading a scrawny donkey nearly collapsing under the load of two huge, obviously ice-filled, canvas sacks.

The scorching midday July sun had us panting, and our canteens were getting low, so I immediately routed my men towards the distant figure. When the men saw the elderly man and his loaded beast, they picked up speed, knowing I would blink at orders and permit them to buy cans of cold drinks. I could hear several digging in their pockets for coins.

When we were but a few yards from the grinning old man, who was undoubtedly congratulating himself on his good fortune and counting up what might be several months' income, I ordered my troops to halt. 'Sergeant,' I commanded, 'take this man prisoner. He is trespassing on government property.' The platoon sergeant, a veteran of a dozen or more Vieques landings, stared at me in disbelief. 'Go ahead,' I barked. The sergeant shook his head, swung about, and, with rifle at the ready, marched toward the old man whose smile suddenly turned to stone.

I commanded my men to 'confiscate the contraband'. Cheering lustily, they did so. While the sergeant tossed cans of chilled fruit juice from the two bulging sacks, the old man squinted at me with doleful eyes. His sacks emptied, we released our 'prisoner'. Shoulders hunched, he rode away on his donkey, perhaps grateful we hadn't strapped him to a tree. (Small wonder that years later 'independence' movements in Puerto Rico agitated for removal of the US military!)

Technically, of course, I had observed military law. Yet I had not given a fleeting thought to the fact that those satchels of juice might have represented the old man's life savings or that my order could mean an entire family might go hungry for months. Rather, I was smugly satisfied, believing that my men were grateful to me for getting them something cold to drink (which they would have happily purchased) and that I had proven I was tough (though my adversary was defenceless). As for the old man, *well*, I thought, *he got what he deserved for violating government property*.

This incident, though quickly forgotten at the time, was vividly brought to my mind years later, after my conversion, as I sat in prison reading from Augustine's *Confessions* the well-known story of his youthful escapade stealing pears from a neighbour's tree. Augustine recorded that late one night a group of youngsters went out to 'shake down and rob this tree. We took great loads of fruit from it, not for our own eating but rather to throw it to the pigs.' He went on to berate himself for the depth of sin this revealed. 'The fruit I gathered I threw away, devouring in it only iniquity. There was no other reason, but foul was the evil and I loved it.'[1]

Contemporary critics, though generous in their praise of Augustine's literary genius and profound philosophical insights, mock him for his seeming obsession with the pear tree episode. Why would one harmless prank loom so large in the saint's mind? By his own admission he had taken a mistress, fathered a child out of wedlock, and indulged in every fleshly passion. Surely any of these were more serious than stealing pears.

But Augustine saw in the pear incident his true nature and the nature of all mankind: *in each of us there is sin* – not just susceptibility to sin, but *sin itself*. Augustine's love for sensual pleasure could be explained as the natural arousing of his human desires, proving inner weakness or susceptibility to sinning. But he had stolen those pears for the pure enjoyment of stealing (he had an abundance of better pears on his own trees). Augustine knew his act was more than weakness; it was sin itself – sin for the sake of sinning.

Alexander Solzhenitsyn discovered the truth of *this individual and universal human condition* following his remarkable encounter with Boris Kornfeld.

During his pain-wracked days and sleepless nights in the grim prison hospital following his cancer surgery, Solzhenitsyn reviewed the strange turns his life had taken. The words of Dr Kornfeld had reawakened in him a hunger for the God he had once known and renounced. Thus, even in his agony Solzhenitsyn could rejoice, for he was spiritually reborn. But Kornfeld's words also made him restless as he tossed about on his narrow cot. The remarkable statement, 'No punishment comes to us in this life which is undeserved', lingered in his mind.

It was an unsettling thought coming from a man who had been unjustly imprisoned and from a Jew, whose race had been mercilessly persecuted. The extraordinary words forced Solzhenitsyn to look back on his own life. And so it was that the then-unknown prisoner saw how he really was and could write, 'In the intoxication of youthful successes I had felt myself to be infallible and I was therefore cruel. In the surfeit of power I was a murderer and an oppressor. In my most evil moments I was convinced I was doing good.'[2]

A bright shaft of light shone into the recesses of his soul, and Solzhenitsyn came face to face with his true self – a sign of genuine conversion.

'And it was only when I lay there on rotting prison straw,' he continues, 'that I sensed within myself the *first* stirrings of good. Gradually it was disclosed to me that *the line separating good and evil passes not through states, nor between classes, nor between parties either – but right through every human heart – through all human hearts*.'[3]

In these few lines Solzhenitsyn captures a truth that has eluded humanity from the beginning. The world is not divided into white hats and black hats; it is not divided into good people and evil people. Rather, good and evil coexist in every human heart.

As I lay in prison and watched the events of my own life – such as the Vieques incident – parade before my eyes, I, too, became aware of this painful reality of the human heart and saw myself: I was a sinner and my sin manifested itself in individual acts of my own making. And worst of all, I had delighted in it.

'Sinner' is not some theological term contrived to explain away the presence of evil in this world; nor is it a cliché conceived by colonial hymn writers or backwoods preachers to frighten recalcitrant congregations.

R. C. Sproul sums it up well: 'We are not sinners because we sin; we sin because we are sinners.' We are not theoretical sinners or honorary sinners or vicarious sinners. We are sinners indeed and in deed.[4]

Man goes to great lengths to avoid his own responsibility. Many blame Satan for every imaginable evil – but Jesus states clearly that sin is in *us*.[5] Others recoil with horror at the sins of the society around them, smugly satisfied that sinful abominations are not of their doing – not realising that God holds *us* responsible for acts of omission as well as acts of commission. Still others believe, as did Socrates two thousand years ago, that sin is not man's moral responsibility, but is caused by ignorance. Hegel, whose philosophy so enormously influenced nineteenth and twentieth century thought, argued that man is 'evolving' through increasing knowledge to superior moral levels.

But what do we see around us in the last third of this twentieth century that has produced such advances in knowledge, technology, and science? Soaring crime rates. Countless shattered families. A globe scarred by continual wars and oppression. All our knowledge has not ushered in a brave new world. It has simply increased our ability to perpetrate evil. History continues to validate the biblical account that man is by his own nature sinful – indeed, imprisoned by his sin.

And we are not reluctant prisoners. Like Augustine, *we actually delight in sin and evil*. What else explains our secret delight in another's fall? What else accounts for our morbid fascination with violence on television or the bloody carnage of horror films? Alypius, Augustine's friend and student who shared his experience in the garden, learned this lesson well.

Alypius was addicted to his day's popular form of entertainment, the bloody gladiatorial games. Frightened by the grip these had on him, he vowed passionately to break his addiction. After avoiding the games successfully for some time, Alypius one day met several friends who, knowing his weakness, dragged him to the arena. Forced into the crowded coliseum, Alypius determined *he would not watch*. So he hunched in his stone seat, jammed among screaming, frenzied fans, his eyes screwed shut and his hands over his ears.

Suddenly, with a single voice, the crowd sent up the loudest blood-curdling cry of delight he had ever heard. Curiosity gripped him. He opened his eyes in time to see one of the fighters fall, covered with blood. He drank in the insane violence. 'And I fell more miserably than that gladiator,' he confided to Augustine later.

Though Alypius thought himself above the enjoyment of such bloodshed, his will was no match for the evil thrill it brought. He became 'drunk on blood and pleasure', and he was again one with his friends and the evil he abhorred.[6]

Who has not found himself at some point slyly boasting of his sins, as Augustine confessed, to earn the 'praise it brought'?[7] So pervasive is the sin in us that we are subject to lonely shame if we cannot share in the sins of our peers.

What causes a man like Alypius to cheer lustily as a gladiator's head is lopped off? Why, in our modern gladiatorial contests played out on a national and international scale, now called war, do we sense a certain spellbinding grandeur in the drama of armies moving across a field of battle?[8] Why do those who find war's allure the most irresistible often become national heroes?[9] (Remember the moment in the movie 'Patton' when the legendary general,

played by George C. Scott, looked over the field of battle from
a command vehicle with undisguised exaltation: 'Look,' he
said to his companion, 'could anything be more magnificent?
. . . I must tell the truth – I love it – God . . . I do love it!'[10])
And why does the same bloody thrill grip a movie theatre
audience when a demon-possessed child gouges out her
mother's eyes?*

What is it? Nothing less than the evil within us, the dark
side of the line that, Solzhenitsyn wrote, passes through each
human heart.

Indeed, that is where the real battle is being fought. It is
not between 'good' people and 'bad' people, like a game of
cops and robbers; it is not between 'good' governments and
'bad', like the US and the Soviet Union. It is not being fought
for mere national or international stakes. The war to end all
wars is a battle for eternal stakes between spiritual forces –
and it is being waged *in* you and *in* me.

When we truly smell the stench of sin within us, it drives us
helplessly and irresistibly to despair. *But God* has provided a

---

* There are those incurable optimists who argue that man visits his
inhumanity on others out of fear and a natural instinct for self-preservation.
They say he acts aggressively and violently out of fear that his fellow-man
will harm him if he does not act first. But consider this example of man's
cruel violence toward helpless animals from an account of the early years of
the great naturalist W. H. Hudson: 'The native manner of killing a cow or
bullock at that time was peculiarly painful . . . One of the two or three
mounted men engaged in the operation would throw his lasso over the
horns, and, galloping off, pull the rope taut; a second man would then drop
from his horse . . . and with two lightning-quick blows of his big knife sever
the tendons of both hind legs. Instantly the beast would go down on his
haunches, and the same man . . . thrust the long blade into its throat just
above the chest, driving it in to the hilt and working it round; then when it
was withdrawn a great torrent of blood would pour out from the tortured
beast, still standing on his fore-legs, bellowing all the time with agony. At
this point the slaughterer would often leap lightly onto its back, stick his
spurs in its sides, and, using the flat of his long knife as a whip, pretend to be
riding a race, yelling with fiendish glee. The bellowing would subside into
deep, awful, sob-like sounds and chokings; then the rider, seeing the animal
about to collapse, would fling himself nimbly off' (From *Far Away and Long
Ago*, E. P. Dutton and Co., 1924, pp. 41–42).

way for us to be freed from the evil within: it is through the door of repentance. When we truly comprehend our own nature, repentance is no dry doctrine, no frightening message, no morbid form of self-flagellation. It is, as the early church fathers said, a gift God grants which leads to life.[11] It is the key to the door of liberation, to the only real freedom we can ever know.

Because it does mean freedom, perhaps it is not surprising that people in prison seem to have an easier time understanding repentance than those on the outside. Prisoners are captives in every sense. They have had their most blatant sins exposed in the blinding light of the courtroom and they have been locked into the midst of every form of evil and depravity.

Thus, it is not surprising that I have found the most vivid illustration of repentance in the Bible beginning in a prison cell . . .

11

Remember Me

By the small square of light from the tiny, high window, the men could tell the sun had risen, but the glimmer barely penetrated the thick darkness of the stone cell where the three prisoners waited.

Since the first hint of dawn they had been standing, pacing, waiting, though each was chained to a guard. The room stank of urine, but it was not fastidiousness that kept them from sinking to the filthy floor. They simply could not sit; they were waiting to die.

The man called Barabbas leaned lightly against the outer wall under the window. While the other two paced and pulled at their chains, cursing the guards, Barabbas stood still, his head lifted as though listening to some far-off sound. He had not spoken to the other men, even when asked a direct question. But like the others, he was waiting.

Despite his resistance, the guards treated Barabbas with a kind of rough respect; he was an important prisoner, almost a celebrity, the leader of a small band of freedom fighters. The government officials hoped his death today would snuff out the tiresome rebellion.

David, the tall, young prisoner with a long and hungry face, had been watching the still, shadowed figure for some time. Now he gestured towards Barabbas and asked, 'What does he hear?'

The third prisoner, a middle-aged man with greying hair and a stoical expression, was called Jacob; he had been a minor lieutenant in Barabbas's insurrectionist band. His answer to David's questions was a shrug of heavy shoulders.

'He hears something,' David insisted, tugging nervously at his chain. 'Look at the way he's listening.'

'Maybe he thinks we're going to be rescued,' Jacob grunted with disdain. 'Maybe he's waiting for Jerusalem to wake up and come to our rescue – throw off the Romans for good and make him king.'

'But you were with him,' David said. 'You were in the same cause.'

'Sure' Jacob confirmed bitterly. 'I've always been a fighter. You start young, choose sides, and fight to the finish. And this is the finish. That's life.'

David's hunger-thin face tightened with suppressed emotions. 'You aren't afraid then?'

Jacob swore. 'Of course I'm afraid. Who wants to die? If you know a way out of here, tell me about it. But I've never had any illusions. We had our moments – now they have theirs.'

Distant sounds filtered into the silence that followed. David strained to hear. 'Sounds like a crowd out there.'

'Sure it's a crowd,' one of the guards said. 'City's packed. It's the Jews' Passover. They're waiting for the good show you're going to put on for them.'

But the sounds were more than ordinary street noises. A chant, muffled by the distance and stone walls, rumbled in the background.

'What are they saying?' David asked.

His guard laughed. 'They say, "Dear, generous, Pilate, please release those nice criminals you're about to crucify. They never meant any harm."' The other two guards joined his mocking laughter, a brief relief from their boring duty.

The chant, whatever it had been, died out. The three men stood, locked together in silent, separate agony. David, like the others, had had his moment before Pilate, had heard the verdict 'guilty' and the sentence 'death by crucifixion'. But it takes time for such words to sink in. Now, the mockery of the guards roused a scream of denial within him. *I can't die. I don't deserve to die. This is unfair. There must be a way out. I've always got away before. There must be a way to escape.*

The guards filled the silence with talk about their families, their bad luck in drawing this duty. To David, their words were like the buzzing of the countless flies the sun had awakened.

'Do you regret anything,' he asked Jacob. He couldn't stand his own silence and sought the consolation of shared fear.

'Yeah, getting caught.'

'No, I mean . . . are you sorry –'

'For what?'

'Well . . . that you didn't lead a more normal life . . . that, well, you've murdered and stolen. Do you regret that – or just getting caught?'

'What about you?' Jacob snapped, refusing the question. 'You did the same.'

'I never killed anyone!' David cried. 'And I only stole what I needed to live. Look at me!' He jerked open his ragged clothing to expose his protruding ribs. 'A man has to eat.'

'Not when he's dead,' Jacob laughed bitterly. 'What are you, a slave?'

'I was. But never again.'

'Sure. I know the story. Your master was cruel. You ran away. Where from?'

'Cyprus.'

'Cyprus, huh. So you lied and got on a ship – bought your passage with money stolen from your master. Right? And somehow got here, half alive. Let me guess the rest. You were begging for food when one of the gangs offered you a living. All you had to do was work as a lookout, warn them when the soldiers were near, carry some messages through the city. No harm in it. Not when you're starving to death. Which gang was it? I know them all.'

David did not answer, stunned by the accuracy of the man's words. Before Jacob could continue, they heard the sound of the outer gate opening and footsteps approaching. The guards' voices came clearly through the small grating of the wooden door.

'Did you know they have that fellow Jesus?' one asked.

'The rabbi?'

'Whatever they call him. They arrested him last night. One of his own men turned him in.'

'What are they doing with him?'

'The Jews want him crucified. Can you believe it? He's the wrong kind of Jew apparently. They've been shouting it out there in the streets for hours. Couldn't you hear them? "Crucify him! Crucify him!"'

'So what does Pilate say?'

'He doesn't know what to say. I think this guy has Pilate scared. I was in the hall when they questioned him. This Jesus talked as though Pilate was on trial. No pleading . . . nothing. I've never seen anyone face Pilate like that. I swear Pilate was spooked.'

'What are they charging him with?'

'They say he claims to be the king of the Jews.'

'King of the Jews? Who cares?'

The door opened and two soldiers looked into the cell, trying to adjust to the darkness. 'Which one's Barabbas?'

Barabbas did not move, gave no indication he had heard his name. His guard rattled the chain between them and laughed. 'Here he is. He's waiting to be rescued.'

'Well, here we are,' one said as they strode over and began unlocking the chain. 'We're the rescue party. We'll send you safely to another world.'

'Do you want to be king, too, Barabbas?' the other laughed. 'Here's your crown.' He placed the palm of his hand on the prisoner's forehead and slammed his head against the wall. 'Hail to the king!'

David listened to their steps as they pulled Barabbas through the room beyond and out to the courtyard. Almost immediately he heard the whip. At each crack, David flinched.

'Pray they give you a lot, boy,' Jacob said quietly. 'Pray they whip you half to death. You go quicker on the cross that way.'

At the twelfth crack Barabbas' grunts became an unearthly cry, a sob, a scream. They took him up to twenty, then the whip hissed no more.

Heavy footsteps crossed the room outside, the door opened, and Barabbas was dumped face down on the floor. In the light from the doorway David could see that the man's back was raw, bloody meat.

They were unchaining Jacob when he took a sudden kick at one of the soldiers, catching him in the groin. The man doubled over, clutching himself, and the other soldier reflexively hit Jacob across the side of the head with the flat of his sword and sent him spinning to the floor. Cursing, the soldiers dragged Jacob to his feet and held him while their injured companion planted a knee into Jacob's groin once, twice, three times. Then they dragged him out. As the whip cracked, Jacob began screaming.

When the fog cleared from David's head after his turn under the lash, his face was in the foul dirt floor, his nostrils filled with it, his teeth gritty. His thoughts came at him in slow motion, framed in a hazy light. He couldn't remember where he was at first. Somewhere in the distance he could hear a crowd calling, 'Barabbas . . . Barabbas . . .' Why were they calling that name? Raising his head from the floor he came back to his surroundings. Jacob and Barabbas were still there. All the soldiers were gone.

'Why are they calling your name?' David asked Barabbas, his voice thick in his throat.

'I don't know.' It was the first David had heard the man speak.

What was it they had chanted earlier? 'Crucify him! Crucify him!' Calling for the death of the man named Jesus, the soldiers had said. David knew a little about the one called Jesus of Nazareth. He had seen the man enter the city last week surrounded by a crowd of followers. Everyone had been talking about him then. Some said he could heal diseases, do magical things. David had even heard rumblings that he was Messiah, the leader many Jews had been waiting for to rescue them from the tyranny of Rome.

Suddenly David felt as though he were up in the sky looking down at his cell and the world outside. From this vantage point he saw his own life clearly as it fit in with all the others. His life, so precious, so special to him was repeated a million times over. His desperate hopes, his desire to be free, were as common as cooking pots. *Everyone has dreams* he thought. *Everyone seizes on any hope, no matter how flimsy.* And slowly the heavy weight of life squeezed those hopes dry. Crushed, people cried for the blood of whoever dared to make them hope. The bigger the dream, the fiercer the anger. That was why the guards had singled out Barabbas for their mockery; he had made people hope. *The man called Jesus must be getting it even worse*, David thought.

The door opened and the soldiers entered again, the ones who had dealt with Barabbas. 'This is your lucky day, Barabbas. You've been pardoned.'

The prisoner sat still, did not acknowledge their presence.

One cuffed him on the side of the head. 'C'mon, wake up. Did you hear me? You're off the hook. Get up.'

Still Barabbas did not move. 'You cannot tempt me to hope,' he said without feeling. 'I am ready to die. Play your torture games with someone else.'

The soldier laughed and poked him in the back with the hilt of his sword. Involuntarily Barabbas opened his mouth to scream, though no sound came. 'Get up. You're free. They always release one prisoner on this day of Passover. You're it this year. The people asked for you. Pilate offered them you or Jesus – they chose you. You're a free man.'

Meanwhile, other guards were removing the chains from David and Jacob. For a second David thought he, too, had been freed. His heart began beating wildly as the shackles dropped from his wrists. Then he was jerked to his feet and hustled out the door, a guard on each arm. Glancing back in terror, he caught a last glimpse of Barabbas in the dark cell, still crouched on the floor.

Then, blinded by the sudden sunlight, David cried out as a heavy wooden beam was thrust onto his raw shoulders.

Hands seized his hands and forced them to grip the rough wood. A heavy palm slapped his face. 'This is your cross, slave. Let's go.'

When David's eyes grew accustomed to the light, he saw that they were surrounded by a pressing, jostling crowd whose attention was concentrated on another prisoner. Jeering, spitting, shaking their fists, they cursed a man gruesomely beaten. A wreath of wicked thorn branches was embedded into his skull, his head and hair caked with blood from the long, sharp spikes. Dark smudges of blood sponged through the garment stuck to his back.

The man turned his head toward David, and for a moment they stared into each other's eyes. David had never seen such a look – quiet, strong – a look of profound peace in the midst of their shared horror.

David realised he had seen the man before. *That's the man Jesus.* His body seemed shrunken, his shoulders weighted by pain, but his face was marked with quiet, absolute authority. Even now David could see why people had followed this man, why they thought he could save them. He had a presence. *Why is this man being executed?* David wondered. *He has done nothing wrong.*

A guard pushed Jesus into motion, and the condemned men began to stumble forward under their crosses, lurching towards their execution.

To the citizens of Jerusalem the crucifixion of thieves and murderers and insurrectionists was rather commonplace. Today, however, the presence of the man called Jesus added a different note, seemed to bring out more venom from the curious and the idle. Hostile faces jammed every space along the route through the narrow city streets, at the gates in the city wall, and along the dusty road leading to the place of execution, a hill called Golgotha. They all seemed concentrated on Jesus – jeering, spitting.

Jesus was ahead of David, weaving slowly under the weight of the wooden burden, stumbling often. Finally the soldiers, impatient to get on with it, grabbed a startled bystander and made him carry the crossbeam for the Nazarene.

I am really taking my last steps, David thought as the procession paused briefly. *These faces are the last I will ever see. This street is the last I will ever walk. My life is over.* Regret and disbelief piled up and spilled over into his entire being. *No. I cannot die. I don't want to die. I have done nothing wrong. Nothing worse than you who stare at me. You would have done the same in my place. Maybe worse. I don't want to die.*

A row of thick poles rose before them now as they left the city walls behind.

'Put your crosspiece down,' a soldier ordered.

In terror David surveyed the crowd that had followed them from the city. It was a strange sampling of society: soldiers, curiosity seekers, officials of the Jewish temple, and an odd little cluster of frightened-looking men and women standing off to one side.

A soldier offered him a cup.

'What is it?' David asked.

'Wine and myrrh. It dulls the pain.'

David gulped greedily until the vessel was pulled away and thrust at Jesus, who tasted it and then refused to drink. Jacob drained the remaining liquid.

The soldiers tugged at David's ragged clothing. When he clutched the cloth, without thinking, his hands were pushed away. 'You have to strip, slave.' In a second he was naked. Nearby, two soldiers were pulling on the ends of the garment they had just taken from Jesus, arguing over it. The commanding officer slapped one of them in the face. 'Let go, you fool. You'll tear it. We'll divide things later.'

The command came, 'Lie down,' and hands pushed David to the ground, his shoulders pressed against the rough beam he had carried. 'Spread your arms.' His right arm was stretched out to full reach and held down. He closed his eyes and felt a sharp prick on his palm. At the same instant he heard a terrible long-drawn scream, and before he had time to wonder whose voice it was, his had joined it as his hand became a fire, pinned to the plank. The soldiers were shouting at him not to move, cursing him; then they had his other hand and that, too, exploded in fire. He filled his lungs with air and screamed.

Now the hands were lifting him up, supporting his legs and lifting his buttocks to rest on a block of wood nailed halfway up the post. They were fastening the crosspiece to the pole with rope. Someone had his feet now, pushing them up so they were bent to the side. Another sharp tip touched his heel – and he was screaming again even before the pain began. With a terrible thud a nail shot through one heel bone and into the other. Hands pressed the fire hard against the post and another hammer blow fastened his feet into place. He emptied his stomach and passed out.

David had too much life in him to stay unconscious for long. The pain that had mercifully sent him into oblivion now cruelly brought him back to consciousness. The fire had spread from his hands and feet throughout his whole body. No description could do justice to such agony.

Yet he could see and hear – and think.

A small crowd was scattered around the crosses. Some, perhaps sickened or fearful, watched from a distance. Others stood close as though to see clearly the expressions on the dying faces. David could hear as they talked among themselves. A few days ago he was mingling with them. Now an invisible curtain closed him from them. *Why don't they help me?* he cried. *Why don't they at least meet my eyes? Why don't they care?*

The pain beyond words was equalled only by his terror of the death he faced and the dying that separated him from every human kindness. Even if he cried out, those people would not hear him. *Oh, God, let me off this cross. Get me out of here. Please.*

They were jeering at Jesus now. The high priest of the Temple, of all people, had started a mocking outcry – 'Come down from your cross, king. You saved others; now save yourself.'

David looked over at the Nazarene. Only a few feet

separated them. Jesus' eyes were staring straight ahead.
Again the thought struck: *This man had done nothing wrong. Why
is he here?*

A muscle spasm moved David's hand, tore the wound, and
the pain stopped all thoughts. He writhed and choked. When
the haze cleared for a moment, he looked at Jesus again,
drawn by the strength in that compelling face. *What has this
man ever done?* But immediately his pain tore him away. *Oh,
God, get me out of this*, he cried.

The religious leaders stood in a small huddle a few yards
from the crosses, talking together, occasionally making loud
comments. Now one of them walked to within a few feet of
Jesus' cross and stood staring up at him.

'Come down, Jesus,' he said. 'Why stay up there and
suffer? You are the son of God, aren't you? Well, then, why
not come down?' Some of the soldiers laughed at the jest.
The priest had probably never spoken to a Roman before,
especially not a soldier. Now he did. 'Isn't that typical. He
saved others, but he can't save himself. He's the king of
Israel. So he says! Let him come down from the cross and we
will believe in him. He trusts in God. Let God rescue him
now if he wants him. He says he is the son of God. Would God
forget his son? Ha!'

David caught at the words, 'He says he is the son of God.'
Did Jesus really say that? He remembered hearing it from
someone. The son of God? Dying? Here? Even Barabbas,
with all his big ideas, never claimed to be the son of
God.

He moved his head to look at Jesus again. The movement
caused excruciating pain: blood slammed through his head
and the pressure he applied to his feet to hold his balance
caused the nail to tear higher into his flesh.

This time Jesus' eyes looked into his. What made his face
so inviting? David had never before seen innocence com-
bined with wisdom. Usually a man was wise from bad
experience and therefore hardly innocent – or innocent but
foolish and therefore not wise. David turned his eyes away;
he could not look at this good man.

That face called up things David did not want to remember. He was a child again with his master's children, playing with them, almost as equals. Until the day his best friend Servius, the master's eldest son, had been separated from him. A teacher had come to instruct Servius, but slaves did not get educated. David had hardened with anger, bitterness, and hatred at losing his friend and being treated as a slave. When Servius had tried, afterward, to make up to him, David had refused to speak to him as a friend. From that moment on he had kept the cautious, distant, polite speech and angry spirit of a slave. On that day his desire to be free had been born.

He had always been proud of that day – looked upon it as the beginning of his manhood. Now, suddenly, looking into the calm, loving face beside him, that bitterness seemed ugly. On that day years ago Servius had become a master and he had hated him for that. Servius had learned to read and he, David, had learned to hate – even his best friend.

There is so much in my life to be ashamed of, he thought, then immediately rejected that thought. *No! No! I have done no wrong, unless it is wrong to want to be free. I do not deserve to die.*

Though it cost him great pain, he moved his head to look at Jesus again. *He said he is the son of God. Why doesn't he say something to those mockers now? Curse them? Why not leave their consciences – if they have any – with his curses. Curse those who curse you.* But the face he looked into was not printed with anger or hatred. The lips moved. David could hear him – he was asking God to forgive them!

David suddenly felt guilty, unclean, naked. *I am ashamed of my life, of the hatred in me,* he thought. Not because he hung there beaten, stripped, and condemned for all to see, but because he felt exposed before some power much greater than any of these who had the power to kill him. Something more painful than the fire consuming his body began to burn within his soul.

The soldiers had taken up the jeering theme of the priests.

Bored, waiting out their duty, they were amused by the thought of a Jewish king. One of them bowed repeatedly before the centre cross. 'If you are the king, save yourself.'

'And save us!' The angry, desperate sound came not from the lazy, teasing soldiers. It was Jacob's voice. 'Aren't you the Christ? Save yourself and us.'

The soldiers had flogged Jacob without mercy; they had given him what he wanted. Now he hung limp, nearer death than the other two. But anger dies last. If Jesus would not go out cursing, Jacob would. Now he turned his anger on one as helpless as he.

Jacob's snarling touched a nerve in David. This man with the quiet face was innocent. How could Jacob – how could he, himself – begin to compare himself with Jesus? They were guilty. This man . . . David burst forth at Jacob, his lungs heaving, his voice choked, 'Aren't you afraid of God? Since you are under the same sentence? You and I deserve our punishment. We earned our death. But this man has done nothing wrong.' The words hung in the air. The effort of speaking was agony, but Jacob's mocking cry had turned the last resisting bolt in David's soul. *This man must be the king he says he is.* And though he could barely gather strength or breath, David whispered what his heart was crying, 'Jesus, remember me . . . remember me when you come into your kingdom.'

And as though he had been waiting for that very plea, Jesus replied, 'I tell you the truth, today you will be with me in paradise.'

I am dying, David thought as the air grew black, but as he tried to focus he realised the darkness was not in his eyes. The sky was growing darker and darker, as though the air was filled with a thick, heavy dust. The sun disappeared. The crowd had become silent – even the soldiers.

It took concentration to suffer his death, to even draw a breath. Spasms of pain tore at David's wounds. But even as the very atmosphere reflected his nightmare of pain, he thought about the last words he had spoken to Jesus and of the promise received in return. He had felt compelled to cry out, believing that somehow Jesus could save him.

Yet how could Jesus save him? Clearly Jesus was dying, too. He was not escaping the cross. Yet he had promised, 'Today you will be with me in paradise.' *His kingdom must be of another world*, the type of world David had ceased to hope for long ago. And if that were true, how could he serve this king? He had nothing left but dying.

The darkness grew deeper, the human figures shadowy. Jesus twitched in the spasm leading to death. He made no cry, but spoke a few words to a woman standing beneath him, weeping, and the man she clung to, apparently one of his followers. Then he cried out words David could not understand. The soldiers ran to place a sponge to his lips. Then another loud cry: 'Father, into your hands I commit my spirit!' And he slumped limp against his impaling bonds. The darkness became thicker ... the ground shook ... the crowd fled ...

David was alone. Utterly alone. Jesus was dead. All he had to hold onto in this endless dying was a promise that he was going to the same place Jesus had gone. But now he knew how to die. He had heard Jesus' last words.

Sounds filtered to him – soldiers talking. The priests wanted the bodies down by sunset. They were asking the soldiers to break the legs so the men would die immediately. Hearing the brutal discussion going on before him, David thought again how cruelly men treat each other. But then came a new thought: *If I was in their position, I'd be doing the same thing.* There was only one person he could not picture acting out that brutality – and he was the son of God.

Barely able to see now, David watched the hazy form of a soldier take a large iron axe and walk to Jacob's cross. With a powerful blow he hit the man's shin with the flat side. Jacob did not scream, just wriggled like a dying creature. The axe fell on the other leg.

The soldier surveyed his work, seemed satisfied, turned and walked toward David.

David looked full into the soldier's face just below him. As the axe lifted, he closed his eyes and whispered, 'Jesus, into your hands I commit my spirit.'

12

We Were There

Golgotha – what a grim set on which to play out the crucial act in the drama of redemption. Golgotha – from the Aramaic meaning 'skull' and the Hebrew implying 'a skull-like mound' – was well-named in light of the bloody business conducted there. The rocky hilltop was chosen as an execution site because of its location near the heavily travelled highway outside the walls of Jerusalem. This assured that people passing by would witness the terrible spectacle of crucifixion, for the authorities believed (even as many so vainly believe today) that public violence would discourage individual violence.

There was a large supporting cast playing out that pivotal day of history, all manner of humanity: the spectators, the scoffers, the soldiers, the mourners. But the central drama of Golgotha was played out upon the crosses themselves.

'Are you not the Christ? Save yourself and us,' cried the one I have called Jacob, angry to the end. He might even have believed that the limp figure beside him was the son of God. But so what? If He couldn't save Himself, He certainly couldn't save anyone else.

The other thief, the one I call David, convicted by the Holy Spirit, realised that he deserved to die. Like Boris Kornfeld, David understood that no matter what he had done or not done, no matter what the circumstances, 'no punishment comes to us in this life on earth which is undeserved'.

And therein lies the crucial distinction between the two thieves. It had nothing to do with their crimes, their moral values, the relative goodness or badness of their lives. In fact Scripture suggests the irrelevance of these criteria by the stark lack of detail describing their lives. The distinction was that David recognised his own sin. His reply to Jacob, 'We are punished justly, for we are getting what our deeds deserve. But this man has done nothing wrong,'[1] is one of the purest expressions of repentance in all Scripture. And his words 'Remember me', are the classic statement of faith. With such simplicity and power this man repented and believed and died trusting in Christ.

How absurd David's words, 'we are getting what we deserve', must have sounded to Jacob. Deserve? Deserve death? For doing what everyone else did in one way or another? He was no worse or better than anybody else, including the ghouls watching him die.

As I consider this scene, I am reminded of the haunting old spiritual, 'Were you there when they crucified my Lord?' I have always understood this refrain in the classic theological sense that we were all there – we were all guilty of putting Jesus to death because of our fallen nature and our need of the atonement His death made. But as I began looking more closely at the crucifixion scene itself and the responses of the two thieves, I did feel cause to 'tremble, tremble, tremble'. For those two men who actually died alongside my Saviour are representative of all mankind. We either recognise our sinful selves, our sentence of death, and our deserving of that sentence, which leads us to repent and believe – or we curse God and die.

But Jacob provides another illustration of the sin that is within us. For if there is anything worse than our sin, it is our infinite capacity to rationalise it away. The Bible tells us this is a fearsome thing. During the period of the divided kingdom, Ahab, described as the most corrupt in a long line of corrupt leaders, became king of Israel. And he 'considered it trivial to commit the sins' of his predecessors.[2] This man who angered God more than all the evil kings considered his sins *trivial*.

Ahab was not unique. So powerful is the human tendency

to trivialise sin that only the Holy Spirit can open our eyes. As John and other writers of Scripture point out, the Spirit must convict us of our sinful nature.[3] I remember this vividly from my own conversion.

I wasn't sure what caused me to visit my old friend Tom Phillips that August night in 1973. I had been impressed by what he told me about his conversion to Christ and by his demeanour; I wished I had what he did. So I suppose I was seeking spiritual answers, but not for any escape from my sin. For despite the daily bombardment of Watergate charges, I saw nothing particularly wrong with myself. I knew what I had done was at least no different from what everyone else had done. Right and wrong were not determined by absolute standards but were relative to people and situations. People in politics played dirty; it was all part of the game.

But that night when I left my friend and sat alone in my car, my own sin – not just Watergate, but the evil deep within – was thrust before me by the conviction of the Holy Spirit, forcefully and painfully. For the first time in my life I felt unclean. Yet I could not turn away. I was as helpless as the thief nailed to that cross, and what I saw within me was so ugly I could do nothing but cry out to God for help.

Without the conviction of the Holy Spirit and the repentance that must follow, there is no way out of our predicament. We have the capacity to change anything about our lives – jobs, homes, cars, even spouses – but we cannot change our own sinful nature.

An episode involving one of Prison Fellowship's seminar instructors, Randy Nabors, illustrates just how true this is.

Randy was conducting an in-prison seminar in a sprawling southern penitentiary. Located in a remote rural area, the prison provided a handsome Victorian guesthouse for those staying overnight on official business. Late one evening when Randy was in his room engrossed in his notes for the next day's lecture, a state-employed psychiatrist, at the prison for one of his routine visits, knocked at his door.

Soon the frustrated doctor was describing his day's cases. 'I'll tell you, Reverend, I can cure somebody's madness, but

I can't do anything about his badness,' he moaned after describing an especially difficult encounter. 'Psychiatry, properly administered, can turn a schizophrenic bank robber into a mentally healthy bank robber; a good teacher can turn an illiterate criminal into an educated criminal. But they are still bank robbers and criminals!'

The doctor seemed near the point of despair. The sultry July evening conspired to add to his discomfort. Pulling a chair next to Randy and wiping his brow with an already soggy handkerchief, the psychiatrist recounted a session that day with a man who, while high on angel dust, had murdered his own child.

'He tells me he's depressed,' the doctor was almost shouting. 'Of course he's depressed! Who wouldn't be? But if I had done that, I hope I'd have more courage and do the only honourable thing – kill myself, too.' He quickly put his hand up, palm outstretched, and added, 'Wait a minute. Of course I didn't tell my patient that.' Then he settled back into his chair with a long sigh.

As Randy Nabors witnessed to the doctor that night, the man admitted that there must be an answer to the dilemma of evil within, because he had seen lives changed among the Christian inmates. But, he added sadly, he had not experienced it himself.

Weary and frustrated prison psychiatrists are not the only ones who cry out in despair over the human condition. Years after his personal encounter with Christ, the apostle Paul posed the eternal question: 'What a wretched man I am! Who will rescue me from this body of death?'[4] He saw that moral precepts could not free him; in fact, paradoxically, they made matters worse while convicting him. 'I would not have known what it was to covet if the law had not said, "Do not covet". But sin, seizing the opportunity afforded by the commandment, produced in me every kind of covetous desire.'[5]

What a desperate plight. Trapped in and by our own sin. Thankfully, there is an answer to the wrenching dilemma. Paul described it in the next chapter of his letter to the

Romans: 'There is now no condemnation for those who are in Christ Jesus . . . For what the law was powerless to do in that it was weakened by the sinful nature, God did by sending his own Son . . . to be a sin offering.'[6] That took place that momentous day on Golgotha nearly 2,000 years ago.

And how is all this part of loving God? Well, when we see the reality of our sin, when we come face to face with it and look into the raging fires of hell itself, and when we then repent and believe and are delivered from that plight, our entire being is filled with unspeakable gratitude to the God who sent His Son to that cross for us.

We must express that gratitude. But how? Simply stated: by living the way He commands. By obedience. That is what the Scriptures mean by holiness or sanctification – believers are set apart for holy living. Therefore, holiness is the only possible response to God's grace. Holy living is loving God.

However, as I began to learn not long after my conversion, and as everyone who has tried to live a holy life knows, holiness is the toughest, most demanding, vocation in the world.

THE HUNGER FOR HOLINESS

Our progress in holiness depends on God and ourselves – on God's grace and on our will to be holy.

Mother Teresa

13
Be Holy Because I Am Holy

The Anacostia section of Washington, DC sits on a bluff overlooking the capital city. Just across the river from the imposing Capitol itself, Anacostia – a ghetto of hunger, crime, drugs, and hopelessness – might as well be a continent away. None of Washington's celebrities and power brokers, nor the reporters who track them, cross that natural divide.

However, one balmy June morning in 1981 proved the exception. Black limousines and television camera trucks lined the kerb in front of the old red brick Assumption Catholic Church in the heart of Anacostia.

Soon after the cameras and reporters were in place, a small group of nuns and priests arrived, clustered about a wisp of a woman in a white muslin sari. The tiny figure moved with unusual grace up the steps of the church, waving at a cluster of children nearby and brushing past the reporters crowding the doorway.

This celebrity who somehow managed to understate her own arrival, an attitude unheard of in a city that thrives on pomp and protocol, was a seventy-year-old Albanian nun named Teresa Bojaxhiu – better known as Mother Teresa. As 1979 Nobel Prize winner and a world-famous figure, she could have commanded an airport welcome by a host of government bigwigs, addressed a joint session of Congress, or attracted thousands at one of the city's great cathedrals. Instead, she went as inconspicuously as possible to a troubled and neglected corner of the city to establish an outpost for nine of her Sisters of Charity.

Since Mother Teresa wouldn't come to them, the power

brokers had come to her. The mayor and city officials trailed the press into the stark church hall with its chipped and cracked plaster walls. The press, which cultivates its irreverence for politicians, were more restrained with this little woman from the streets of Calcutta. Still, she had to dodge the boom mikes coming at her like spears.

'What do you hope to accomplish here?' someone shouted.

'The joy of loving and being loved,' she smiled, her eyes sparkling in the face of camera lights.

'That takes a lot of money doesn't it?' another reporter threw out the obvious question. Everything in Washington costs money; and the more it costs, the more important it is.

Mother Teresa shook her head. 'No, it takes a lot of sacrifice.'[1]

The press was bewildered. Everyone who comes to Washington has grand plans, usually involving the creation of agencies with armies of bureaucrats. That's what the city is for: setting agendas, passing laws, organising departments – and trumpeting it all to the press. But this woman with her leathery, wrinkled face talked about 'sharing suffering' and 'caring that people can live and die with dignity'.

No grandiose scheme, her message: Do something for someone else ... for the sick, unwanted, crippled, heart-broken, aged, or alone. Strange words indeed for Washington's sophisticated commentators who left the conference shaking their heads.

Like them, the world cannot understand the source of Mother Teresa's power. Though her words sound naive, something extraordinary happens wherever she goes. For *what* Mother Teresa does, whether in Washington or Calcutta, is what the Bible calls 'religion ... pure and faultless'.[2] But *why* she does it is our point here.

A few years ago a brother in the order came to her complaining about a superior whose rules, he felt, were interfering with his ministry. 'My vocation is to work for lepers,' he told Mother Teresa. 'I want to spend myself for the lepers.'

She stared at him a moment, then smiled. 'Brother,' she

said gently, 'your vocation is not to work for lepers, your vocation is to belong to Jesus.'[3]

Mother Teresa is not in love with a cause, noble as her cause is. Rather, she loves God and is dedicated to living His life, not her own, This is holiness. It is the complete surrender of self in obedience to the will and service of God. Or as Mother Teresa sums it up, complete 'acceptance of the will of God'.[4]

Mother Teresa's definition may sound rather nebulous to many Christians who have from childhood associated holiness with a long string of do's and don'ts. But seeing holiness only as rule-keeping breeds serious problems: first, it limits the scope of true biblical holiness, which must affect every aspect of our lives. Second, even though the rules may be biblically based, we often end up obeying the rules rather than obeying God; concern with the letter of the law can cause us to lose its spirit.[5] Third, emphasis on rule-keeping deludes us into thinking *we* can be holy through our efforts. But there can be no holiness apart from the work of the Holy Spirit – in quickening us through the conviction of sin and bringing us by grace to Christ, and in sanctifying us – for it is grace that causes us to even *want* to be holy. And finally, our pious efforts can become ego-gratifying, as if holy living were some kind of spiritual beauty contest. Such self-centred spirituality in turn leads to self-righteousness – the very opposite of the selflessness of true holiness.

No, holiness is much more than a set of rules against sin. Holiness must be seen as the opposite of sin. Sin, as the Westminster Confession defines it, is 'any want of conformity to, or transgression of, the law of God'. Holiness, then, is the opposite: 'conformity to the character of God and obedience to the will of God'[6] (precisely Mother Teresa's point to the recalcitrant brother). Conforming to the character of God – separating ourselves from sin and cleaving to Him – is the *essence* of biblical holiness, and it is the foundational covenant, a central theme running throughout Scripture.

The earliest call to holiness came soon after Moses had led Israel out of Egypt and through the parted waters of the Red

Sea. Safe at last from the Egyptian army, this unruly horde of humanity – 600,000 men accompanied by women and children – camped at the foot of Mount Sinai. There, God called Moses to the mountaintop and instructed him in the laws by which His chosen people were now to live. These laws ranged from the all-encompassing Ten Commandments (the first four of which demand unconditional, reverent worship of a holy God) to such detailed ordinances as the means of restitution for stolen animals.[7]

When the Israelites accepted God's covenant with the words, 'Everything the Lord has said we will do . . . we will obey,'[8] God again called Moses to the mountaintop where He made one of the most remarkable promises in the Bible: 'I will consecrate the Tent of Meeting and the altar and . . . I will dwell among the Israelites.'[9] What a staggering thought! The sovereign God of the universe promised to pitch His tent, *actually* to dwell in the midst of His chosen people.

Many are tempted to skip over these chapters of Exodus and Leviticus that describe in such detail the construction of the tabernacle, the forms of worship and the like. Altars and acacia wood and cubits sound irrelevant today, superseded by the atonement of Christ. But this is a perfect example of the necessity of taking the Word of God in its entirety. For the prescriptions for the place wherein God was to dwell and be worshipped reveal the very character of God Himself.

The tabernacle reflects a holy God, a God set apart, unique, utterly unstained by the sin of the world. No wonder God specified rules of cleanliness for those who worshipped there. It was not because He had some obsession with personal hygiene, but because in every way possible His people were to be clean, set apart – holy – as they entered to worship in the place where He, a holy God, *actually* dwelt.

This is indeed the very heart of the relationship God demands with His people, expressed in the covenant: 'I am the Lord your God; consecrate yourselves and *be holy because I am holy.*'[10] Understanding this basic covenant, the character of God, and what He expects is essential to understanding the New Covenant. For the character of God has not changed, nor has His expectation of holiness from His people.

In fact, the same remarkable promise that God made to Moses – that He would *pitch His tent* and dwell in the midst of His people – is a central theme throughout Scripture. In the familiar passage of John's gospel, 'The Word became flesh, and *dwelt* among us',[11] the Greek word for *dwelt* literally means to 'pitch a tent'. So now, through Christ, God comes to 'pitch His tent' among His people. And to carry the theme to its conclusion, John, in describing his apocalyptic vision of the new heaven and new earth, writes, 'The tabernacle of God is among men, and He shall dwell among them, and they shall be His people.'[12] Again the word *dwell* is literally translated to 'pitch a tent'.

Thus, from Exodus to Revelation we find the identical imagery, a holy God 'pitching His tent' among His people: first in the tabernacle, then in Christ and Christ in us, and ultimately in His kingdom.

Salvation, therefore, is not simply a matter of being separated from our past and freed from our bondage to sin; salvation means also that we are joined to a holy God. By pitching His tent in our midst, God identifies with His people through His very presence. The reality of a 'God who is here' – personal and in our midst – is an extraordinary assurance, one which distinguishes the Judaeo-Christian faith from all other religions.

But God demands something in return for His presence. He demands that we identify with Him – that we be holy because He is holy.

Holiness is not an option. God will not tolerate our indifference to His central command.* It is the central covenant and command of Scripture, the 'cardinal point on which the whole of Christianity turns', William Wilberforce

---

* Moses and Aaron were not permitted to lead the Israelites into the Promised Land because they failed to treat God as holy (Numbers 20:12). Then a long succession of kings failed to respect God's holiness and the Israelites ended up in captivity again.

wrote.[13] It is not just for well-known saints like Mother Teresa, but for every believer.

What does this mean for us, then, in the real world in which we live every day?

14

The Everyday Business of Holiness

When we think of holiness, great saints of the past like
Francis of Assisi or George Müller spring to mind – or
contemporary giants of the faith like Mother Teresa. But
holiness is not the private preserve of an elite corps of
martyrs, mystics, and Nobel prize winners. Holiness is the
everyday business of every Christian. It evidences itself in the
decisions we make and the things we do, hour by hour, day by
day.

The following few examples, drawn from the lives of
Christians I've encountered in recent years, might help make
the point.

It was a quiet December evening on Ward C43, the oncology
unit at Georgetown University Hospital. Many of the rooms
around the central nurses' station were dark and empty, but
in Room 11 a man lay critically ill.

The patient was Jack Swigert, the man who had piloted
the Apollo 13 lunar mission in 1970 and was now Congress-
man-elect from Colorado's 6th Congressional District. Cancer, the great leveller, now waged its deadly assault on his
body.

With the dying man was a tall, quiet visitor, sitting in the
spot he had occupied almost every night since Swigert had
been admitted. Though Bill Armstrong, US Senator from
Colorado and chairman of the Senate subcommittee handling Washington's hottest issue, social security, was one of
the busiest and most powerful men in Washington, he was
not visiting this room night after night as a powerful

politician. He was here as a deeply committed Christian and as Jack Swigert's friend, fulfilling a responsibility he would not delegate or shirk, much as he disliked hospitals.

This night Bill leaned over the bed and spoke quietly to his friend. 'Jack, you're going to be all right. God loves you. I love you. You're surrounded by friends who are praying for you. You're going to be all right.' The only response was Jack's tortured and uneven breathing.

Bill pulled his chair closer to the bed and opened the Bible. 'Psalm 23,' he began to read in a steady voice. 'The Lord is my shepherd, I shall not want . . .'

Time passed. 'Psalm 150,' Bill began, then his skin prickled. Jack's ragged breathing had stopped. He leaned down over the bed, then called for help. As he watched the nurse examining Jack, Bill knew there was nothing more he could do. His friend was dead.

Politicians are busy people, especially Senate committee chairmen. Yet it never occurred to Bill Armstrong that he was too busy to be at the hospital. Nothing dramatic or heroic about his decision – just a friend doing what he could.

Holiness is obeying God – loving one another as He loved us.

When Orv Krieger, a hotel broker with a friendly mid-westerner's grin, received a call about a choice piece of property for sale in Spokane, Washington, he was thrilled. He knew the 140-unit Holiday Inn – minutes from the airport and perched on thirteen acres of firry hillside overlooking the city – was a buy, despite its multi-million-dollar price tag. So instead of listing it for sale to someone else, Orv took the plunge and bought it himself.

Only one problem. The Inn's restaurant was the big money maker, and no wonder – the bar grossed an average of $10,000 a month. But Orv wasn't going to keep the bar. Not that he wanted to impose his own views on others, but as a Christian he chose not to run a business subsidised by alcohol sales.

The motel manager argued that if guests couldn't get a drink at the Inn they'd be out the door to a competitor in a flash. He also gave Orv some convincing statistics that showed the motel couldn't make it without the bar. Orv listened politely – and closed the bar. He must stick to his convictions. The manager promptly quit.

Orv continued with his plans. He remodelled the hotel lobby and replaced the bar area with a cosy coffee shop brimming with greenery. In his first five years of business, food sales went up 20 percent, room bookings up 30 percent. Still, profits aren't what they could be. If the bar were open, the hotel would be a real money machine.

But, as Orv says, his grin as big as ever, 'Beliefs aren't worth much if a fella's not ready to live by them.'

Holiness is obeying God – even when it's against our own interests.

When she arrives at the prison gate each weekday at noon, the guards wave her through. Prison officials stop to ask her how her kids are doing or about her work at the office. After all, Joyce Page is family; she's been spending her lunch hour at the St Louis County Correctional Institution just about every weekday since 1979.

Joyce began going to the prison with her supervisor, also a Christian concerned for prisoners. When the supervisor was transferred, Joyce continued by herself, leaving her office alone with a peanut butter sandwich while other secretaries bustled off in clusters for the cafeteria.

Each day Joyce meets with a different group of inmates, from the men in isolation and maximum security to a small group of women prisoners. 'What we do is up to them,' she says. 'Sometimes we have a worship service, or a time of testimony and singing, or in-depth Bible study and discussion. It depends on their needs.'

When she slips back to her desk at one o'clock, one of her co-workers is usually already bemoaning her lunchtime excesses and loudly proclaiming that she really will have the diet plate tomorrow. Joyce laughs to herself. She knows exactly what she'll have for lunch tomorrow – another peanut butter sandwich at the wheel of her car on the way to prison.

For many, meeting with inmates every day in the middle of a hectic work schedule would be an unthinkable chore. Joyce, in her matter-of-fact way, sees it differently. 'For me it's a real answer to prayer,' she says. 'You see, I don't have time to go *after* work – I have six kids of my own that I'm raising by myself.'

Holiness is obeying God – sharing His love, even when it is inconvenient.

No one in his right mind would pick the village of Duvalierville on the island of Haiti as the location for a factory, especially if he lived in North Carolina. But retired businessmen Kenneth Hooker and Donald Adcox did just that.

It all began in the mid-1970s when Donald Adcox was contacted by a Haitian pastor for help; the pastor had found Adcox's name in a magazine article about Christian laymen. As a result, Donald and several other Christian businessmen visited Haiti and were appalled at what they found. Entire villages subsisted in huts with barely enough to eat; disease was rampant and medical care scarce.

Don enlisted the help of his long time associate, Ken Hooker, and some other businessmen. Government aid, they discovered, was a slow and cumbersome process and might never reach those it was intended to help. And they realised that the people in Haiti wanted opportunity more than welfare. So they linked up with the pastor of the Duvalierville church and got to work.

Along with two other Christian businessmen, Robert Vickery and Don Crace, Ken and Don bought a small rug factory in Pennsylvania and shipped the machinery and supplies to Haiti to set up the plant. This completed, they brought two young leaders, chosen by the Haitian church, to North Carolina for training.

Today the Duvalierville plant is the centre of a thriving community of a thousand people. The church consists of six hundred people, and the church school enrols seven hundred children. Don, Ken, and others have helped the

Haitians build a clinic and guesthouse on the factory grounds and are setting up a programme for Christian doctors and dentists from the States to donate their services.

The busy factory is a tangible encouragement, and the villagers' pride in their plant comes from a sense of ownership, for the plant *does* belong to them. Don and Ken and the other businessmen who participated quietly gave the business to the church a few years ago.

The establishment of the Haitian plant has also brought new hope to another unlikely place – North Carolina prisons. When Don and Ken set up a prototype factory to learn the rug business, they needed a few people to run it. Ken had been volunteering with Prison Fellowship for several years, so he and Don began hiring prisoners on work release to run the rug-braiding machines. In fact, several inmates had their sentences shortened because they had the promise of a steady job. The factory isn't large, employing only three or four at a time, but a nearby plant has followed their example by providing work for prisoners on work release and for ex-offenders.

Meanwhile, Ken Hooker and Don Adcox are busy cooking up other ideas to expand the Haitian ministry and are working with Christian laypeople in other projects. They still claim they're retired, but the past few years have been their busiest.

'We try to put people and available resources together,' Ken says. 'We just do what we can,' adds Donald.

Holiness is obeying God – finding ways to help those in need.

Heroism is an extraordinary feat of the flesh; holiness is an ordinary act of the spirit. One may bring personal glory; the other *always* gives God the glory.

These illustrations can be helpful as practical examples, but the sure standard for holiness is Scripture. There God makes clear what He means by holy living or, as theologians call it, the process of sanctification.

The Ten Commandments, from which all other commandments flow, are the beginning; they apply today as much as they did when God engraved them on tablets of stone for Moses. Next, the life of Jesus provides holiness in the flesh; in His persevering self-denial, His unqualified obedience of the Father's will, and the fullness of the Holy Spirit in His daily life, Jesus remains our example.

Then Paul gives explicit guidelines. Consider just this sampling of injunctions:

Lay aside falsehood and speak the truth.
Do not let the sun go down on your anger.
Let him who steals, steal no longer but work.
Let no unwholesome word come from your mouth.
Be rid of bitterness and wrath and malice.
Be kind to each other, forgiving.
Walk in love.
Be careful so you will not even be accused of immorality, greed, or any impurity.
Engage not in silly or coarse or filthy talk.
Do not practise idolatry in any form nor associate with those who do.
Abstain from sexual immorality and conquer lustful passions.
Do not lead weaker brethren to sin.[1]

In Galatians 5, Paul gives a summary of the fruit of the Spirit along with the contrary sins of the flesh. What a check list!

Love	Immorality
Joy	Impurity
Peace	Sensuality
Patience	Idolatry
Kindness	Sorcery
Goodness	Strife
Faithfulness	Outbursts of anger
Gentleness	Drunkenness
Self-control	Jealousy

The apostle's picture of life by the Spirit versus desires of the sinful nature is graphic. Having set forth the contrast, he exhorts the faithful not to 'become weary in doing good. A man reaps what he sows.'[2]

The quest for holiness, then, should begin with a search of the Scriptures. (The few verses above are but samples of the rich treasure that awaits.) We next begin applying what we find, seeking His will for our lives. As the nineteenth-century Scottish theologian John Brown put it: '*Holiness* does not consist in mystic speculations, enthusiastic fervours, or un-commanded austerities; it *consists in thinking as God thinks and willing as God wills*.'[3]

That thinking and willing is a process requiring discipline and perseverance and is a joint effort: God's and ours. On the one hand, the Holy Spirit convicts of sin and sanctifies.[4] But that doesn't mean that we can sit back, relax, and leave the driving to God. God expects – demands – that we do our part. As Mother Teresa says, 'Our progress in holiness depends on God and ourselves – on God's grace and on our will to be holy.'[5]

Understanding this joint responsibility makes clear what is otherwise one of the most troublesome areas for many Christians, found in Paul's letter to the church at Rome where on one hand he says we are dead to sin and in the next verse exhorts us not to let sin reign in our mortal bodies.[6]

Why should we turn away from sin that is already dead? The answer to this seeming contradiction underscores the joint responsibility for sanctification. We are dead to sin because Christ died to sin for us. He settled the ultimate victory. But as we live day by day, sin still remains a constant reality. Though God gives us the will to be holy, the daily fight requires continuing effort on our part.

In his marvellous book, *Pursuit of Holiness*, Jerry Bridges likens this to nations at war: one defeats the other, as at Calvary Christ defeated Satan. But the losing army, though vanquished, then takes to the hills and fights on as a guerrilla movement. Fighting off sin, he says, is like beating back continuing guerrilla attacks.[7]

Holy living demands constant examination of our actions and motives. But in doing so we must guard against the tendency to focus totally on self, which is easy to do – especially as the culture's egocentric values invade the church. In fact, this self-indulgent character of our times is a major reason the topic of true holiness is so neglected today by Christian teachers, leaders, writers, and speakers. We have, perhaps unconsciously, substituted a secularised self-centred message in its place. For when we speak of 'victory' in the Christian life, we all-too-often mean personal victory – how God will conquer sin *for us* (at least those sins we'd like to be rid of – those extra ten pounds, that annoying habit, maybe a quick temper). This reflects not only egocentricity but an incorrect view of sin.

Sin is not simply the wrong we do our neighbour when we cheat him, or the wrong we do ourselves when we abuse our bodies. Sin, all sin, is a root rebellion and offence against God, what R. C. Sproul calls 'cosmic treason'.

We must understand that our goal as believers is to seek what we can do to please God, not what He can do for us. Personal victories may come, but they are a result, not the object. True Christian maturity – holiness, sanctification – is God-centred. So-called 'victorious Christian living' is self-centred. Jerry Bridges puts it well:

> It is time for us Christians to face up to our responsibility for holiness. Too often we say we are 'defeated' by this or that sin. No, we are not defeated; we are simply disobedient. It might be well if we stopped using the terms 'victory' and 'defeat' to describe our progress in holiness. Rather we should use the terms 'obedience' and 'disobedience'.[8]

So we have come full circle – back to where we started. The Christian life begins with obedience, depends on obedience, and results in obedience. We can't escape it. The orders from our commander-in-chief are plain: 'Whoever has my commandments and obeys them, he is the one who loves me.'[9]

Loving God – really loving Him – means living out His commands no matter what the cost.

A young woman in a suburban Washington church recently demonstrated this truth.

No one was surprised when Patti Awan stood during the informal praise time at the Sunday evening service. A young Sunday school teacher with an air of quiet maturity, she had given birth to a healthy son a few months earlier, a first child for her and her husband Javy. The congregation settled back for a report of the baby's progress and his parents' thanksgiving. They were totally unprepared for what followed.

Hanging onto the podium before her, Patti began. 'Four years ago this week, a young girl sat crying on the floor of a New Jersey apartment, devastated by the news of a lab report. Unmarried and alone, she had just learned she was pregnant.'

The congregation grew completely quiet; Patti's tear-choked voice indicated just who that young woman was.

'I considered myself a Christian at the time,' she continued. 'But I had found out about Christ while in the drug scene. After I learned about Him, I knew I wanted to commit myself to Him, but I couldn't give up my old friends or my old habits. So I was drifting between two worlds – in one still smoking dope every day and sleeping with the man who lived in the apartment below mine; in the other, going to church, witnessing to others, and working with the church youth group.

'But being pregnant ripped through the hypocrisy of my double life. I had been meaning to "get right with God", but I kept slipping back. Now I couldn't live a nice, clean Christian life like all those church people.

'I felt the only answer was to wipe the slate clean. I would get an abortion; no one in the church would ever know.

'The clinic scheduled an abortion date. I was terrified, but my boyfriend was adamant. My sister was furious with me for being so stupid as to get pregnant. Finally, in desperation I wrote my parents. They were staunch Catholics, and I knew they would support me if I decided to have the baby. My mother called me: "If you don't get an abortion, I don't want to see you while you're pregnant. Your life will be ruined and you'll deserve it."

'I had always been desperately dependent on other people. But I knew this was one decision I had to make alone. I was looking out my bedroom window one night when I thought clearly for the first time in weeks. I realised I either believed in Christianity or I didn't believe it. And if I believed in Christ, then I couldn't do this. *God is real*, I thought, *even if I've never lived like He is*.

'That decision was a point of no return. I put my faith in the God of the Bible, not the God I had made up in my head. I was still everything I never wanted to be – pregnant, alone, deserted by family, and rejected by the one I had loved. Yet for the first time in my life I was really peaceful, because I knew for the first time I was being obedient.

'When I went to an obstetrician and told him of my decision to have the baby and why I had made that choice, he refused to charge me for the pre-natal care and delivery. I confessed my double life to the church, and through the support of Christians was able to move away from my old friends to an apartment of my own. I began going to a Christian counselling agency and felt God leading me to give the baby up for adoption.

'I had a beautiful baby girl and named her Sarah. She was placed with a childless Christian couple, and we felt God's hand in the decision.

'And so that's why I praise God this evening. I thought in the depths of my despair that my life was ruined, but I knew I had to at least be obedient in taking responsibility for my sin. But today, because of that very despair and obedience, I have what I never thought I could – a godly husband and now a baby of our own. But what matters more than anything is

that I have what I was searching for so desperately before –
peace with God.'

Holiness is obeying God.

15

And *His Righteousness*

William Wilberforce, eighteenth century slave trade abolitionist, wrote in his diary: 'God Almighty has set before me
two great objects, the suppression of the slave trade and the
reformation of manners.' The latter did not refer to table
etiquette, of course, but to the moral standards of professing
Christians.

Wilberforce believed holy living, what he called the 'reformation of manners', would inevitably foster righteousness in the land and end the injustice of slavery; conversely,
the end of slavery would uplift the moral character of the
nation.

That is precisely what happened. Slavery was abolished as
a great spiritual awakening swept England clean of its
indulgent apostasy.[1]

If only that lesson of interdependence could be learned
today! Churches, particularly evangelical ones, are packed
with people attempting to practise personal piety, to establish moral lifestyles, and 'to witness'. Yet they seem oblivious
to the need to work for those same standards in their society
and world. At times the church seems schizophrenic: pious
and righteously aroused in the safety of pews and prayer
groups, but indifferent in the world outside.

From the beginning God made plain the standard He
demands of His people. Following His commission to Moses
that Israel was to be a 'kingdom of priests and a holy
nation',[2] God carefully prescribed the just way the affairs of
this nation were to be managed. Exodus 21 through 23 set
forth standards for justice for individuals, personal injury

claims, rights of private property, restitution, and care for the poor, orphaned, widowed, and foreign.

For God holds man responsible not only for his individual sins but for the corporate sins of society. Wrongs such as aggression, inflation, injustice, racism, and economic oppression are manifestations of man's sin just as much as our individual transgressions. The great impersonal entity called 'society' is not responsible for these sins – we are. These conditions grieve the heart of God, and He clearly calls us to account for them and to repent.*

In Leviticus, Numbers, and Deuteronomy the pattern for God's people is established: repentance and restitution prescribed for offences against God and society; cities of refuge ordered to protect those who had committed manslaughter; strict safeguards for imposition of capital punishment.†

God's command is clear: 'Follow justice and justice alone, so that you may live and possess the land.'³ Centuries later when Saul was removed from the throne of Israel, God chose a man 'after his own heart' the young David, to be the king who 'administered justice and righteousness for all his people.'⁴

Following David came his son Solomon whose wisdom has become a political cliché. At every swearing in, from county dog-catcher to president, someone ritualistically prays that the newly elected one be endowed with 'the wisdom of Solomon'. Unfortunately, few bother to look up the source of their quote. If they did, they would probably be startled to

---

* Examples of responsibility and repentance for corporate sins are found throughout Scripture. Moses often went before God in earnest repentance for the sins of his people. Moses might have counted himself blameless; after all, he had told the people the right thing to do. They were the rebels. Yet Moses repented for the corporate sins of his people. See also Nehemiah 1:6. Throughout the prophetic literature, there is consistent call by God for His people to repent for the sins of their nation.

† Many Christians cite Genesis 9:6 as the biblical justification for capital punishment but fail to cite the protection for the accused that God *also* demanded – such as two eyewitnesses, and the requirement that an accuser participate in the execution (Deuteronomy 17:6–7). Nothing comparable to those biblical safeguards can be found today in any of the state statutes that call for the death penalty.

find that when God asked Solomon what one thing he wanted, the young man replied, 'Give your servant a discerning heart to govern your people and to distinguish between right and wrong.'[5] God was so pleased with Solomon's request – not for himself, but in order to dispense justice to others – that He rewarded him with wisdom never given before or since.

However, following this bright spot the record descends into one of shameful apostasy. King after king committed idolatry and did evil in the sight of God. Judah was divided from Israel, and both became weaker as justice disappeared.

Since the kings could not be trusted to do justice, God raised up a new breed of servant: the prophets. The line began with Elijah and Elisha, through the great evangelical prophet Isaiah, to Jeremiah and Ezekiel.[6] Each repeated the same three-pronged message: condemnation of unrighteous kings and people; a call to justice and holy living; and the promise of miraculous intervention of God in history to bring judgment to the wicked and blessing to the obedient.

Significantly, justice is seen not through the eyes of the powerful but through the eyes of the powerless. (In fact, many of the prophets were men God raised up from among the peasant class.) The moral worth of a society, the prophets declared, is measured not by life in the palace but by life in the streets. For the former to prosper at the expense of the latter violates God's standard for the humanity He created in His image. *To know the all-powerful God, one must know the powerless.*[7]

The angriest judgments come from the lips of the men we call the Minor Prophets. One of these, the prophet Amos, brought a message that was particularly devastating to the powerful elite of Israel. Every time I read and study Amos, I am chilled by some parallels with today's culture; it is a book with special and powerful insights for twentieth century Christians, for it reveals a view of God's justice that today's society often ignores to its peril.

Amos was a shepherd living in the rugged terrain south of Jerusalem. One day while about the regular duties of sheep-tending, he was dramatically confronted by a vision of God's fearsome judgment. Knowing this vision was from God, Amos left his flock to deliver the stinging rebuke to Israel.

He was received as a pariah – an occupational hazard for prophets. For like a doctor ripping gauze bandages off a putrid sore, Amos laid bare Israel's ugliest sins, including pagan rituals and immoral sexual practices such as temple prostitution.[8]

Blatant as these sins were, Amos exposed something even more offensive. Under Jewish law, a man's coat might be held as collateral for his debts during the day when the temperature was usually warm, but had to be returned in the evening for protection against the cold night air. However, the wealthy were ignoring this and were keeping the pledged coats. And heaping sin upon sin, they were then using the coats as bedding for sex acts in the temple, thus desecrating the temple twice: by sexual immorality and by flouting God's law intended to protect the poor.

Amos also exposed the practice of selling wheat on the Sabbath, cheating with dishonest scales, and selling the refuse of wheat remaining after the harvest which under Jewish law was to be left at the edges of the field for the poor.[9] This was God's welfare plan, but the Jews had become so greedy profiting at the expense of the poor and powerless that they were depriving them of the crumbs needed to stay alive.*

Amos pronounced God's judgment upon Israel because 'they sell the righteous for money and the needy for a pair of sandals', a reference to the common practice of the wealthy who could bribe judges with as little as the price of a poor man's sandals.

Greed had replaced justice, money had triumphed over mercy, and the judicial system was merely a pawn of power

* It should be noted that God does not attack the rich for being rich but rather for being unjust in the use of their riches. For example, all these offences cited had to do with profit, but there's nothing wrong with making a profit – elsewhere it can be argued the Bible legitimises it. But profit must be made honestly and in accordance with God's standards. The problem here was the method and the motive. Materialism had become Israel's god.

and privilege used to oppress the very people it was intended to protect. The righteousness of God was no longer the standard in the land.

And so, speaking through Amos, God demanded that the nation repent. 'Hate evil, love good; maintain justice in the courts.'[10] And then, in one of the grandest declarations of Scripture, he thundered, 'Let justice roll down like waters and righteousness like an ever-flowing stream.'[11]

Let those who believe that 'God helps those who help themselves' read Amos. The Bible teaches exactly the opposite of that hallowed American maxim: God cares *especially* for those who can't help themselves – the poor and needy, the forgotten and helpless. Amos warned that the nation whose vested interests manipulated power structures for their own gain, at the expense of the poor, must face the judgment of an angry God.

That's why a leading Christian lawyer, Jay Poppinga, writes: 'When we speak of justice in the biblical sense we . . . are talking about meeting need wherever it exists and particularly where it exists most helplessly.'[12]

Some will say, however, that these standards for corporate holiness are no longer in force. Applicable to Old Testament times, yes. In force today, no.

That is tempting to believe – tempting, but not biblical. For while it is true we now live under grace since Jesus came to fulfil the law, Jesus did not repeal the law.[13] A perfect, just God cannot change His perfect standards of justice.

Jesus' first sermon reflects this: Walking into the synagogue, He picked up the parchment with the words of the prophet Isaiah and read:

The Spirit of the Lord is on me,
    because he has anointed me
    to preach good news to the poor.
He has sent me to proclaim freedom for the prisoners
    and recovery of sight for the blind,
    to release the oppressed,
    to proclaim the year of the Lord's favour.[14]

Jesus put down the scroll and said, 'Today this scripture is fulfilled in your hearing.'[15]

Jesus went on to demonstrate in His ministry a deep compassion for the suffering and forgotten. He fed the hungry, healed the lame, gave sight to the blind. He was concerned not only with saving man from hell in the next world, but delivering him from the hellishness of this one. Thus, the Son reflected the Father's passion for mercy and justice. And His message of social justice was just as unsettling and convicting as it was in the time of Amos – and as it is today.

Consider just one of Jesus' last admonitions to His disciples and to us. The setting is the Mount of Olives and Jesus is giving His followers a glimpse of the future – His eventual return and the faithfulness expected of them in the meantime. Then He describes the final judgment before the throne of the Lord, where with a wave of His hand the righteous and unrighteous will be separated. With terrifying finality, Jesus says, the unrighteous will hear God's final judgment: 'I was hungry and you gave me nothing to eat, I was thirsty and you gave me nothing to drink, I was a stranger and you did not invite me in, I needed clothes and you did not clothe me, I was sick and in prison and you did not look after me.'[16]

This is not hellfire and brimstone evangelism. This is justice. And, yes, this is love as well. God loves us so much that He holds us accountable; for by judging us according to how well we live out His holy standards of justice and righteousness, He ascribes meaning to our daily actions. He ensures that what we do matters.

So Christianity is not just a high-sounding ritual we perform on Sunday mornings. Christianity is abiding by biblical standards of personal holiness and in turn seeking to bring holiness into the society in which we live. And that's why Jesus called us 'salt and light'.[17] It is what He meant in the magnificent words of the Sermon on the Mount: 'Seek ye first the kingdom of God, *and* his righteousness.'[18] (Too many Christians glibly quote the first part of this verse, 'seek ye first the kingdom of God', forgetting the demanding command to which Jesus gives equal emphasis, 'and his righteousness'.)

The path of personal holiness can be a tough one, but hacking out a holy pathway in society brings us face to face with the cost of discipleship. It means making moral judgments by God's standards not man's, sometimes pitting the believer against the state. That can raise sticky questions in a democracy where, as Supreme Court Justice Oliver Wendell Holmes put it, 'Truth is the majority vote of that nation that could lick all others.'[19]

As a politician I not only believed that, but fervently worked for it; and in the Korean War I would have laid down my life in its defence. But that is not the way of the kingdom of God. Because something is legal does not make it right. Nor can the will of the majority be confused with the will of God. They may be very different; in fact, they often are.

Let me tell you what happened to a judge who found himself caught between this government of man and the justice of God . . .

16

Contra Mundum

The handcuffs chafing Fred Palmer's arms had rubbed his wrists raw. Heavy chains connected the cuffs to a steel belt circling his waist. The dark holding cell, into which he was packed along with twelve other men waiting to be sentenced, stank from the heat of unwashed bodies despite the cold February wind outside.

When the electronic lock clicked and the heavy cell door swung open, armed officers herded Fred and a few others towards a barred elevator. After a short wait, they pressed together into the tiny cage to be transported up two flights. The guards then took them to a small, bleak room where they were to wait until called into the courtroom as each of their cases came up.

Fred Palmer leaned against the wall. He was a rather short man, in his mid-twenties, with thick dark hair, blue eyes, and a muscular build. He carried himself well, though now the chains held his aching arms in a supplicant position. Not that pleading would do any good, he thought. He had heard about the man he would face in the courtroom. Bontrager. The hanging judge.

Down the hall from the courtroom Judge William Bontrager, his long frame stretched in a reclining leather swivel chair and his booted feet propped on a gleaming walnut desk, stared at the snow-covered trees outside his corner office. At thirty-six his face was unlined, his crew cut sandy. His brown eyes focused intently on whatever had his attention, and at the moment his attention was on the morning's court schedule and the men to be sentenced. *Fred Palmer*, he thought as he inhaled deeply on a cigarette, *that's the case.*

He got up, took the black robe from the closet, slipped the garment over his head, and took a final drag before crushing the cigarette out in a heavy marble ashtray. Then Judge William D. Bontrager, Superior Court 2, Elkhart, Indiana, went to take his place at the bench.

It was a modern courtroom, especially for Elkhart. Built only ten years before, it was carpeted, had recessed lighting, a sophisticated sound system, and polished walnut furniture. The judge's elevated platform had the witness stand, attorneys' tables, and jury box all in sight, designed so the man presiding could exercise control over his courtroom without turning his head.

And Bill Bontrager was in control, though he never used his gavel. His deep voice carried through the sensitive sound system with an intensity and authority commanding respect.

Today the courtroom was nearly empty, with just a few relatives and observers dotted throughout the public seating area. But one row, right in the middle, was full. These people waited with a common expectancy, for they were the victims of one of the men to be sentenced, Fred Palmer.

Randy Brown sat in the centre of that row. He and his wife had been on their honeymoon when Palmer broke into their small house and stole all their wedding presents. They had come home to find a window smashed, wrapping paper strewn everywhere, and their gifts gone. Even thinking of the mess made bile rise in Randy's throat. He couldn't wait to see justice done.

Finally a deputy sheriff escorted Fred Palmer into the courtroom where he took a seat beside his attorney. When Fred looked back to the spectator section, he could see his wife Loretta, her face tight with anxiety. *She looks like I feel*, he thought. *She must have left Jamie with a babysitter*. Then he turned back and lifted his head towards the unsmiling, robed figure at the front of the room.

Judge Bontrager looked piercingly at the young defendant,

then picked up the pre-sentence report. Harry Fred Palmer, age twenty-five, involved in drugs and alcohol; charged with house burglary; arrested, pleaded guilty, confessed to eleven similar crimes. At the time of arrest, mid-September, 1977, Palmer's offence drew a mandatory sentence of ten to twenty years. However, Indiana legislators had recently passed a new penal code designating a lesser penalty for this particular crime and giving the judge discretion in sentencing; unfortunately for Palmer the new code did not take effect until October 1, eighteen days after his arrest. Therefore, he must be sentenced under the old statute to no less than ten years imprisonment.

Fred's prior offences included marijuana possession, auto theft, possession of stolen property, but all except one of public drunkenness were committed after returning from service in Vietnam. Bontrager had looked over the impressive list of entries in the report pertaining to Palmer's war record: Bronze Star, National Defense Ribbon, Air Medal, Vietnam Service Medal, Vietnam Campaign Medal, Honorable Discharge.

It was also noted that Palmer had a young wife, Loretta, and a one-year-old daughter, Jamie, and that the defendant said he had committed his life to Jesus Christ while sitting in the Elkhart County Jail for five-and-a-half months awaiting trial. Bontrager had taken somewhat passing note of the last item. A lot of cons claimed jailhouse conversions. Only time would tell whether Palmer's was sincere.

Now the judge cleared his throat and leaned on one elbow into the microphone. His index finger jabbed the air as he spoke.

'Mr Palmer,' he thundered, 'you are aware that under Indiana state law you must be sentenced according to the mandatory strictures of the old penal code, since your crime was committed before the new code went into effect. And you are aware that the penalty of no less than a ten and no more than a twenty year sentence is, under Indiana law, not suspendable. And perhaps you know that the victims of your burglaries have written letters to this court suggesting that the maximum penalty of twenty years will not be long enough to keep you off the streets of Elkhart.'

There was a heavy pause of anticipation as Bontrager launched into his sentencing. 'It is the opinion of this court, however, that fixed sentences themselves do not deter crime; what deters crime is that which the offender himself perceives as punishment. I am aware, of course, that you have spent five-and-a-half months in the Elkhart County Security Centre, Mr Palmer – but that is not sufficient punishment. It is the opinion of this court that what you would most likely perceive as punishment is a solid dose of maximum security incarceration.

'I am also aware, Mr Palmer, that you claim a religious change of heart. If true, it is that which will sustain you as you are exposed to what we call the therapeutic shock value of the hellholes of the Indiana state prison system.'

The words slowly tumbled through Fred Palmer's mind. He turned his head sharply to see Loretta's face completely white, her dark eyes panic-stricken. But something told him to hold on; this judge wasn't finished with him yet.

Bontrager paused, looking at the row of victims. His voice grew softer and his face, if possible, sterner.

'However, this court recognises that the Indiana State Constitution is unique in that its penal code is founded on a principle of reformation, and not vindictive punishment. So this court is going one step further and declaring the mandatory and non-suspendable ten-to-twenty-year sentence in violation of that Indiana constitution. For to send Fred Palmer – in light of his individual case, post-Vietnam syndrome, and never having been in prison before – to a ten-year sentence in a maximum security prison would in fact be vindictive, cruel and unusual punishment that would ruin him unavoidably for life.

'Therefore, in the interest of society, as well as Mr Palmer, this court holds that he serve 205 days in a state maximum security facility – one year, less the 160 days already served – that he then be released and make all reasonable restitution to his victims, engage in drug and alcohol therapy as needed, and remain on probation for a five-year period.'

The judge leaned toward Palmer and added a final word: 'Further, Mr Palmer, as those who have spent time in my courtroom can tell you, I do not give people a second chance.'

The victims, subdued while the judge spoke, now erupted. Their anger was no longer focused on Palmer, but on the judge. Bontrager looked calmly over the sputtering row of enraged spectators as the deputy sheriff approached to escort Fred Palmer back to the cell. Palmer shot a quick glance at his wife, noticing that her shock had been replaced by a glimmer of hope. On his way through the side door, he looked up at the young judge whose face was as hard as ever, but who somehow also seemed to flash him a look of challenge.

Bill Bontrager's decision to overturn an Indiana mandatory sentencing law surprised no one who knew him. Though he had been a judge for only slightly more than a year, that year had been marked by his aggressive, often controversial style. He was restless, idealistic, driven.

He came by this naturally. His father, prominent in state Republican politics, had been a stern, hard-working attorney who ruled his three sons with an iron will. He had favoured black suits and crisp white shirts, perhaps because of his upbringing among the Amish 'plain people'. A self-made man who studied law by correspondence, the senior Bontrager had reached his political summit as the Republican nominee for the US Senate, running on the same ticket that Barry Goldwater led to defeat in 1964. If by national standards he never reached great recognition (though a stand he took in the state legislature was written up in a 1954 *Readers' Digest*), in Indiana his name meant hard work, strong principles, and stubborn independence.

To his middle son, Bill, he was a pair of eyeglasses behind a newspaper, or an incensed listener to evening news broadcasts, too busy to show much interest in or warmth towards his sons. As Bontrager remembered years later, 'In one sense I idolised my father and doted upon the possibility of a compliment or the acknowledgment of my existence. In another sense I hated him with everything I had, and hated myself more for allowing him to totally dominate my life.

'But my father taught me that morality is an absolute and not situational; he taught me that a man must be true to God, the Creator; he taught me that the rules we must live by can be found only in the Bible; he taught me to have the courage of my convictions and the willingness to speak them regardless of the personal cost. Unfortunately, he did not teach me to be tactful.'

Reacting to this domineering presence, teen-age Bill Bontrager swore four oaths, meant to make him as unlike his father as possible. He vowed he would never be an attorney, he would never return to Elkhart, he would never enter politics, and he would be a better father and husband than his father had been.

The first oath was kept through one year of college. Bill had planned to be an engineer. Then, without really understanding why, he decided to leave Purdue and study pre-law at the University of Colorado. Perhaps because, as his Aunt Grace pointed out, all lawyers were frustrated actors, and Bill certainly had a flair for the dramatic. He also loved the Rocky Mountains which seemed to offer a size and scale to match his own ambitions and drive. While there he began to wear cowboy boots and string ties, a style as unlike Elkhart (and his father) as possible.

One Saturday afternoon in 1960 while handing out Nixon/Lodge stickers to football fans before the game, he noticed a tiny girl with a wide smile, also dispensing Nixon buttons. Her name was Ellen, and she was a freshman. Five months later they were married. Nine months after that they had their first child. With a family to support, Bill had to work every kind of menial job to pay his way through school.

His second vow – never to return to Elkhart – went out the window when he graduated from law school. He had accepted a position as a law clerk in the Supreme Court of Idaho. Then on New Year's Eve, having drunk a good quantity of rum-laced eggnog, he roared into a fierce con-

frontation with his father over why he was not returning to
Elkhart. Typically, his dad couldn't simply ask him to come
home because he wanted him in his law office, for that would
show warmth and love; he had to argue on principle. But
ten days later Bill called Idaho and told them he wasn't
coming, then called home and asked for a job in his father's
firm.

Bill and Ellen settled into Elkhart, and over the next ten
years life flowed somewhat predictably. Bill's caseload was
steady and their income good, giving them a new home in a
pleasant suburb.

Bill's third vow – to stay out of politics – lasted four years.
He decided to run for the state House of Representatives, but
his father talked him out of it. Four years later, after his
father's death, Bill ran for the state senate and lost. But his
involvement in Republican politics won him an appointment
by the governor to the State Board of Corrections, which
recommended policy for prisons. Bill knew nothing about
prisons, but dug into the job with his usual fervour, studying
the subject, visiting prisons, and gradually developing a
philosophy about correction and criminal justice.

He was, however, more interested in politics than in
prisons and spent most evenings in political or community
meetings. Thus, his fourth vow to be a better father and
husband than his own father nagged at him, for he spent little
time at home with his wife and children.

Bill Bontrager knew about the God who made the heavens
and the earth, who was all-powerful and had given an
exacting standard of justice for men to live by. He knew
nothing about a God who loved, who could weep, who sought
intimacy with His human children. God was, in short, made
in the image of his father; Bill respected and feared Him but
could never come close to Him.

Ellen had even less background in the Christian faith.
However, she became involved with a group of women who
gathered weekly to study the Bible. Bill noticed that she
began to change. She quit drinking, and she took consider-

ably more interest in church. She even managed to drag him in occasionally. Bill was pleased that she had found an outlet that kept her busy and happy, but had no interest himself. Nothing was further from his mind than his need for God.

Then tragedy struck. The Bontragers' sons, Danny and Richard, were playing in the garage with a chemistry set when their concoction exploded. Flames enveloped ten-year-old Richard's face, chest, and right leg, covering him with third-degree burns. After several days, visitors could be admitted to his hospital room only if they removed clothing, scrubbed down completely, and suited up in surgical garb and facial masks. In spite of this laborious process, usually taking at least half an hour, one visitor came every day: Rev. Fred Finks, pastor of Winding Waters Brethren Church in the Bontrager's neighbourhood. Fred would sit working puzzles with Richard day after day; also, each day he would ask a riddle and come with the answer the next. Richard looked forward to the minister's visits almost more than his parents'.

During his son's recovery, Bill found in Fred Finks, and in his congregation, religion that was more than moral principles; it was life lived compassionately with strength and joy. That attracted him.

Perhaps that explains why one day in early 1976 Bill took the highly unusual step of stopping by the pastor's office in the middle of the afternoon to seek some personal advice about a judgeship in Elkhart's Superior Court 2 that would soon be available. Several colleagues had suggested that Bill run for the office.

At first the idea seemed ludicrous. Not yet thirty-five, Bill was already earning much more than a superior court judge. Moreover, he had good political opportunities ahead. But as he thought about it, the idea became more appealing.

Rev. Finks listened to Bill's pros and cons, but gave little advice. He simply told Bontrager to discuss it with his wife and pray for guidance from God. Bill went home, talked it over with Ellen, but didn't bother to pray. He announced his candidacy.

As a Republican in Elkhart County with the name of Bontrager, he knew he could not lose. He was right.

January, 1977, found Bill Bontrager, thirty-five years old with the crew cut he had worn all his life and the cowboy boots and string ties he had worn since his Colorado days, residing in the plush judge's chambers of Superior Court 2, County Court Building, Elkhart, Indiana. Unknowingly, it seemed he had been heading toward this vocation all his life. Here he found the natural outlet for his training and talents, and an arena in which to exercise his beliefs about law, order, justice, absolute morality, and individual accountability. He couldn't help thinking that his dad would finally be proud.

Bill had thought a judge's hours would leave much-needed time for his family (that fourth vow again), and that had been part of the post's attraction. But the caseload increased dramatically from month to month and his passionate involvement made the choice between family and work more difficult. Soon he was spending twelve and fourteen-hour days in the courthouse, coming home late and exhausted.

One October weekend Ellen planned to attend a conference at the Winding Waters church. Bill didn't intend to go; praying and sharing feelings with a group of church folk wasn't his idea of relaxation. But that Friday night his juvenile court cases, which ordinarily went to 8:00 P.M., wound up early at 6:30. So he stopped by the church to explain to Ellen that he was going home to fix himself dinner, stare at the TV set, and fall into the sack. As he walked around looking for his wife, different members kept greeting him so warmly that he got talked into staying. At first he merely listened. Then, to his amazement, he found himself sharing his own struggles. At last, as he said later, 'I split open like an overripe tomato,' and for the third time in his life wept openly.

That night Bill Bontrager realised he needed more than iron principles. He needed Jesus. So he opened his heart to Christ and remarkable joy and peace flooded over him. He felt drained of everything rotten and filled with the Spirit of God. Judge William Bontrager had become a Christian.

This new life in Christ did not change Judge Bontrager's view of the law; nor did he surrender to the Lordship of Christ at that time. It did, however, strengthen his sense of compassion. His image of a judge was not a blind official mechanically weighing evidence, but a sensitive, open-eyed justice applying the law to individual cases, aware of the entire legal system and people caught in it. He also believed that his role involved more than meting out penalties.

With these principles, he attacked the criminal justice system in Elkhart with all his energy, though not always with tact. He soon offended people in the Probation Department, the Prosecutor's Office, the Welfare Department, the Juvenile Court, the County Council and County Commissioners, and the Elkhart school system – the many agencies that try to help troubled families. He demanded that these agencies change their procedures, and some slowly did. When he came to the bench, many trials were taking place eighteen months after the crime committed; he cut that time to under five months. For the first time in many years the juvenile arrest rate fell, at least partly because Judge Bontrager insisted that school truancy not be ignored but treated as a serious problem.

But mandatory sentences were a growing part of the legal system, and he had no power to change that. While he had a reputation as a tough, no-nonsense judge, Bill believed that mandatory sentencing destroyed the concept of individual justice. For instance, anyone convicted of two felonies had to serve at least two years in prison. In general, that sounded reasonable. But the way the law was stated, that meant that someone convicted of two shoplifting offences twenty years apart would have to go to prison for two years; the judge had no discretion to consider the particular crime and the individual. Knowing the prisons as he did, Bontrager did not take two years inside lightly. He believed there was no more certain way to ruin a person's life, for most who went in for more than a year came out embittered, hardened, and violent criminals. So he was just waiting for an opportunity to challenge the mandatory sentencing laws and in February, 1978, Fred Palmer's case presented that opportunity. But when Bontrager sentenced Palmer to only one year, he also knew he was confronting the plain language of the law; and he knew the prosecuting attorney would take the case to the Indiana Supreme Court. Bontrager hoped his boldness would encourage the Supreme Court to uphold a person's right to be treated as an individual under the law.

When Fred Palmer left the courtroom that February day after sentencing, he was whisked by police van to the Indiana Reception and Diagnostic Centre for processing where he found himself in line behind a kid who confided his panic at the prospect of prison. Fred felt much of the same terror, but he believed the same God who had entered his life in the Elkhart County Jail would be with him in prison. Concerned for the terrified boy, Fred prayed, *Lord, send me where this guy ahead of me goes.* He strained forward and heard the choice offered the young prisoner: Michigan City or Indiana State Reformatory at Pendleton – equally tough joints, equally crowded. He heard the kid opt for Michigan City, so when the officer in charge asked Fred's preference, after filling out the necessary forms, Fred said, 'Michigan City.'

Palmer's time in prison was tough, but he studied his Bible, got involved with Christian volunteers through Prison Fellowship, and stayed in touch with the young man he had followed there. Through Fred's ministry that young man, along with many other prisoners, became a Christian.

Seven months later, Fred was released and went home to Loretta and Jamie in Bristol, Indiana. He got involved in a solid church fellowship, found a job, and scheduled appointments with his victims to pay them back for the money and goods he had stolen. Most were eager to confront him, but as they met the new Fred Palmer, they, too, were changed.

Randy Brown was particularly anxious to face Palmer, for he had watched in helpless rage as Palmer got off with a mere year of time. At least this victim-restitution programme offered a chance to meet Palmer face to face and tell the worthless con what Randy thought of him.

But the Fred Palmer he confronted was no monster. Fred asked the Browns' forgiveness, told them about his time in Vietnam, his struggles with alcohol, the needs of his wife and child at the time of his crimes. Now he wanted to make restitution.

Randy found him 'a guy just like me'. And he was ready to pay them back, not knowing what kind of revenge they might want. That took guts. Randy watched from inside while Fred began by chopping firewood on their lot. Soon he was out the door giving Fred a hand.*

The year following the Palmer decision was fairly uneventful for Bill Bontrager. His work load increased, as did his crusade to reform the system. He and Ellen and the boys went camping and spent a lot of time together at church. Bill even began teaching Sunday school.

Usually he prepared his Sunday school lesson on Saturday evening, but one week he chose to begin on Sunday afternoon right after church. He read through Amos, the short Old Testament book they were to study. It meant nothing to him –just a dry, dusty sermon preached to an insignificant nation almost three thousand years ago. The study guide didn't help either. So Bill kept picking the Bible up at odd moments during the week, trying to get a meaningful lesson out of it before the next Sunday.

Then early one evening as he sat in his chambers with the words of Amos before him, the pages suddenly came alive with a howl of rage against the injustices in the courts and palaces of Amos's land. Bill grabbed the pen he had parked behind his ear and began scribbling on a legal pad. Soon the

---

* An additional interesting result of the restitution made by Fred Palmer: Another of his victims was Randy Yohn, who was also present at Fred's trial because he was a deputy sheriff. As a result of his meeting Fred Palmer during the restitution time, Yohn realised that there was a 'better way' than prison. He later became chairman of the Victim-Offender Reconciliation Advisory Board.

long yellow sheets were filled with his own paraphrases of the Lord's words to Amos:

> I demand righteousness and a right relationship with you.
> I demand justice and a compassionate integrity toward all.
> I demand that you stick by My standards and insist that you do the right thing toward others for the right reasons. The picture of Me that you make in your own mind so that you feel complacent and secure is idolatry. You think justice blind, but My justice is open-eyed. It passionately seeks out wrong and tries to right it. It is dedicated to other people's needs, and especially the needs of those less able to care for themselves.

His heart racing with exhilaration, Bill threw down his pen, leaned back and lit a cigarette. *What I've been fumbling around trying to say all my life is right here*, he thought. *It's really what God says . . . 'let justice roll down . . .'* In his own small way in the Palmer case he had been trying to do his part to uphold God's standards of justice, even though it meant opposition to the laws of the state.

As the events of the next three years crashed about him, Bill Bontrager returned often to Amos. The words of the ancient peasant prophet became his own – as did the howl of rage.

The wheels of justice in America grind slowly. A year passed. Palmer was out of prison, establishing a credible new life, and most people had forgotten the case. But Bill Bontrager still waited, knowing that the Supreme Court of Indiana would either overturn the sentencing law or overturn his decision.

Then on Friday, March 23, 1979, his secretary, Eloise, brought in the day's mail with a bulky brief from the state supreme court on top. It confirmed his worst fears: the court had not only reversed his decision but ordered him to send Fred Palmer back to prison for the remainder of his ten to twenty year mandatory sentence.

In the outer office, Eloise jumped as she heard the judge's fist crash down on his desk. Coffee cups and ashtrays rattled as he stormed around like an enraged bull. 'That does it,' she heard him utter in increasing volume . 'THAT DOES IT!'

Bill Bontrager was hurt and angry. He did not like to be told he was wrong. But his reaction was more than hurt pride. He was infuriated at the tyranny of a mechanical court. A group of men in Indianapolis who had never met Fred Palmer were willing to mete out their version of justice and ruin Palmer's life to satisfy the letter of a law no longer even on the books, and furthermore, without considering the rehabilitation that had taken place in Palmer's life. To Bontrager that was not justice.

Bontrager reached for the phone and called Fred at his trailer home in Bristol. Fred was speechless. He could not believe the news. 'I served my sentence,' he kept saying. 'I'm paying my victims back. Why in the world would the court want to send me back to prison?'

'Don't worry,' Bontrager assured him. 'We're going to fight this.'

With those words, Bontrager crossed a line, though he did not realise it at the time. He was no longer an impartial judge dispensing justice; he had joined Fred Palmer's side.

Bontrager made the twenty-minute drive home in half the usual time. He was taking a troop of Boy Scouts to Ohio for the weekend and hadn't packed yet. He slammed into the house, up the stairs to the bedroom, and began flinging jeans, shirts, and boots into an old suitcase, shouting his news to Ellen who stood in the doorway.

'That does it!' he said for the umpteenth time that day. 'The Supreme Court wants to send Fred back to prison! I'm resigning my judgeship!' Socks flew through the air from the dresser to the suitcase. 'I've called a press conference for Monday morning,' he continued. 'I want you to be there. I can't continue in this kind of a system.'

Bill slammed the suitcase shut and bounded down the stairs, Ellen behind him. 'Bye,' he yelled. 'Handle any calls. Okay?'

On Monday morning the Elkhart courthouse was humming. Clusters of curious secretaries and court clerks gossiped excitedly; attorneys paced the second floor hall like expectant fathers. Inside Judge Bontrager's office, klieg lights, TV cameras, microphones, and reporters from newspaper, radio, and TV jammed the overheated room.

Bontrager sat at his desk, fingers interlaced behind his head. On a small couch nearby Ellen sat with a young couple.

Bontrager told the press that he was going to resign his judgeship. He described the Palmer case and said he could not in conscience send Fred Palmer back to prison.

'When God's law and man's law come into conflict,' he said, 'we must choose God's law. Christ cared for the individual. So must we.' He paused. 'If I have to be true to something, I will be true to God and not the law.' The man who in the past could not, like his father, show emotion had gravel in his voice and bit his cheek to stifle his tears.

The reporters knew they had a great story: small-town Republican judge throwing his career away because of concern for an individual abused by the system. What a 'one man standing alone' headline.

For Bontrager it was not that simple. Still angry, still hurt, he knew his flair for drama was playing on his passion for justice. His motives were mixed up just as this case was mixed up. But he was certain of one thing: while the news media would focus on Bontrager and the Supreme Court and the wording of the law, somebody ought to be caring about Fred Palmer and his family. In all the legal manoeuvrings, lives were at stake.

Bontrager stood and walked over to the couch, took a seat beside his wife, and put his arm around the young man seated there. 'This is Fred Palmer,' he said, 'I wanted you all to meet him. He is the story, not me. Bill Bontrager will survive; I'm not the one going back to those prison hellholes.'

By evening the story was a major item on the local news. By the next day, it was national. Calls came from across the nation, even across the ocean. But friends in Elkhart hounded Bill for a different purpose. They didn't want him to quit. Even some of the folks he had offended asked him to stay on, trying to convince him that he could do more to fight injustice as a judge than he could through the dramatic gesture of resigning.

So after two weeks of turmoil, Bill announced he would stay. That decision made, he launched himself back into his work the way he always had – long hours, heavy caseload. But he did not stop thinking about the Palmer case. He investigated legal strategy Fred could use to avoid returning to prison. After all, the man had served his sentence. If the Supreme Court said he, the judge, had mistakenly judged the case, why should Palmer suffer for it?

In June, the Supreme Court's decision was made official. Palmer was to appear in court immediately to be sent back to prison. Bontrager ordered him in, but then granted delays to his lawyer. Then he went further. He began to work with Palmer's lawyer, guiding his legal strategy and helping him gather evidence about the Indiana prisons Palmer would be sent to. This move took Bill beyond acceptable standards of judicial involvement in a case.

The prosecuting attorney burst into Bill's office one day, shut the door, and told him in no uncertain terms that he was a flaming idiot. He was risking contempt of the Indiana Supreme Court and was too emotionally involved in the case.

'It isn't too difficult to see that you are wrong when someone hits you between the eyes with a four-by-four,' Bontrager confessed later.

So Bill removed himself from the case and a local attorney, Richard Sproull, was selected as Special Judge. He made a decision that Palmer would have to be sent back to prison but then ruled that such punishment would be manifestly unjust and cruel. He was practically inviting another appeal of Palmer's sentence, and Palmer's lawyer made it. Palmer stayed out of prison while the case went back to the Supreme Court.

The wheels of justice rolled on for two more years while the court made a full investigation of the case. Fred Palmer continued to grow as a Christian and as a responsible father and husband and continued meeting with his victims and making restitution. He and Loretta also were expecting a second child.

Bontrager also grew as a Christian during this time, often returning to the Book of Amos. He regretted stepping over his bounds in the Palmer case, but believed that the Indiana Supreme Court would overlook his exuberance in light of the right judgment he had made. He told Palmer not to worry; the court would never send him back to prison.

On January 30, 1981, a Friday evening, Bill and Ellen and the boys were eating a late dinner and discussing plans for an upcoming ski trip when the phone rang. Ellen reached to answer it, then handed the receiver across the table to Bill.

Bill took the phone; it was the prosecuting attorney in the Palmer case. He listened for a moment, made no reponse, and hung up, his face drained of colour.

As Ellen and the kids watched, wondering what had happened, the doorbell rang. Ellen opened the front door to an abashed state trooper and escorted him to the dinner table.

'I'm really sorry to have to give you this, Judge,' said the officer, handing Bill a stiff sheet of paper. The document confirmed what the attorney had called to tell him: the Indiana Supreme Court had dismissed Fred Palmer's case, ordered Palmer back to prison, and charged both Judge William Bontrager and Special Judge Richard Sproull with criminal contempt of court.

Bill was dumbfounded, to say the least. The Supreme Court had caught him in a vice. The legal battles for Fred Palmer were over; his own were just beginning. But the hardest thing facing him at that moment was how in the world he was going to call Fred and tell him he would have to go back to prison. He had reassured Fred a hundred times that justice would be done.

He could not sleep, and early the next morning made the dreaded call.

The phone rang several times in the Palmers' trailer. Fred was still asleep, Loretta was in the shower, and Jamie was watching cartoons on TV. Still half asleep, Fred picked up the bedroom phone and heard Jamie pick up the kitchen extension at the same time.

His voice choked with tears, Bill did not mince words. 'Fred,' he said, 'the Supreme Court's made a decision. They dismissed your appeal – and they've ordered you back to prison.'

Fred felt his stomach turn over, then realised that his little girl had heard Bill's words, for she had dropped the extension and was screaming hysterically.

'Wait,' Fred shouted into the phone. 'Bill, hold on.' He ran to the kitchen and picked up his daughter, trying to quiet her. He began praying out loud and gradually her sobs ceased. By this time Loretta was out of the shower, tears streaming down her face as she heard the news.

Jamie eventually lifted her head from Fred's soggy shoulder. 'It's going to be all right, daddy,' she said. 'Jesus told me so.'

When Fred got back to the phone, Bill continued, 'Fred, you need to turn yourself in.'

'I'll be there,' Fred replied. 'Give me until six o'clock this evening. I need to help my family get ready.'

When they had hung up, a shaking Fred called some friends. Within an hour the small trailer was full of people from church. They prayed, sang, read Scripture, and cried.

At 5:30 that afternoon Fred Palmer walked into the Elkhart County Jail and turned himself in.

A week later Fred Palmer appeared in court for final senten-cing. The courtroom was packed with members of the press, members of the Palmers' and Bontragers' churches, friends, and supporters. Several of the victims, including Randy Brown and Randy Yohn were again in court – this time on Fred's behalf. Ellen and Loretta sat together, their faces, like many others, wet with tears.

The proceedings were brief. Fred was led in from the

holding cell in chains. Bontrager didn't allow himself to say much, knowing he would break down. He simply read out the sentence – no less than ten and no more than twenty years – enacting the will of the state. Then the guards took Palmer away, back to prison for at least nine more years.

Ellen went out to meet Fred in the back hallway as he was being led away. The man in chains and the wife of the judge stood quietly holding hands. 'It's okay,' Fred said. 'Tell Bill I understand.'

A month later, February, 1981, the Supreme Court of Indiana found Judge William Bontrager in contempt of court. They sentenced him to thirty days in prison and fined him $500, then suspended his prison sentence. They also ordered a complete investigation of his four years as a judge, with a possibility of removing him from the bench and taking away his licence to practise law. By November, 1981, ten charges had been filed against him.

For Bill and his family, 1981 was agony. He continued to serve as a judge while the legal threat and mounting legal costs hung over him. Besides the contempt finding, a computer error in his pay cost him $700 a month in income; Ellen injured her knee and spent the year in physical therapy; Richard had unsuccessful skin-graft surgery.

Bill contemplated resigning several times, but decided to let the legal battle run its course, whatever the outcome. His sons also urged him to stay and fight, for they, too, had learned the need to stand on principles.

Ironically, the very system he had tried to change was now bearing coldly and mechanically down on him, threatening to take away his livelihood and his sense of worth.

His reputation was shot. He had been a promising politician, a successful lawyer. Now gossip pictured him as a troublemaker, a man with unquenchable thirst for drama, a maverick who loved to make waves and tilt with windmills. He could see a kernel of truth in the gossip, too; he had made mistakes, big mistakes. Had he ultimately helped the cause of justice or harmed it? Had he helped Fred Palmer or hurt him? He was uncertain. All he knew for sure was that his current dilemma had come about because he had cared about Harry Fred Palmer, cared that he be treated justly under the law, and believed that was how God meant him to feel. By the letter of the law, however, he had cared too much.

The Bontrager case ended unexpectedly and rather undramatically. While the charges stood before the Supreme Court, an unrelated controversy grew in the juvenile courts. Bontrager foresaw a fight that could only hurt the reputation of the court. Rather than fight and see the court harmed, he resigned in December, 1981. His staff wept at the news. The Supreme Court dropped their charges.

Fred Palmer served twenty more months of his sentence before being released by a special clemency order of Governor Robert Orr. After an additional six months in a work-release centre, Palmer finally returned home.

'Sometimes in prison,' he says, 'people would ask me, "If God's so good, why did He send you back to prison?" and I would tell them, "God didn't send me back here. He allowed me to send men back to tell people like you about Jesus Christ."

'Since I came to Christ,' he continues, 'I view all those things from a different perspective. God is sovereign. When I was in prison, I was still living within my Father's house. Prison had nothing to do with rehabilitating me. It was the Word of God that did that.'

Bill Bontrager operates a struggling law practice from a small house in Elkhart. Business is scarce and reporters don't come around any more. They have moved on to other stories.

Bill often feels he is wasting his time. Once he was Judge Bontrager, sweeping the courts clean, making justice just. Now many in Elkhart think of him only as a chapter in history. And yet he still sometimes daydreams of different outcomes. He ponders his own mistakes, his personal shortcomings, and he surely does not think of himself as a saint or martyr.

Bill sees his own experiences as part of God's plan: 'I met

and accepted Christ in 1977, but I continued in control of my own destiny. It wasn't until November, 1981, after becoming an emotional wreck, that I let go and turned the future over to Him. I surrendered myself. Since then He has continued to teach me submission and patience, the need to study His Word and seek Him in prayer. He has removed much of my anger; in short, I am at peace today, *knowing Him* – and that makes me count as gain all that the world might count as loss.'

His court reporter, Zo Ann Myers, thinks she understands Bill's decisions: 'He became a Christian while on the bench, you know, and that made it harder for him. He was a judge who had compassion. I've seen him rule on a juvenile case, then rip off his robes and run out to the hall and put his arm around the kid as he was being led away. "I care about you," he would say. And they knew he did. Sometimes he would get choked up during a case, right there in the courtroom.

'He stood on his convictions. When he felt the legal system was at odds with God's law, he knew he had to obey God. And he loved his job. But near the end, when he was so emotionally drained from the whole thing, I heard him say many times, "I've just got to do what I know to be right, even if I lose my job over it."'

Which he did.

So whatever you think of Bill Bontrager and his stand, however you sum up his passionate personality and the mistakes he made, what he did remains clear: he saw something he believed was wrong under God's standards and he did something about it. He took the risk of action.

And he paid dearly for that action. Obedience to God does not always mean a happy ending. But why should we think it would?

17
The Radical Christian

Whenever old-timers – lawyers, court officials, and reporters – gather around the Elkhart County Court house, it is not unusual for the conversation to turn to Bill Bontrager. Some understand what he did; others still can't, and wonder why the judge got so worked up over 'the kid who just got what he had coming'. Old political cronies have the hardest time, for they can't figure out why a conservative Republican would go against his fellow conservatives on the State Supreme Court. 'Bontrager,' one office holder shrugs, sighing in resignation, 'well, he's just gone radical, that's all.'

Gone radical. What a great term for it. Unfortunately, 'radical' has taken on unpleasant, even nasty connotations in modern times. It suggests something un-American, like the violent protesters of the 1960s who blew up campus buildings, or fiery-eyed extremists of the right. But the word 'radical' comes from the Latin *radix* meaning 'the root' or 'the fundamental'. So it simply means going back to the original source or 'getting to the root of things.'

Indeed, in a world where values are being shaped by the fleeting fantasies of secular humanism, it is radical to stand for the fundamental truth of God, to go to the 'root', the Word of God.

Believers today have many ancestral radicals in their family tree. In fact, the kingdom of God is full of them.

John Wesley passionately argued that there could be 'no holiness but social holiness . . . [and] to turn [Christianity] into a solitary religion is to destroy it'.[1] Wesley was branded a radical for his famed St Mary's speech, an angry, but accurate denunciation of his fellow Oxford faculty members for their weak-kneed faith (he was never invited to speak there again). Later he captured the essence of radical holiness when he wrote: 'Making an open stand against all the ungodliness and unrighteousness, which overspreads our land as a flood, is one of the noblest ways of confessing Christ in the face of His enemies.'[2]

Anyone who has read my books or heard me speak knows the profound impact William Wilberforce has had on my Christian life. That's why I refer so consistently to his radical stand for Christ in his culture and why I quote so often from a letter written by John Wesley to Wilberforce – then a recent convert. Wesley, who was to die only days later, commissioned Wilberforce to lead the radical campaign against slavery. I've carried this excerpt from Wesley's letter in my Bible for the past seven years:

> Unless the Divine Power has raised you up to be as Athanasius, *contra mundum*, I see not how you can go through your glorious enterprise in opposing that execrable villainy which is the scandal of religion, of England, and of human nature. Unless God has raised you up for this very thing, you will be worn out by the opposition of men and devils, but if God be for you, who can be against you? Are all of them together stronger than God? Oh, be not weary in well doing. Go on, in the name of God and in the power of His might, till even American slavery, the vilest that ever saw the sun, shall vanish away before it.[3]

Wilberforce took his stand, at first but a single, lonely voice against a business that was the mainstay of the lucrative West Indies trade, employing some 5,500 sailors and 160 ships worth 6,000,000 pounds sterling a year. For twenty years the radical Wilberforce, later joined by a small group of Christian friends known as the Clapham Sect, fought the economic and political might of the British Empire. In the end, righteousness prevailed, and for the next half century a mighty revival swept across England and the Western world.

Contra mundum. Against the world. Radicals.

Certainly that describes believers like Dietrich Bonhoeffer and other German Christians who had the audacity to stand against Hitler and his super-race monstrosity, and whose stand led many of them to imprisonment and death. And certainly it describes Bill Bontrager.

Radical stands do, however, lead us into the briar patch of thorny questions about the Christian's role in government and politics.

First comes the issue of civil disobedience.

The Bontrager case suggests that Christians must disobey their government when it directs them contrary to God's law. Yet Scripture plainly commands us to obey civil laws and to be in subjection to governing authorities.[4] Isn't this a clear conflict?

No. But to resolve it requires understanding a major biblical purpose of government. The origin of government goes back to humanity's first sin, when to keep rebellious Adam and Eve away from the Tree of Life, God stationed an angel with flaming sword at the entrance to the Garden; this was, so to speak, the first cop on the beat. Thereafter the Bible makes clear that government was established as God's means for restraining man's sin.* God's people are enjoined to submit to those in authority not because governments are inherently sanctified, but because the alternative is anarchy. In its sinfulness, humanity would quickly destroy itself.

Government, then, is biblically ordained for the purpose of preserving order, but, as Francis Schaeffer writes, 'God has ordained the State as a *delegated* authority; it is not

---

* Avaricious as it is by nature, government has today strayed far from its biblical purposes; it is hard to imagine how subsidising college professors or controlling tobacco crops, laudable though such ventures may seem, can be considered as necessary for preserving order and maintaining justice. So the Christian, when weighing his biblical responsibility towards governments, may draw ethical distinctions between a government's exercise of a clear biblical mandate and the exercise of some illegitimate function.

autonomous.'[5] So when government violates what God clearly commands, it exceeds its authority. At that point, the Christian is no longer bound to be in submission, but can be compelled to open and active disobedience. Dr Carl Henry sums up the Christian duty: 'If a government puts itself above the norms of civilised society, it can be disobeyed and challenged in view of the revealed will of God; if it otherwise requires what conscience disallows, one should inform government and be ready to take the consequences.'

John Knox, the great Scottish lawyer and theologian, advocated Christian revolution under such circumstances – to the shock of the Christian world of the sixteenth century.[6]

Furthermore, the Bible provides clear precedence for civil disobedience. Moses' parents are cited approvingly for their decision to hide their child from Egyptian officials, as are Daniel and his friends for their refusal to bow before the statue of Nebuchadnezzar. In the days following Pentecost, Peter and John defied the orders of the Sanhedrin, the Jewish governing body, who ordered the disciples to stop speaking of Jesus.[7]

Most cases are not this clear-cut, of course, and therefore the Christian's response can never be made lightly or automatically. Only after seeking every other remedy, after prayer, consultation with Christian brothers and sisters, and a thorough search of Scripture should civil disobedience be employed.

The second thorny question is whether men and women who seek to be faithful to Christ can serve in public office.

My answer is yes. For if Christ is not only truth, but *the* truth of life and all creation, then Christians belong in the political arena, just as they belong in all legitimate fields and activities, that 'the blessings of God might show forth in every area of life', to quote the great Puritan pastor Cotton Mather. Indeed, it is the Christian's duty to see that God's standards of righteousness are upheld in the governing process. This may be accomplished from within the structures themselves or from the outside by organising public pressure to influence the system.

LOVING GOD

Or, it may have to be done as Bontrager did by taking a
stand in open defiance of the system.

This, then, leads us to the third and perhaps the thorniest
question: can Christians be vigorous advocates for justice
and morality without destroying the separation of church
and state?

The New Testament is clear: there is to be no merger of
church and state until Christ returns and the kingdoms of
this world become 'the kingdom of our Lord and of his
Christ.'[8] As Schaeffer writes, we must not 'confuse the
Kingdom of God with our country . . . or wrap Christianity
in our national flag.'[9]

Yet Christians sometimes do just that, using God to
sanctify their own political prejudices, becoming arrogant
and divisive in equating their favourite form of government
or their political hobbyhorse with Christianity.

Politicians are willing partners in this process, all too often
deftly turning the tables so that the religious leader who
thinks he is influencing the government may suddenly discover he's the one being manipulated – for the politician's
gain. (As one whose job it was to woo religious leaders for the
Nixon White House, I can testify that they are no more
immune than anyone else to the blandishments of power.)

Or as one clear-sighted writer warns: 'History has shown
that when society embraces religion, religion usually hugs
back. Accommodation is often followed by assimilation and
amalgamation. We accept some popularity and, craving
more, we discard the convictions we have that might be
unpopular . . . our identity as Christians is threatened.'[10]

The key to answering this question is to understand that
the Christian's goal is not power, but justice. We are to seek
to make the institutions of power just, without being corrupted by the process necessary to do this. It requires a
delicate balance, and Deity is our role model:

God in His sheer power could have crushed Satan in his
revolt by the use of that sufficient power. But because of
God's character, justice came before the use of power

alone. Therefore Christ died that justice, rooted in what God is, would be the solution . . . Christ's example, because of who He is, is our standard, our rule, our measure. Therefore power is not first, but justice is first in society and law.[11]

But, say some, it's just common sense that to be in a position to exercise justice one must acquire power first. How often that rationale has been used to justify the most awful abuses committed in the name of religion. Though it is one of the most baffling paradoxes of the Christian faith, often precisely the opposite seems true. Malcolm Muggeridge helps explain it: 'It is in the breakdown of power rather than in its triumph that men may discern its true nature and in an awareness of their own inadequacy when confronted with such a breakdown that they can best understand who and what they are.'[12]

Bontrager learned that lesson. So did I . . . in prison.

All my life I sought wealth, success, and fame because they were the keys – or so I thought – to security and power. I was influenced, like most children of the Great Depression, by memories of breadlines and parents worrying whether there would be enough money for food and rent. The vision of the American dream drove this immigrant's grandson, and I believed with determination and hard work I could make it to the top. Money and property were the keys to the kingdom where I could lock the door against want, fear, and insecurity.

Law school only deepened my convictions about the importance of private property. (In the post-war era, property courses in law school outnumbered courses about individual rights by at least 4 to 1; there were, incidentally, no courses on ethics.)

Then, I discovered that practising law was like most businesses: the most desirable clients were those able to pay the most. So I began to spend my time almost exclusively with corporate executives or individuals with resources. (Like 98 percent of all lawyers, my only brush with criminal

law or the poor and disadvantaged were those dreaded
occasions – once or twice a year at most – when my number
was called in one of the local courts and I was assigned an
indigent client.)

I became convinced that law – justice, that is – functioned
to protect the individual's property and to act as the ultimate
arbitrator in a mercantile society. Thus I saw my mission to
be one of using my persuasive abilities in Congress or in the
courts on behalf of those whose economic interests I represented (and by whom, not incidentally, I was very well
paid). Justice was, in short, the sum of the rules and policies I
tried to shape.

When I moved into politics, my task was not really any
different, except that my clients became the politicians I
served, the political convictions I had formed, the party
platform, and those whose campaign contributions or influence could get them through the imposing security of the
White House gates. (I used to scoff at the protesters who
couldn't get through those gates. 'Law is not made in the
streets but in the halls of government', was a favourite
expression. A nice way of saying that justice was determined
by those of us who controlled the levers of political power.)

Ultimately, of course, I saw justice as the instrument for
removing from society, and punishing, those who refused or
were unable to live by the rules people like myself made. To
be sure I had fundamental convictions about individual
liberty and, as a student of Locke and Jefferson, believed
deeply in man's inalienable rights and the preservation of
individual freedoms. But my basis for judgment (as well as
the causes and individuals I fought for) was almost entirely
subjective, hence dangerously vulnerable to every whim and
passion. The brighter I became, the more dangerous I was;
the more power I acquired, the more power acquired me.

I was blind. Indeed, only in the 'breakdown of power' did I
finally understand both it and myself. For my view of life was
through such narrow openings as the elegantly draped windows of the White House, and my vistas were of lush green
lawns, manicured bushes, and proud edifices housing the

corridors of power. But looking at the world from the underside through the bars of a dark prison cage and the barbed wire of forced confinement, I could, for the first time, really *see*.

Lying on the next cot, three feet away in the crowded, noisy dormitory, was a former small-town bank president doing three years for a first offence conviction of $3,000 tax fraud. So deep were the wounds of years of fruitless appeals that his face was drawn and gaunt. He was the first flesh-and-blood casualty I met of the great economic wars I had fought. *Maybe*, I thought, *he ran afoul of one of those quirks or loopholes I'd engineered in the Internal Revenue Code.* (Prison was full of people prosecuted under laws I had written or enforced; that's why my life was threatened during those first days in prison.)

Next I encountered a man in his twenties whose face reflected perpetual pain. A filling station owner, he was doing six months for having cashed a customer's $84.00 cheque which later proved to be stolen. First offence, too. His harsh sentence was the result of some ambitious prosecutor making a name for himself and a judge with a mean streak and a reputation for impulsiveness.

A moon-faced black lad with doleful eyes came to talk with me, insisting he did not know what his sentence was. Certain he was playing dumb to win my sympathy and legal assistance, I brushed him aside. Some days later, to my astonishment, I discovered he was sincere. A court-appointed lawyer had given him twenty minutes, persuaded him to plead guilty to a charge of knowingly purchasing stolen property, and marched him terrified and handcuffed before a judge who mumbled something about four years and cracked the gavel with that sound no defendant ever forgets. This young man, who had never been in jail before, had spent the next thirty days fending for his life, crouched in the corner of a holding cell in a Tennessee jail. For weeks after arriving at our prison he cowered like a dog who had been beaten.

These men were not exceptions. Most of those in prison with me were poor; or if they had had any money, it had been wiped out by their enormous trial costs. Though folklore has

it that minimum security prisons, like the one I was in, are
full of wealthy 'white-collar criminals' doing a few months of
'easy' time, I met but a handful who could have afforded to
hire me as their lawyer only a year earlier.

So it was there, surrounded by such despair and suffering,
that I began to see through the eyes of the powerless. I began
to understand why God views society not through the princes
of power, but through the eyes of the sick and needy, the
oppressed and downtrodden. I began to realise why in
demanding justice God spoke not through easily corrupted
kings, but through peasant prophets who in their own
powerlessness could see and communicate God's perspective. As a result, I learned to say with Solzhenitsyn, 'bless
you, prison' for coming into my life. For only in the breakdown of my own worldly power did I see what power is, what
it had done to me, and what it had done through me to others.
I learned that power did not equal justice.

But the Christian who breaks radically with the power of
the world is far from powerless – another kingdom paradox.
For example, some might think that in surrendering the
power of his judgeship, Bill Bontrager forfeited any chance to
influence the justice system in his state. But the verdict on
that is not in yet, and reform efforts are actively underway in
Indiana. At the very least, his move revealed a system of
injustice to eyes that might never otherwise have seen it. In
my own life it is certainly clear that my powerlessness has
been used by God to influence the criminal justice system far
more than anything I did from my office of worldly power.

If we would love God, we must love His justice and act
upon it. Then, taking a holy, radical stand – *contra mundum* if
need be – we surrender the illusion of power and find it
replaced by True Power. That was certainly one of Alexander Solzhenitsyn's greatest discoveries in the Soviet gulag.

Like other prisoners, Solzhenitsyn worked in the fields,
his days a pattern of backbreaking labour and slow star-
vation. One day the hopelessness became too much to bear.
Solzhenitsyn felt no purpose in fighting on; his life would

make no ultimate difference. Laying his shovel down, he walked slowly to a crude work-site bench. He knew at any moment a guard would order him up and, when he failed to respond, bludgeon him to death, probably with his own shovel. He'd seen it happen many times.

As he sat waiting, head down, he felt a presence. Slowly he lifted his eyes. Next to him sat an old man with a wrinkled, utterly expressionless face. Hunched over, the man drew a stick through the sand at Solzhenitsyn's feet, deliberately tracing out the sign of the cross.

As Solzhenitsyn stared at that rough outline, his entire perspective shifted. He knew he was merely one man against the all-powerful Soviet empire. Yet in that moment, he also knew that the hope of all mankind was represented by that simple cross – and through its power, anything was possible. Solzhenitsyn slowly got up, picked up his shovel, and went back to work – not knowing that his writings on truth and freedom would one day enflame the whole world.

Such is the power God's truth affords one man willing to stand against seemingly hopeless odds. Such is the power of the cross.

THE HOLY NATION

They love one another. They never fail to help widows; they save orphans from those who would hurt them. If they have something they give freely to the man who has nothing; if they see a stranger, they take him home, and are happy, as though he were a real brother. They don't consider themselves brothers in the usual sense, but brothers instead through the Spirit, in God.

Aristides describing Christians
to the Emperor Hadrian

18

The Holy Nation

At the height of the energy crisis in 1977, the governor of
Virginia ordered energy use restricted in non-essential buildings. No one seemed particularly surprised that churches
headed his list. In the eyes of the world, as well as many
church-goers, the church is only a building, and an expensive, under-used one at that; except for a few hours on
Sunday and an occasional mid-week service or function, the
building sits empty. So why use scarce resources to heat
it?

These same people consider the church just another institution with its own bureaucracy, run by ministers and
priests who, like lawyers and doctors, are members of a
profession (though not so well-paid). And while this parochial institution fulfils a worthwhile social and inspirational
function, rather like an arts society or civic club, most people
could get along fine without it.

In many ways, of course, the church has allowed itself to
become what the world says it is. (This seems to be a
common human bent – to become what others consider us to
be.) But that sad fact has not dulled or changed God's
definition of, and intention for, His church. For biblically the
church is an *organism* not an *organisation* – a *movement*, not a
monument. It is not a part of the community; it is a whole
new community. It is not an orderly gathering; it is a new
order with new values, often in sharp conflict with the values
of the surrounding society.

The church does not draw people in; it sends them out. It
does not settle into a comfortable niche, taking its place

alongside the Rotary, the Elks, and the country club. Rather, the church is to make society uncomfortable. Like yeast, it unsettles the mass around it, changing it from within. Like salt, it flavours and preserves that into which it vanishes.

But as yeast is made up of many particles and salt composed of multiplied grains, so the church is many individual believers. For God has given us each other; we do not live the Christian life alone. We do not love God alone.

To believe Jesus means we follow Him and join what He called the 'kingdom of God' which He said was 'at hand'.[1] This is a 'new commitment . . . a new companionship, a new community established by conversion.'[2]

Consider how Aristides described the Christians to the Roman Emperor Hadrian:

> They love one another. They never fail to help widows; they save orphans from those who would hurt them. If they have something they give freely to the man who has nothing; if they see a stranger, they take him home, and are happy, as though he were a real brother. They don't consider themselves brothers in the usual sense, but brothers instead through the Spirit, in God.[3]

Aristides was describing the kingdom of God made visible by believers.

Paradoxically, it was Peter, the most Jewish and parochial of all the apostles – the one who argued with Paul over circumcision and who was reluctant to preach the Good News to the Gentiles at Caesarea – who grasped most clearly this vision of a new kingdom. He addressed the young church, made up of believers of every country, race, and language of the then-known world as 'a holy nation'.[4]

This was no catchy phrase Peter thought up to describe the church; he took the words from the Scriptures – from the words God spoke to Moses when He called the Israelites to be His 'holy nation'.[5] In those days God literally pitched His tent and lived among His people. Now the kingdom is evidenced through those in whom Christ dwells. As John Calvin said, it is the first duty of the Christian to make the invisible Kingdom visible.

Can it happen? Can we be not only a holy people but a holy nation? Yes, we *must* be. But to do so requires an understanding and practice of certain truths – what might be considered basic principles for the church. I have found some of these best illustrated by a church in what might at first seem an unlikely place – Seoul, Korea.

The Republic of Korea, a country of 37,000,000 people, is predominantly Buddhist; there are only 7,000,000 Christians, of which perhaps 2,000,000 are evangelical. Yet I was astonished during my first visit to Seoul in 1981 to see signs of Christian influence everywhere: thriving churches, Christian values, and complete openness to the Gospel. I was given access to the prisons, even those with political prisoners, preaching three times to packed prison halls, where many inmates made profession of faith. I was permitted to meet with American inmates held on Korean charges and was even allowed unmonitored visits with leaders of dissident groups.

The highlight of the trip was a Sunday morning service at the Full Gospel Church in Seoul – again to my astonishment. I was wary. I had read about this church's phenomenal growth from a tiny mission with a handful of members in the early 1960s to the largest congregation in the world twenty years later – over 150,000 members.

I have never believed growth should be the prime goal of the church and certainly not proof of its spirituality. So I mumbled a bit to myself about super-hype when I arrived and saw the mobs being herded in and out, buses lined up for blocks, TV cameras and technicians everywhere. *They must not preach the Gospel* I thought, judging that only Madison Avenue and Hollywood transplanted to Seoul could do this – not the Holy Spirit. I was also apprehensive because I'd heard the crowd was even more demonstrative than most Pentecostal churches in the US. I like amen corners, but . . .

Though I've spoken to large crowds many times, it was

electrifying to look out over the more than 10,000 people packed wall-to-wall and be told there were 15,000 more in overflow halls watching on closed-circuit television. And this was only one of six Sunday services!

As I began to preach, the Senior Pastor Cho at my side translating rapidly, I sensed a genuine warmth radiating from the congregation, a powerful surge of the Spirit. My speaking became effortless. The language barrier, often evident through even the best interpreters, vanished as the pastor and I developed immediate rapport. And though I couldn't understand the words during the rest of the service, there was excitement and, to my delight, real reverence. It was a holy time.

Afterward, I met with Pastor Cho in his study. A pale and slender man, the pastor seemed shy and withdrawn until he began to speak; then there was a fire about him.

'Fantastic church you lead, Pastor,' I said.

'Oh, no,' he waved aside the compliment. 'This is not the church. This is only where we all come together once a week. The church is in the home – 10,000 cell groups which meet regularly all around this city.'

My mistake was a natural one. I figured a church so phenomenally successful must be the result of the leader's charisma and personality, for so often our American churches and parachurch movements grow because of the personality of the pastor or leader. This pattern is merely another Christian adaptation of the celebrity cultism of our society.

But a charismatic leader is not the secret of the vitality and size of the Full Gospel Church in Seoul. Cho *is* dynamic and brilliant; but the growth of the church resulted from his brokenness, not his strength. Cho has been ill most of his life, has had TB diagnosed in its terminal stages, has suffered a nervous breakdown from fatigue, and has had repeated severe ulcer attacks. The cell concept was developed as necessity because Cho was so weak he couldn't manage the church; thus, he commissioned elders to take responsibility for the people in each of their neighbourhoods. (Breaking customs deeply rooted in his Oriental culture, Pastor Cho named many women to head cell groups.)

Those cell groups, really home churches, evangelised their neighbourhoods, provided a way neighbours could help each other, encouraged spiritual discipline, and began to mushroom.[6]

I silently chastised myself for my judgmental attitude as Pastor Cho told me that though he had a carefully organised system for maintaining appropriate pastoral authority and providing structured sermons and teaching materials for the groups, from 1964 to 1973 he never once totalled the membership of the church. When he finally discovered that through the quiet evangelisation of the home church the membership had jumped during that time from 8,000 to 23,000, Cho was stunned.

This raises what I believe is the first principle for the church: *the body of believers called the church is to grow from the inside out in response to the Spirit.* Built that way, the church prevails against anything.

Ever aware that an army of North Korean divisions is poised at the DMZ, twenty-six kilometres north of Seoul, Pastor Cho is quick to point out that he could be arrested, the church doors barred, his staff removed overnight, and the church would still grow. (That's exactly what happened in China, where the Church multiplied several times over during the dark years of the cultural revolution and the great purges.)

What would happen if your pastor was removed and your church building closed or destroyed? Most churches are totally dependent on the pastor and church staff. Youth for Christ president, Jay Kesler, sometimes quips, 'The western church is like a pro football game on Sunday afternoon: 100,000 people sitting in the stands watching 22 men knock their brains out on the field.' Take away the 22 and there is no game.

Cho has not allowed that to happen in Seoul. He believes God at one point ordered him 'to let my people grow', so he has taken his mission 'to equip the lay people, so the lay people can carry out the ministry both inside and outside the church.'[7]

Beloved pastor and Chaplain of the Senate, Dick Halverson, agrees that 'equipping the saints' – which of course means all believers – is the central thrust of any pastor's calling. 'Nowhere in the Bible,' he writes, 'is the world exhorted to "come to church". But the church's mandate is clear: she must go to the world . . . the work of ministry belongs to the one in the pew, not the one in the pulpit.' So, he says, the church comes together on Sunday mornings principally to be prepared to carry out its ministry the rest of the week in every walk of life.[8]

And that is the second principle for the church: *it must equip the laity to take the church into the world.*

If practised, this principle would cure the schizophrenia so many Christians have. Ask a church layman, 'What is your ministry?' and the reply is invariably the same: 'Oh, I'm a computer programmer by day, but every Thursday night I work with the Gideons. That's my ministry.' Halverson calls this a false dichotomy between the sacred and the secular. The believer's ministry is being Christ's person right where he or she is, in the marketplace or the home, every moment of every day. This is part of the everyday business of holiness. This is the very nature of loving God.

The church in Korea has problems, of course – and in some cases the criticism that it is in an unholy league with the government may be valid. Despite this, its people are characterised by an intense commitment to spiritual discipline. Many of the cell groups from Cho's church and prayer groups from other churches meet in the early morning hours for Bible study and prayer. Few serious Korean Christians would begin their day without a devotional time. Because of the pervasiveness of this commitment, many employers permit prayer and study groups to meet in factories and office buildings during lunch breaks.

The Full Gospel Church has a retreat centre called Prayer Mountain where on any given day a thousand or more believers may be found kneeling on straw mats in tiny caves hollowed out of a mountainside. The overflow fills one of the centre's large halls. Workers will often take the first half of their two-week vacation at this place for fasting and prayer.

Is it any wonder that though outnumbered 5 to 1 by Buddhists, the Christian church is the most powerful influence in the Korean culture? While in sad contrast, the Christian church in America, outnumbering other religions 10 to 1, is far from the dominant influence in our culture.

The third key principle for the church, then is *spiritual discipline – fervent prayer and serious study of God's Word*. This is the life or death principle, for churches that neglect the Word and the prayer life quickly wither. But churches that exercise spiritual discipline can be mightily used.

The great revivals have been born in times when Christians were intent on prayer. The lay revival of 1858, which affected the Western world for half a century, began when businessman Jeremiah Lanphier started a weekly prayer meeting with a handful of people in a small room of the Old North Dutch Church in New York City. The group grew, then meetings were held daily. Several churches followed the pattern, and soon all public meeting places in the city were regularly packed. Within a few months 10,000 people gathered daily at noon for open prayer meetings in New York streets. In two years, 2,000,000 converts entered American churches.

Like flood waters, the revival spread through the Hudson River Valley and on to Chicago, where Dwight Moody was just beginning his work with young people. Then it jumped the Atlantic to Ireland, Scotland, England, Wales, and danced like fire across much of Europe, then to South Africa and India. There was no elaborate evangelistic organisation. Communication was slow; word had to spread from one prayer cell to the next, from church to church, from city to city. It was movement inspired by the fervour of thousands of Christian laypeople.

Similar evidence can be found about the other mighty spiritual movements of recent centuries.

This evidence also makes clear that revivals are not confined geographically. For the church of Jesus Christ is not American or Korean or English or Dutch. It is one church, one body, one holy nation transcending man's arbitrary geographic and political boundaries.

This leads us to the fourth key principle for the church: *as one holy nation, we must break free of any provincialism and work for unity in Christ.*

Before my conversion, I confess, some ugly prejudices lurked in the darker corners of my heart, particularly toward those nations which America had fought against in the wars of this century. But in my travels as a believer among fellow believers of other races and nationalities, the Lord has given me some of His richest fellowship in those very countries. The Holy Spirit can break down every barrier.

Thus, what happens in the church on the remotest continent is as important as the life of our local congregation. The rest of the world is as far away as the nearest fund-starved ghetto church in our town or as close as the underground cell in China.

'If one part suffers, every part suffers with it.'[9] The great exodus to the suburbs in the last three decades makes this scriptural truth especially urgent in America. Thriving new middle-class congregations now ring centre-city ghettos where the older, almost-abandoned churches are starving to death. Like an army retreating from the battlefield, prosperous suburban congregations have left the wounded to die in the core of great metropolitan areas – both physically and spiritually.*

Congregations that continue to look inward will find their field of vision ever-narrowing. Those that recognise, as Peter

* One simple solution to this problem would be for each suburban church to adopt one centre-city church, sharing resources and teaching. The impact can be dramatic and the giving church is greatly blessed. A fine Christian movement known as STEP is dedicated to this vision: STEP Foundation, 2429 Martin Luther King Blvd., Dallas, TX 75215 (214-421-9210). Prison Fellowship is also working to mobilise inter-city communities, matching need with resources. Contact Prison Fellowship, Community Mobilisation, PO Box 17500, Washington, DC 20041.

did, that the church of Christ is one holy nation will discover unimagined spiritual treasure.

Eastminster Presbyterian Church in Wichita, Kansas, has experienced this. Though pastored by a gifted minister, Frank Kik, responsibility for the church is shared by strong laypeople and the saints are being well-equipped. Christian scholars from around the country frequently lecture there; laypeople are involved in serious theological study; many in the church are involved in prayer groups; and the congregation actively supports overseas missions and mercy ministries around the country.

All this is, I believe, the direct result of the conscious decision at Eastminster to break from its natural provincialism and put the unity of the holy nation principle into practice.

During 1975 the church, then 850 members, had raised $500,000 for an addition to its always-crowded sanctuary. The architect's drawings were nearly completed and the members were excited about the imminent construction.

Then a missions conference was held at the church, and a missionary from Guatemala showed slides of the terrible devastation from the massive earthquake which had hit that country two weeks earlier. Villages were totally wiped out; everything was in rubble, including what had once been small but growing mission churches.

When the slide presentation was over, there was a long, uncomfortable silence, as if each member had been seized with the same thought. One man spoke for everyone: 'All of this has gone on and here we are planning to spend half a million dollars on a new building.'

Another added in hushed tones, 'How can we build a Cadillac when our brothers and sisters in Guatemala haven't even got a Volkswagen?'

Eastminster scrapped its plans and drawings, scaled down its expansion to $100,000 for a multi-purpose fellowship hall, and voted that the remaining $400,000 be sent to Guatemala along with a credit line for $500,000. Pastor Kik and two elders travelled to Guatemala to oversee the building of twenty-six village churches and twenty-eight parsonages.

But the requirement for individual cells within God's holy nation goes far beyond sharing financial resources; the church is called to give itself, to share in the hunger and pain of those in need.[10]

Jesus Himself shared the pain of the needy; He suffered for the entire world. As God's visible presence in the world today, should not His people also participate in the suffering of the world?

Most emphatically, yes. Not until we go where need is and share in the suffering of the poor, alienated, isolated, and downtrodden will the holy nation of God's people also become the loving nation.

As a small group of Christians in Jefferson City, Missouri, illustrates, this is indeed how the church loves God.

19
Shared Suffering

The shadow people made no noise in Jefferson City. They appeared for a day or two, spent little money, then drifted away. They slept under bridges, on park benches, in empty parking lots; in fact, they slept anywhere they could.

While the citizens of Jefferson City knew about these shadows, they didn't think much about them, for they had no real link to the 'normal' life of this city in the middle of Missouri in the middle of the Midwest.

Jeff City is a state capital of neat shops, quiet streets, area universities. The shining legislature building, modelled after the US Capitol, sits on a high bluff overlooking the Missouri River. The town of 35,000 is sprinkled with churches.

But if you follow East High Street for a few blocks from downtown, then turn left, you come face to face with a high, grey wall spiked with guard towers. This wall encloses the forty-seven acres of the Missouri State Penitentiary; along with the three other prisons in Jefferson City, this maximum security facility holds half of Missouri's prison population.

Most of these prisoners never see a visitor. They are lost to the world, hidden from sight and memory. The few whose families do visit have the best chance of staying out of prison once they're released. So prison authorities encourage visitation.

The shadow people were the wives, children, girlfriends, parents – the families who did come to visit. They came from St Louis and Kansas City, miles away, or from smaller towns scattered across the state. Most of them lived on welfare cheques, and if they used up their meagre funds just getting to Jeff City, they certainly couldn't afford to pay for lodging.

So those who managed to come invented ways to pass the night. Like the woman who took the last possible Greyhound from Kansas City so she arrived at Jefferson City's grimy bus station at two in the morning. She then carried her six-month-old baby a few blocks to a downtown hotel, sneaked through the lobby into a rest room, wedged herself and her baby into a toilet stall, and passed the hours until eight in the morning when the prison opened for visitors. As long as she kept the baby quiet, nobody bothered her, and she felt safe. As safe as a shadow.

Others were not so safe – like the two women who, with their two small children, timed their drive from a tiny upstate town so they arrived a little after nightfall. They then drove to one of the area's many bridges – four rivers converge in Jeff City – and pulled under the shelter of the arches. Out of sight of the highway, with all four doors locked, they felt fairly secure. But they took turns sleeping in two-hour shifts, just in case.

For the most part, the shadow people weren't molested. But they felt thoroughly unwelcome in a strange city, without a place to sleep, a warm meal, or a place to shower and change clothes. They felt they were being punished along with their imprisoned loved ones.

But shadows aren't really invisible, and someone had begun to notice them as more than a nuisance or necessary evil. A group of concerned individuals from some of the area churches and civic organisations began wondering what they could do to help these obviously needy people. A study group began meeting once a month to discuss the problem, but a year passed without action.

Meanwhile, another group – Prison Fellowship volunteers already involved working with prisoners – was talking about the biblical mandate to help 'the strangers among us' and were concerned about Jeff City's shadow people. So they began inviting inmates' families to their homes. It was a start, but soon proved inadequate for the need; there were just too many visitors.

Then one volunteer, Janice Webb, began to get big ideas. A Baptist laywoman active with Prison Fellowship for several years, Janice had learned about a West Virginia hospitality house for inmates' families. Used to mobilising people for action, Janice thought, 'Why couldn't a house like that work in Jefferson City?'

About the same time, Sister Ruth Heaney, a nun who served on a criminal justice commission and was also in the civic study group, contacted Janice Webb. In Sister Ruth's opinion, Janice was 'the only logical person to get the job done'.

In May, 1980, the two women formed the Agape House Board, deciding on a name before they had any place to put it: *Agape* because they wanted to 'show the unconditional, caring love of Jesus'; and *House* because they wanted a 'place that would show that love.'

The board was made up of Catholics, Presbyterians, Episcopalians, Methodists, and Baptists; they united to attack the problem with gusto. Gusto was all they had at the time, for as Janice wryly recalls, 'We didn't have a nickel in the bank; the whole thing was a venture of faith.'

But faith along with enthusiasm got the job done. First they stumbled across an old rooming house just two blocks from the Missouri State Penitentiary; the place had nearly a dozen bedrooms, three kitchens, and a price tag of $46,000. In just six weeks the board raised the $5,000 down payment and a Christian attorney donated his legal services to manage the transaction.

The board members and their churches and families moved into the musty old house like a liberating army – hammering, sawing, painting, patching, cleaning. Five churches divided up the upstairs bedrooms. The Presbyterians' fresh wallpaper and rocking chair in one were rivalled by the Methodists' respackled ceiling, bright trim, and dried flower arrangements in another.

Downstairs, Sister Ruth coaxed hanging plants into life to

fill a bright bay window. The long stairwell was festooned with big banners brightly decorated with Scripture verses; a huge family Bible graced the foyer sideboard. Two youths from an area Catholic high school arrived one Saturday armed with a rug shampooer that attacked the acres of ancient carpet. A group of fourth graders sent freshly baked cookies to treat the troops. And one small church made a particularly significant contribution – a continuing supply of toilet paper for Agape House.

But the board knew that creating their house of love was more than just a matter of appearance. Scripture verses on the walls would not bring Scripture alive. The home would live up to its name only if the people who ran it lived up to its name.

Sister Ruth Heaney was willing to serve as the first assistant manager, and for the crucial role of house manager the board found Mildred Taylor, a small, quiet, thoroughly Southern Baptist lady waiting at her home in South Carolina for God's call to service. She was ready for whatever He had for her in Missouri.

On November 2, 1980, Mildred Taylor welcomed the first guests to Agape House, warmly offering them New Testaments along with clean sheets and towels and room keys. The charge was $3.00 a night – if they could afford it. If not, they could stay for free.

Without money, detailed studies, proposals, conferences, or government grants, the people of God reached out to the poor and those in prison. Though initially sceptical, most of the citizens of Jefferson City were happy about the house. And soon the word began to spread to the people who were no longer shadows.

New smells filled the old rooming house: fresh paint, beans or macaroni or hot dogs cooking on the kitchen stove; cigarette smoke and nail polish. New sounds filled it, too: women talking, laughing, crying; children playing and giggling.

And at night the murmur of conversation could be heard in the small apartment at the back of the big house. For from the beginning, manager Mildred Taylor made it clear to guests that the door to her quarters was always open. As the months passed, increasing numbers sought her out for a cup of tea and a quiet chat.

One weekend guest who tapped on Mildred's door was a young mother visiting her son at one of the prisons. Sara didn't talk much, but seemed comforted just to sit with Mildred. As she prepared to leave on Sunday afternoon, Sara stopped at Mildred's apartment to give her a hug. 'Thank you for having me here,' she said. 'You can't know how much this house means.'

A few days later, Mildred received the following letter from Sara:

Dear Sister Mildred,

I told you how much staying at your house meant to me, but I did not tell you the most important thing. I read the Bible you gave me the very first night but was too sick and heavy-eyed to finish. I had been trying to reaffirm my faith for months. The next night I had $13 left to get home on and I saw that Shirley there was in greater need than I was so I gave her half of it because I knew God would provide . . . Well, I went to bed feeling good that I could, with God's help, do something for someone. I read more of the Bible and got to the page where you say the prayer to get saved, and I prayed and was washed clean of my sins! I prayed a lot before I went to sleep.

Then the next day I told the Lord how sick and tired I was, and if it was His will that I might have a dry road home so it would not take me six hours. Before I went a mile the rain had stopped and I had sun all the way. I sang and praised God all the way home. The country had never looked so good.

Mildred Taylor eventually returned to South Carolina, hoping to start a ministry like Agape House in her hometown of Columbia. Because of her heavy workload with the justice Commission, Sister Ruth also left, but remained on the

board. They have been replaced by Marietta Borden, a lay
volunteer with the Southern Baptist Home Mission Board,
and Lunette Bouknight, a former nun who spent thirty-eight
years in a Catholic convent.

When Marietta was called to come to Agape House, she
left her home in New York and drove straight to Missouri
with $500 in her pocket and everything she owned packed in
her car.

Lunette first came to the house when her life-long friend
Mildred was still there – to help for a month. 'I got hooked,'
she explains. 'I knew I could stay in the convent and save my
soul. But if I wanted to do the perfect will of God, I knew I'd
have to come out and minister to His people.'

Lunette and Marietta share the house's small apartment
and nearly everything else. They rise every morning at five to
pray and study the Bible – first individually, then together.
The rest of the day they respond to the needs around them –
gathering soiled linens, emptying garbage, cleaning bath-
rooms, keeping finances straight, buying supplies, and regis-
tering guests. And they keep their apartment door open, just
as Mildred Taylor did.

'We're in the business of planting seeds,' Lu will say. 'We
don't know when a lot of them will be harvested, but that's
God's business. We just do what we can.'

Lu and Marietta don't see many dramatic conversions,
and not everyone who comes to Agape recognises their
sacrifice and love for what it is. Some take the house simply as
a cheap place to sleep. They pay – sometimes – and leave.
Others wonder what the angle is, but accept the clean, warm
comfort.

No matter, Lu and Marietta and all the others involved in
the Agape House ministry want to provide love and care, not
to calculate results. They are loving God.

The following vignette tells it all:

Sherry, a tall young woman with thick red hair and a serious
manner, first heard about Agape House from her husband
Al. She was getting ready to leave the prison visiting room

early so she could catch the bus back to St Louis before dark, when he mentioned a rooming house he had heard about from some other inmates whose wives and girlfriends had stayed there. 'It's sort of a rooming house, but cleaner, with kitchen privileges,' he said.

So Sherry walked over to the house, and though the place was just about full, the ladies in charge made a place for her. Now she was here for her third weekend and it seemed like home. Lu and Marietta welcomed her warmly, asked about Al, and bustled around with clean sheets and a readiness to talk and laugh. Sherry had put her things in a room upstairs, made up her bed, then started her dinner. She was sitting with a group at the big dining room table, engrossed in writing her nightly letter to Al while the others ate and chattered, when Jane's shrill voice called to her from the kitchen.

'Sherry,' Jane screeched, 'you'd best get out here and turn the heat down on them beans if you're serious 'bout eatin' 'em.'

Sherry flicked her hair out of her eyes, threw down her pen, and got up from the table. Jane was right; the pork and beans were stuck to the bottom of the pan, but she was so hungry she didn't care. She ladled the unburnt beans onto a large plastic plate from the cupboard, grabbed her Pepsi from the refrigerator, and rejoined the group in the dining room.

Patty, her blond hair coiled on bright pink curlers, was telling a story while she finished applying the dark red polish to her pointed fingernails. Marcia held her daughter on her lap and spooned carrots and mashed potatoes into the small mouth, while next to her Brenda plaited little LaVon's wiry black hair.

Sherry finished her beans, pushed the plate away, and lighted a cigarette. *You'd think this was Saturday night at a neighbourhood gathering if you didn't know every last person here has a husband or father two blocks away locked up in the state pen*, she laughed to herself. And even these women were a tough bunch. Patty had served a couple of prison terms and now tended bar at a beer joint in Kansas City. Her husband was a lifer. Marcia's son was in for dope. Sherry didn't know much about Brenda yet, for in the prison visiting room the blacks and whites kept pretty much apart. But she might find out more later that night when she shared a room with Brenda and her little girl.

Sherry watched Marietta come through the room carrying clean sheets and stop to compliment Patty on her neat nail-polish job. Sherry couldn't figure out what made these two ladies tick; she knew they were religious, of course. There were Bible verses everywhere, and they gave paperback New Testaments to everyone who came in. She hadn't looked at hers yet. With all the other things going on in her life she wasn't getting involved in religion. Not now anyway.

I do know one thing, though, she mused as she crushed out her cigarette. *If God is real and He is good, He must be something like these ladies at Agape House.*

20

The Church on the Front Lines

Agape House wonderfully illustrates the description once
given the church by Archbishop of Canterbury and Bible
commentator, William Temple: 'the only cooperative society
in the world that exists for the benefits of its non-members.'*
Too often, though, the church's strategy for reaching those
who 'don't belong' is exactly backward. Priority goes to
constructing an attractive edifice in a location near a growing
suburb and as far from crime-infested downtown as possible.
Next come the committees organising concerts, covered-dish
suppers, Bible studies, slide shows, and the like. Then, with
fresh welcome mat at the door, the members enthusiastic-
ally wait for all the lost and needy souls to come and join
them.

Of course they never do. What the church attracts are the
neighbours who are bored with their old church anyway, or
those looking for a group with a bit more 'status'. The folks
'out there' have no interest in the handsome sanctuary and
progressive programmes and wouldn't feel comfortable inside
no matter what wonderful attractions were offered. (And
probably the church members wouldn't feel comfortable if
they did come.)

* An unexpected affirmation for the Agape House staff and board came
in April, 1982, when President Reagan singled out Agape House as an
example for the nation. Addressing a White House gathering of 150 religious
leaders, the President commended the House as a prime example of
volunteerism at work and captured the spirit of the Agape ministry when he
summed up, 'They provided bed and bath, but something deeper – the
certainty that someone cares.'

The cultural barriers in American society are imposing. Millions live in conditions unimaginable to the typical white, middle-class American congregation. The family in the ghetto, for example, lives a day at a time, often one welfare cheque away from disaster; and odds are it's a one-parent family with one or more of its members victims of one of the plagues epidemic in America's inner cities – child abuse, alcoholism, drug addiction, prostitution.

But when the church fails to break the barrier, both sides lose. Those who need the gospel message of hope and the reality of love, don't get it; and the isolated church keeps evangelising the same people over and over until its only mission finally is to entertain itself.

Isn't it interesting that Jesus didn't set up an office in the temple and wait for people to come to Him for counselling? Instead, He went to them – to the homes of the most notorious sinners, to the places where he would most likely encounter the handicapped and sick, the needy, the outcasts of society.

I am not naive enough to think the church can bridge the cultural chasms overnight. But I do know we can come out of our safe sanctuaries and move alongside those in need and begin to demonstrate some caring concern. Our presence in a place of need is more powerful than a thousand sermons. *Being there* is our witness. And until we are, our orthodoxy and doctrine are mere words; our liturgies and gospel choruses ring hollow.

Agape House and ministries like it are taking the gospel to people wherever they are, meeting them at their point of need as Jesus taught us to do. As we love God through our love for others, seemingly insurmountable barriers fall before us, as I saw dramatically demonstrated during my first visit to the Indiana Penitentiary in 1981.

After speaking to more than two hundred inmates in the auditorium for a Prison Fellowship seminar,* I asked the warden to let us visit death row. I knew things were tense there because Stephen Judy had just been executed (electrocuted). But I wanted to see two Christian inmates with whom I'd been corresponding. The warden agreed and invited a group of our volunteers to come along as well. So about twenty of us made our way through the maze of concrete cellblocks to the double set of barred doors that led into the most despairing of all places – death row – the end of the line where men live for years from appeal to appeal. The only way out is a new trial or death.

The warden opened the individual cell doors, and one by one the men drifted out, slowly mixing with our volunteers and gathering in a circle on the walkway.

I was especially glad to meet Richard Moore, whose wife had written me such moving letters, and James Brewer, a young black man who though seriously ill with a kidney disease, was a powerful witness to the others on death row. Whether his death would come swiftly by several thousand volts of electricity or slowly by uremic poisoning, James was at perfect peace with God and his warm smile showed it.

Nancy Honeytree, the talented gospel singer who often goes with us into the prisons, played the guitar and sang a few songs. I spoke briefly. Then we all joined hands and sang 'Amazing Grace'. (Nowhere do the words of that hymn have richer meaning than among a group of society's despised outcasts condemned to die for the most awful crimes.)

My schedule was extremely tight, so after we finished 'Amazing Grace' we said our good-byes and began filing out. We were crowded into the caged area between the two massive gates when we noticed one volunteer had stayed back and was with James Brewer in his cell. I went to get the man because the warden could not operate the gates until we had all cleared out.

'I'm sorry, we have to leave,' I said, looking nervously at my watch, knowing a plane stood waiting at a nearby airstrip

---

* We constantly encounter cultural obstacles in prison, too. For example, we draw twice as many inmates if we meet in the auditorium or mess hall instead of the chapel. Some of it is peer pressure, of course, and fear of being tagged 'religious'. But much of it is the association of the chapel with an 'insensitive' church.

to fly me to Indianapolis to meet with Governor Orr. The
volunteer, a short white man in his early fifties, was standing
shoulder to shoulder with Brewer. The prisoner was holding
his Bible open while the older man appeared to be reading a
verse.

'Oh, yes,' the volunteer looked up. 'Give us just a minute,
please. This is important,' he added softly.

'No, I'm sorry,' I snapped. 'I can't keep the governor
waiting. We must go.'

'I understand,' the man said, still speaking softly, 'but this
is important. You see, I'm Judge Clement. I'm the man who
sentenced James here to die. But now he's my brother and we
want a minute to pray together.'

I stood frozen in the cell doorway. It didn't matter who I
kept waiting. Before me were two men: one was powerless,
the other powerful; one was black, the other white; one had
sentenced the other to death. Anywhere other than the
kingdom of God, that inmate might have killed that judge
with his bare hands – or wanted to anyway. Now they were
one, their faces reflecting an indescribable expression of love
as they prayed together.

Though he could hardly speak, on the way out of the
prison Judge Clement told me he had been praying for
Brewer every day since he had sentenced him four years
earlier.

After we left the prison, the judge cancelled his court
calendar for the next morning and spent the day in the Prison
Fellowship seminar. His testimony – and the story of his
meeting with Brewer, which quickly spread through the
prison grapevine – brought dozens of men to Christ.

Taking the gospel to people wherever they are – death row, the
ghetto, or next door – *is frontline evangelism.* Frontline love. *It is
our one hope for breaking down barriers and for restoring the sense of
community, of caring for one another,* that our decadent, imper-
sonalised culture has sucked out of us. It is the most urgent
challenge for the holy nation, the fifth and perhaps most
important principle.

One other story from our ministry underscores this point.

In November, 1981, Prison Fellowship brought to Atlanta, Georgia, six inmates from Florida's Eglin Prison. The six were on two-week furlough and stayed in the homes of Fellowship volunteers. (Significantly, none of the families who agreed to take inmates into their homes asked the colour of their skin or the nature of the crimes of which they had been convicted. Two of the men were black, two were white, and two were Hispanic.)

Each morning the six men gathered with Fellowship instructors in a small room at the Georgia Avenue Presbyterian Church, a red brick Victorian structure that only a generation ago towered over the quiet tree-lined streets of the Grant Park area; now the old church was nearly abandoned, a victim of Atlanta's sprawling urban decay.

After their Bible study the men descended upon the homes of two elderly widows in the neighbourhood. Crawling in the mud underneath the small frame houses, they put in insulation; they did weatherstripping, caulking, and painting. Their work was part of our community service project programme, initiated to show that non-violent inmates could be used to perform worthwhile community projects rather than sitting in a prison cell at a cost of $17,000 per year per inmate to the taxpayer. For we believe restitution, not prison, is the biblical prescribed form of punishment for these kinds of offences.*

The programme was a great success and without incident. Two widows' homes were winterised for a fraction of the estimated cost of $20,000 and without government red-tape

---

* See Exodus 21. The Bible continually mandates restitution for property offences. The Old Testament contains repeated references; and in the New Testament is found the example of Zacchaeus giving back fourfold what he had wrongly taken. Nowhere in Scripture are prisons instituted as punishment for crimes. They are referred to as places for detaining people and for political purposes. The use of prisons for rehabilitation or punishment following conviction is a very recent invention, the result of Quaker-initiated reforms two centuries ago. The word 'penitentiary' comes from the Quaker idea that the criminals needed to be penitent and repent and reform themselves. The first state prison in America was the Walnut Street Jail in Philadelphia, Pennsylvania, opened in 1790.

and bureaucratic bungling.* But the real significance of the project went far beyond a demonstration of a useful alternative to prison. The real story is what happened in the lives of the people and the community . . .

One of the widows, Roxie Vaughn, eighty-three years old and blind, was elated when informed that her tiny two-room house had been chosen for the project; the thin, shingle-covered walls barely kept out the chilling winter winds, and each month half of her social security cheque went to pay for fuel for the one space heater in her living room.

But, when Roxie learned the work was to be done by six inmates, she was terrified; her home had been broken into four times in the prior two years. One can only try to imagine what fear that would mean for an elderly blind woman living alone. However, she finally agreed to have the men come.

By the second day, Roxie had invited the men in for cookies and milk. Then they began to pray together each day. And before the first week was over, Roxie and the six men were fast friends. An Atlanta TV crew, having heard about the project, captured an unforgettable scene: Roxie playing her small electric organ with the six convicts standing behind her, singing. The song? 'Amazing Grace', of course.

Georgia Avenue Church hosted the closing services from which the men were to be returned to prison. People came from all over Atlanta, black and white, rich and poor, famous and forgotten. Folks were there from the twelve churches of different denominations and four local Christian groups that had sponsored the project with Prison Fellowship, most of them working together for the first time. The gathering was like a fresh breeze blowing through the musty, dark sanctuary.

There were some tears. The youngsters of one host family kept saying, 'Mommy, don't let Bob go back to prison.' And when the men told the congregation what the two weeks had

---

* The programme drew national attention and has been duplicated many times since. For further information contact: Justice Fellowship, P.O. Box 17500, Washington, DC, 20041.

meant to them and when the widows were introduced and some of the volunteers spoke, eyes throughout the audience were wet.

The dilapidated, neglected old church seemed to stand tall against the grey November sky that Saturday afternoon, as if swelling with pride and joy because at last it was doing what it was meant to do.

It is the nature of man to organise. Probably since the Tower of Babel we have been setting up hierarchies, organisational flow charts, orders of authority, and all the other structural schemes dreamed up through the ages. The more advanced the civilisation, the more refined the organisational schemes.

However, though structures are essential to hold society together, they are there to serve, not be served. The marvels of modern technology have produced a sophistication in systems and structures that encourages what Jacques Ellul, the French historian, calls the 'political illusion', the misguided belief that all problems can be solved by structures – namely, institutions.[1] So for each new problem, a new institution is created.

Unfortunately this mentality has invaded the church, and we treat it as a structure (and just another one of many in society at that) dependent on charts and manuals and plans and computer print-outs.

But the true church is not held together by any structure man creates; it is not an organisation. It is alive, its life breathed into it by a sovereign God. Its heart beats with God's heart. It is one with Him and moves as His Spirit moves – where He chooses and often against the designs of man.

The life function of this living organism is to love the God who created it – to care for others out of obedience to Christ, to heal those who hurt, to take away fear, to restore community, to belong to one another, to proclaim the Good News while living it out. The church is the invisible made visible.

I witnessed this when I was in prison. A few of us began meeting each night to pray, read the Bible, and support each other. From that grew a Bible study. Others became involved, men gave their lives to Christ, and attendance in the prison chapel increased. This was not the clever strategy of men, but the Spirit of God at work – and in a place where faith and religion are mocked, believers sometimes persecuted.

My experience pales beside that of the believers in my next story. But perhaps because of my prison experience, and the evidence of the power of the Spirit, without human intervention, I have been inspired by this group of men who found that, indeed, the gates of hell itself cannot prevail against His church . . .

21

This Is My Body

This was Captain Jeff Powell's forty-second career mission. He was flying about thirty miles southeast of Hanoi in an F-105 Thunderchief, a supersonic aircraft carrying almost half its weight in munitions. His target was a bridge, a vital North Vietnamese supply line between the Haiphong harbour and the Ho Chi Minh Trail.

Powell let down through a 10,000-foot cloud ceiling, sighted the objective, did a roll-in, and released his stores. Half the cement span distintegrated. When he tried to pull out of the manoeuvre, the controls wouldn't respond.

This isn't possible, he thought, *I didn't hear anything*.

The sky around him turned a bright white as the fuel tank under the left wing exploded. He was forced to eject before he could radio anyone.

A month later, stripped of his survival gear, blindfolded, trussed with wire, Jeff Powell was being marched through the jungles and rural villages of North Vietnam by night, his captors travelling under cover of darkness to avoid being spotted by American bombers or rescue planes. At one point, nauseous and feverish, he was hung from a banana tree in a large village as the star attraction in a circus of mockery. He was stoned and urinated on by the villagers. Later propaganda movies and photographs were taken of him being marched under the gun-toting guard of a little girl dressed in pyjamas.[1]

THE GULF OF TONKIN, ONE MONTH LATER . . .

Captain Terry Jones had survived the destruction of his F-4 Phantom II by a surface-to-air missile, ejecting only after trying every emergency procedure to regain control of his plane. As he floated downward he knew that his only injury was a cut on the arm, but he was terrified. Beneath him, excited villagers and miltiamen were gathering in a rice paddy. Some brandished what looked like sticks or machetes; others carried guns.

As Jones looked upward at his parachute and the sky, he wondered, *Did the flight leader see me go down?* Below him, the shouts grew louder.

Six weeks later, Terry Jones was in a bamboo cage in the jungle, lying on his stomach with his feet in wooden stocks, his arms tied behind him with wet ropes. Following this torturous confinement he was taken to a temple near a rice paddy where he was turned over to a North Vietnamese officer who had with him another American pilot dressed in native garb. Jones' countryman had obviously been on the road longer than he – was heavily bearded and emaciated.* The officer told the two prisoners that they would be taken to Hanoi and that if they tried to communicate with each other, they would be executed.

HANOI, THE SAME YEAR . . .

Thus Jeff Powell and Terry Jones, and many others like them, came together to a place the American airmen called the Hanoi Hilton. It was a triangular building the size of a city block, surrounded by a dry moat and twenty-foot walls studded with sharp hunks of glass and topped with electrified barbed wire. The prison had been built by the French during their occupation of Vietnam; there was still a guillotine in the basement.

* At that point, Captain Powell weighed about 110 pounds and Captain Jones had already lost about forty pounds.

On the streets surrounding the prison, bicycles darted back and forth and truck horns blared. Inside, from the cellblock called Heartbreak, a prisoner in solitary confinement could be heard crying, 'Oh God!' Because he would not give his captors information beyond his name, rank, serial number, and date of birth, he had been bent over backwards and tied so that his spine threatened to snap like a dry stick at any moment.

Jeff and Terry both went through Heartbreak – everybody did – were classified, then moved to another area of the Hilton. Some prisoners were sent to outlying prison camps. The frequency and severity of the torture depended on a prisoner's rank and the quality of information he could give the enemy.

ALONE, 1966–1970 . . .

Major James Kasler arrived at the Hilton with a broken thighbone sticking into his groin. He was beaten from 6:00 A.M. to 10:00 P.M., each hour, for days on end. His head was smashed and his buttocks ripped to hamburger with fan belts. His mouth was so badly bruised that he could not open it, and one of his eardrums was ruptured. But Kasler found that when he recited the Lord's Prayer, concentrating intently upon it, he was able to block out the pain for a time.

Norman McDaniel knew that it was 5:30 A.M. because the morning gong had sounded and the camp's p.a. system was blaring the 'voice of Vietnam' broadcast, nicknamed Hanoi Hannah by the Americans. McDaniel folded his mosquito netting and blotted out the propaganda with a verse he remembered from his youth: 'Lo, I am with you always, even unto the end of the world.'

Captain James Ray, shot down on Mother's Day, 1966, had been in solitary confinement for two years. Each day's menu consisted of two servings of pumpkin soup with a lump of pig fat in it. He shared his cell with ants, lizards, mosquitoes, and flies. It would have been easy to lose his

faith, but sometimes, mysteriously, he felt he was not alone.
His family and the people in his church back home in Texas
were praying for him.

THE BODY INVISIBLE . . .

From inside his cell at Heartbreak, Howard Rutledge
could hear the guard walking through the corridor and
methodically unlocking the thick teak doors of the cells.
Rutledge counted to three, and then it was his turn. The key
turned and the door swung open. Rutledge knelt down, as if
to genuflect in front of his captor, and grasped the two bowls
of rations that were placed on the grimy cement floor in front
of him. After receiving the food, he stood at attention in front
of the guard; he would be punished if he did not. When the
door closed, a waft of air bearing the odour of excrement took
away what appetite he had. He sat on his cement-slab bed
and kept one hand over his bowl of sewer greens to keep the
cockroaches out of it. When he chewed on the hard bread,
bits of sand embedded in the dough crunched between his
teeth.

The guard came to the door again and the first of
Rutledge's two daily meals was finished. A gong sounded,
signalling that it was time to lie down for two hours. Periodi-
cally a guard pacing the corridor would open the Judas hole
in the cell door to make certain he was prone. He dozed until
another gong sounded, the one that forbade him to lie down;
now he had to stand or sit for seven more hours.

Rutledge heard a soft whistle from the cell across from his. It
was Harry Jenkins whistling 'Mary Had a Little Lamb', the
signal that he wished to communicate.

Rutledge placed his bare feet on the cement slabs on either
side of his cell and boosted himself up to the metal-barred
window above the door.

'Howard,' Jenkins whispered.

'I'm here,' whispered Rutledge.

'I remembered another story,' said Jenkins quickly.

'What is it?'

'Ruth and Naomi. How Naomi lost everything she had – her husband, her sons, and her land.'

'I remember some of it.'

'Ruth was Naomi's daughter-in-law. Ruth was faithful to Naomi and stayed with her. They went to a foreign land.'

'What happened?' Rutledge asked.

'I can't remember that.'

A prisoner in a neighbouring cell coughed, signalling that a guard was near. Rutledge climbed down from his perch.

He paced his cell, thinking of Jenkins' story. He tried to remember the name of the person who had helped Ruth and Naomi. Three hours later he was still going over the story in his mind. He had learned it in Sunday school when he was ten. He meditated on the story throughout the second and final meal of the day – seaweed soup and sowbelly fat.

'Hanoi Hannah' crackled to life on the loudspeakers at 8:30 P.M. for a bedtime propaganda story which lasted half an hour. When it was over, Rutledge climbed up to the opening again and whispered, 'Jenkins'.

A pause. Then, 'What?'

'Boaz.'

'I know. I just remembered.'

Gradually communications between the prisoners improved. They made up a code based on Morse Code and communicated that way, with their ears to the walls and their bodies wrapped in blankets – if they had them – to keep the noise levels down. The alphabet was translated into a 5×5 dot matrix in which each letter was represented by the placement of vertical and horizontal wall taps. Once a prisoner knew the code, he was 'on line'. Via this network, the men recalled and taught each other Scripture and learned the names and serial numbers of every prisoner in the cellblock. They learned who had been transferred and who was being tortured; in this way they shared each other's pain.

On Sunday morning, when the guards gave them a

chance, the senior officers in each cellblock thumped on the
wall five times, alerting the prisoners in solitary as well as
those who had cellmates, that it was time to worship. This
signal was 'church call'.

Each man recited to himself the Lord's Prayer or the 23rd
or 100th psalm. Then they had silent hymns and private
prayers.

A new prisoner was stuck in solitary at the end of the
building. Each morning he ran in place to keep in shape,
shaking the entire structure. After the new man was taught
the tap code, he began running in an odd, jerky way. Seven
men at the other end of the cellblock deciphered the jogger's
message: 'I will lift up mine eyes to the hills from whence
cometh my help. I will lift up mine eyes . . .'

THE BODY VISIBLE . . .

After an unsuccessful American rescue attempt on
November 21, 1970, the North Vietnamese decided for
security reasons to move all the airmen in the outlying camps
back to the Hanoi Hilton with the other prisoners. To make
room for the influx, new cells were partitioned off; men were
moved out of solitary into large, open, bay-typed cells that
could accommodate forty, fifty, and sixty prisoners. The new
cellblock was named Camp Unity. Unlike the cells in
Heartbreak, the cells in Camp Unity had huge, high, barred
windows that let in rivers of daylight.

Conditions improved somewhat. Occasionally the prisoners were let out for reasons other than interrogation or
torture. Sometimes they did chores – anything was a relief to
the boredom; they emptied the two-gallon toilet bucket,
washed dishes and cleaned the courtyard. If they bathed or
washed their own clothes, they usually had to use sewage.

For years these prisoners had asked for a Bible. Not until
December, 1970, did they even see one. Then the English-
speaking interrogator brought one into cell 4 and the men
gathered around. Jeff Powell read the Christmas story aloud,

then several psalms, then the Sermon on the Mount. The men were not sure how long they would have the Bible or whether they would ever see it again, so James Ray turned to 1 Corinthians 13 and memorised the chapter. The Bible was in the cell for two hours.

On the condition that the prisoners follow an approved format, the North Vietnamese allowed as many as twenty men at a time to gather for formal church services. This had to take place out in the courtyard, behind bamboo screens which obstructed their view of the other cells. There they worshipped while the English-speaking interrogator monitored everything they said and did.

On more than one occasion, the prisoners digressed from the 'format' by reciting Scripture that had not been previously approved by the interrogator. When this happened, he pushed into the circle shaking his head furiously, and thrust the men back into their cells.

One Sunday morning James Ray called the men to order by leading them in singing the Doxology. He prayed, 'We thank You, Lord, for Your protection and mercy. For bringing us together.' Eight of the men then assembled in front of the group and sang, 'Holy, holy, holy, Lord God almighty, early in the morning, my song shall rise to Thee.'

The prisoners' obvious determination to worship caused repeated confrontations with their captors.

For example, a guard would hear the men singing hymns in their cell and would run for the English-speaking interrogator, who would order, 'No political meetings.'

'It isn't political.'

'There are too many of you. You cannot hold a political meeting.'

'Join us. Find out. This isn't a political meeting.'

'We will throw you in solitary if you continue.'

'Join us and see. This isn't a political meeting.'

'No.'

Eventually, despite solitary confinement, threats of torture, and harassment, the captives were down their captors and more freedom was given to those in Camp Unity.

In the spring of 1971 the North Vietnamese permitted three prisoners to copy the Bible for one hour a week. James Ray was one of the three. He sat on a wooden chair at a wooden table and began copying the Sermon on the Mount. The guard standing close by, watching, repeatedly placed his elbow on the verse Ray was trying to copy. When the guard moved his elbow, Ray wrote so fast his hand cramped. When the guard wasn't holding his elbow on the page, sometimes for up to fifteen minutes at a time, he was trying to distract Ray with inane questions. During the five weeks the programme lasted, James Ray managed to copy much more than the Sermon on the Mount.

Each day when he brought the precious words back to the cell, Ray's cellmates recopied the words in the crude fashion they had devised for other writing: on toilet-paper rations with brick-dust ink and quill pens. They recopied the verses because each week Ray had to return his previous week's copy before he could transcribe more. The verses were also immediately memorised by different prisoners.

EASTER SUNDAY, 1971 . . .

Captain Tom Curtis woke up early and studied the notes and verses that he and James Ray had assembled the previous evening. Curtis looked at the roomful of sleeping prisoners around him. Twenty-eight men. All of them flyers. How had they managed to survive in this place?

The morning gong sounded just as sunlight struck the western wall of the cell. Several of the men limped or stretched painfully while getting up. Old wounds had not healed.

At about ten o'clock Curtis stood in front of the drab eastern wall and called the service to order. The men gathered in a semi-circle before him. It was Easter Sunday.

A quartet sang 'The Old Rugged Cross' and then everyone

joined in 'Amazing Grace'. Curtis recited the version of the passion of Christ that the men had patched together from somewhat faulty memories. 'And when they had bound Him, they led Him away and delivered Him to Pontius Pilate. And they stripped Him and put a crown of thorns on His head, and spit on Him and hit Him. And they said, "Crucify him".'

As he listened to the familiar words, Curtis thought of the experiences they all had shared: being bound, chained, spat upon, whipped, lashed to trees, stoned . . .

Then someone handed Curtis several pieces of bread that had been saved from the previous day's rations. 'And He took the bread, and when He had given thanks, He broke it and gave it to His disciples, saying, "Take, eat, this is My body that is broken for you. Do this in remembrance of Me."'

The bread was passed and quietly eaten.

Then Curtis repeated the verses about the cup – 'This is My blood shed for you.'

These men know about blood, Curtis thought. Their own blood flowing from open wounds, from lacerations and ruptured eardrums, from torn-out fingernails – blood that seeped through every makeshift bandage. Now they thought about Christ's blood shed for them.

The cup of carefully saved seaweed soup was passed. Someone quietly hummed 'Amazing Grace'.

As Curtis brought the cup to his lips, he began to weep. He wondered if they had any right to identify their suffering with Christ's. But then wasn't their presence in this place, alive against all odds, a sign of Christ's continuing presence with them? He remembered that Christ had said He would found His church and the gates of hell would not prevail against it. They were part of that church, a part of the broken body of Christ in every way.

Yes, Christ had prevailed; for here they were, worshipping Him in the jungles of a world gone mad. Relying on Him, they had nothing less than the privilege of showing the Lord's death, burial, and resurrection – His presence, the church – in what otherwise was a living hell.

LOVING GOD

For whoever wants to save his life will lose it, but
whoever loses his life for me will find it.

Jesus, to His disciples

22

Life and Death

And so the church of Jesus Christ is vital and alive and changing the world – wherever individual believers obey Him, live out His Word, and love Him, whether it be in the Hanoi Hilton or in a dreary Georgia nursing home where I met a remarkable woman . . .

I had first heard about Myrtie Howell from an inmate in a New Hampshire prison when he wrote to ask those of us at Prison Fellowship headquarters to join in prayers for her health. The Fellowship had matched this man and Mrs Howell up as pen pals, something we do with thousands of inmates and volunteers.

'Please pray for Grandma Howell,' pleaded his childlike scrawl, 'cause she's sick and may be going to die. Nobody has ever loved me like she has. I just wait for her letters, they mean so much.'

Our office staff began praying for Mrs Howell. Then some months later, I received a letter from the woman herself reporting on the inmates she was corresponding with and telling me how each one was doing, about their morale and their problems.

She concluded: 'Writing to inmates has filled my last days with joy.' That was a cheerful thought. But then she added the ominous request that I come to speak at her funeral. She had instructed her pastor to notify me when the day came. 'It won't help me,' she wrote, 'but it will wake up my church to the need of taking part in prison ministry.'

I wrote back to Mrs Howell, reminding her that the days of our lives are numbered by, and known only to, the Lord.

Therefore I didn't feel I could make a commitment to preach at her funeral since nobody knew the date . . . To say the least, it was a most awkward letter.

Over the next year, Myrtie's letters kept coming – always upbeat and usually enclosing what was literally her widow's mite (once she simply endorsed over a $67.90 US Treasurer's cheque that was her supplemental income). In each letter she reported on 'her boys' and frequently asked for more names to add to her correspondence list. At one point we tallied that she was actually writing to seventeen inmates. No small task for a ninety-one-year-old woman.

No small task for anyone, for just the thought of writing to prisoners scares most people, including Christians, half to death. They have visions of dangerous criminals getting their names and addresses and, once out of prison, tracking them down for nefarious purposes. Why was this elderly, obviously frail, woman different? Why, at ninety-one, did she care at all, yet alone so much?

I thought I might get my answer when a Prison Fellowship seminar and community rally was scheduled for Columbus, Georgia, in June, 1981. Columbus was Myrtie's home town. So I wrote and invited her to attend the rally. She replied immediately, explaining that since her hip had never healed from a fall, she couldn't move without a walker and wouldn't dare attempt a crowded auditorium.

'But,' she wrote, 'I have a great desire to meet you and I am claiming Psalm 37:4.'* I stuck the letter in my briefcase without looking up the Scripture and kicked myself for being so insensitive as to suggest she attend a big public rally.

The day of the seminar and rally was a full schedule, as always, but that morning I knew I had to make time for one more thing. I just had to meet Myrtie Howell, this woman whose letters could call forth such concern from incarcerated men she had never met.

When I tracked her down, I found that Myrtie lived in an old soot-covered brick high-rise in downtown Columbus, an

* 'Delight yourself in the Lord and he will give you the desires of your heart.'

apartment building converted a few years earlier into a home for the aged. Inside, the lobby resembled the waiting room of a hospital, except more depressing. There were no ringing words of encouragement to break the tension of the place, no reassuring banter, no youthful voices, no hopeful expressions. Instead, I saw rows of wheelchairs lined in front of a blaring television set; bodies hunched about on pea-soup green plastic couches and overstuffed chairs with worn upholstery patterns long since erased. The sit-com soundtrack bounced harshly off garish yellow walls. Most of those turned to the set were either dozing or staring blankly. Others thumbed idly through magazines or watched the lobby door like sentries at their post. I felt chilled just walking across the lobby.

After signing in at the front desk, I rode the elevator to Myrtie's floor. The hallway was carpeted with a rippling, colourless, thread-bare strip that had seen years of scuffling footsteps.

At her door I knocked. 'Come in, come in,' a firm, strong voice shouted.

As I opened the unlocked door, I was greeted by a broad, welcoming smile as Myrtie leaned back in her rocker in satisfaction, her white fleecy hair neatly parted at the side. Her blue eyes sparkled behind thick, black-rimmed spectacles and her cheeks glowed with life. *This woman is not preparing to die*, I thought.

'S'cuse me for not getting up,' she said, gesturing toward the walker alongside her chair. 'Oh, I don't believe you are really here . . . I just don't believe it. It's so . . . the Lord does give us the desires of our heart.' She kept grinning and rocking and I just had to lean over and hug her, experiencing that familiar affinity believers so often have on first meeting.

I took the armchair opposite her with its doily-decorated arms. Myrtie's apartment had one window and was no larger than a modest hotel room. It contained a bed, a 12-inch television set, a dresser, a mirror, the two chairs we sat in, and a fragile desk crowded with Bibles and commentaries and piled high with correspondence. Photographs lined the edges of the mirror hanging just above the desk. I'd seen cells with more amenities.

Unlike her surroundings, Myrtie looked almost regal, her hands folded in her lap and her shoulders proud beneath her shawl.

I started to thank her for her faithful ministry, but before I could finish my first sentence, Myrtie waved her hand, started grinning again, and interrupted with a protest.

'Oh, no, you've helped me. These last years have been the most fulfilling of my whole life. I thank you – and most of all I thank Jesus,' the last word pronounced with great reverence.

And I knew that Myrtie, despite living alone in this dreary place, crippled and in continuous pain, really did mean what she said. I was already sensing a spiritual depth to this woman that I'd not often encountered. I asked her to tell me about her life and her spiritual journey.

Born in Texas in 1890, Myrtie was brought to Columbus, Georgia, at the age of three; at ten she went to work in the mill for ten cents a day.

'We was raised poor,' she said, explaining that she had had only one year of schooling. Her parents gave her little in the way of religious education, but from the age of ten on she knew there was a God, felt He had His hand on her, and knew she would 'do best to obey Him'. At the age of sixteen she joined a Christian church.

Married at seventeen, she had her first child the next year and two more in rapid succession. Her middle child, a son, died at the age of two. Indeed, the deaths of her closest relatives proved the crucible for Myrtie's faith. During the late 1930s, Myrtie's mother and her husband's father lived with them. In mid-December of 1939, Myrtie's mother died. Then in mid-January Myrtie's husband was killed in an accident; two weeks later her father-in-law died as well.

Tears brimmed in Myrtie's eyes as she recalled to me, 'I felt like Job. I just felt like old Satan had a conversation with the Lord and said if the Lord would just let him get that Myrtie he'd make her give the Lord up. But it only made me lean more closer, more to Him.'

The death of her husband resulted in the loss of her home also, and Myrtie had to go back to work to support herself. At first she did 'practical work', piece work from the mill, and then 'for two years I run a dress shop. And then I run a little café. I always been doin' somethin' to take care of myself. I didn't want to get on with the children or nothin' like that.' So Myrtie worked until her advanced age and declining health forced her to move into, as she put it, 'this old folk's home'.

The death of her youngest son, her 'baby boy', the declining health of her oldest, and her own move into the home sent Myrtie into a spiritual depression. So many of her loved ones had died and she 'couldn't do' for those who remained; she felt she had nothing left to live for. She wanted to die.

'Lord, what more can I do for You?' she prayed with all her heart one day. 'If You're ready for me, I'm ready to come. I want to die. Take me.'

'I knew I was dying,' she continued. 'But then He spoke to me as clear as can be: WRITE TO PRISONERS. Three words: WRITE TO PRISONERS. Imagine that! I want to die, figure I'm about to, and the Lord say, "Okay now, Myrtie, you go back and write to prisoners."

'He couldn't of spoke to me any clearer if'n He'd been standing before me. And I was afraid at first. I said, "Lord, me write to prisoners? I ain't got no education, had to teach myself to read and write. And I don't know nuthin' bout prisons."

'But there wasn't no doubt. I would have squirmed out of His hand if I hadn't obeyed. I had to.'

Myrtie's call became even more miraculous to my mind when she told me that at the time she'd never heard of Prison Fellowship or any other prison ministry. She had never given such a task the merest thought.

But she was faithful to God's command and acted on the best plan she could think of. She knew there was a penitentiary in Atlanta, so she wrote there, the envelope addressed simply, 'Atlanta Penitentiary, Atlanta, Georgia'. Inside her message read:

Dear Inmate,

I am a Grandmother who love and care for you who are in a place you had not plans to be.

My love and sympathy goes out to you. I am willing to be a friend to you in correspondent.

If you like to hear from me, write me. I will answer every letter you write.

A Christian friend,
Grandmother Howell

The letter must have been passed on to the prison chaplain, for Myrtie received eight names of prisoners to whom she was invited to write. Chaplain Ray, who carries on an extensive prison ministry, sent her additional names, as did Prison Fellowship when we were put in contact with her.

Myrtie has subsequently corresponded with hundreds of inmates, up to forty at a time, becoming a one-woman ministry reaching into prisons all over America.

Her strategy is simple: 'When I get a letter, I read it, and when I answer it, I pray: "Lord, You know what You want me to say. Now say it through me." And you'd be surprised sometimes at the letters He writes!

'His Spirit works. I obey. I don't put anything in there that I feel's of self, of flesh. As He give me, I write it.

'But the real blessings, they're in the answers,' she said, reaching over to the stack of letters piled on her desk, within arm's reach of her chair. 'Just look at these,' she said, grinning and handing me a packet. As I scanned the pages, phrases leaped out at me:

Dear Grandmother . . . was very happy to get your letter . . . the guys kidded me when they said I had a letter . . . I didn't believe them, but it was true . . . I don't have anyone to care about me but the Lord and you . . . I'm in the hole now, that's why I can write letters . . . Why am I so afraid, grandmother? Why doesn't God answer my prayers about this? . . . I am really glad to know that there is someone out there who cares . . . I will remember you in my prayers every night starting now and for the rest of my life . . . please write back soon . . . love, Joe . . . in the love of Jesus, David . . .

One letter, signed 'Granddaughter Janice", read:

Dear Grandmother,

I received your letter and it made me sad when you wrote that you think you may not be alive much longer. I thought that I would wait and come to see you and then tell you all you have meant to me, but now I've changed my mind. I'm going to tell you now.

You've given me all the love and concern and care that I've missed for years and my whole outlook on life has changed. You've made me realize that life is worth living and that it's not all bad. You claim it's all God's doing but I think you deserve the credit.

I didn't think I was capable of feeling love for anyone again but I know I love you as my very own precious grandmother.

'Bless you, Myrtie,' I said, putting the stack of letters back on the desk.

'Oh, the Lord has just blessed me so wonderful, Mr Colson. I've had the greatest time of my life since I've been writing to prisoners.

'And you know, once I turned over my life to Him – I mean, really did it – He took care of all my needs. Things go right before I even think about 'em.'

After I asked about the Bible commentaries on her desk, Myrtie told me how she spends her days. She said she doesn't 'do much of anything' but write to prisoners, read and study the Bible, pray, watch a few religious programmes on TV and 'be carried' to and from the common dining room where she takes her meals. Myrtie insisted that time passed faster and more joyously for her now than it ever did before.

As our time together drew to a close, Myrtie gave me a final bit of advice: 'So, now, Mr Colson, you just keep remembering the Lord don't need no quitters. Once in a while old Satan tells me I'm getting too old, don't remember things good . . . had to agree with him there . . . But we mustn't listen to him. First thing you know he'll turn us around every which way. So I just keep remembering what the Lord told me and I can't quit,' quickly adding with an admonitory gesture toward me, 'and neither can you.'

With that, Myrtie Howell gave me her wonderful grin again, exuding the joy of life lived to the fullest.

We prayed together, hugged one more time, and I promised we'd see each other again, holding to that marvellous thought C. S. Lewis was so fond of: Christians never have to say good-bye.

Two Prison Fellowship volunteers were waiting at the desk downstairs to take me to my next meeting. As we reached the front door, I felt compelled to turn and take one more look at that lobby. No, the scene hadn't changed.

Keeping my voice low, I said, 'Look at that. Nothing left –'

'But to wait for the bodies to be carried out,' one of my companions added, his expression quickly turning sombre as he realised his bad joke was no joke at all.

All at once I was overwhelmed by the sad scene before me – the mirthless pit of depression, despair, emptiness. There was no joy in any of their expressions. Instead, their sunken eyes seemed to reflect a raging anger: anger that their families had left them there; anger that fate had dealt them cruel blows; anger that their minds were weak and their bones brittle; anger that their favourite TV programme was interrupted or that someone else was served ahead of them at lunch. And jealousy, too, that someone less deserving than themselves might survive and watch them being carried off through that lobby door – unless, that is, they could hold on long enough to relish the sight of that someone being carried out first.

My heart ached for these pathetic figures, clinging so desperately to something they never had, seeking to save a life that for so many had been only a cruel hoax; seventy or eighty or ninety years of joy, defeat, pain, and pleasure and then just sitting, waiting, for darkness to come. Waiting. Waiting – for this meaningless existence to end. And what was beyond? Nothing? Or more of this hell? If there is no God, or if He can't be known, then why live at all?

Meanwhile, upstairs, sat Myrtie Howell with her wide ninety-one-year old grin of joy and triumph. Ready to live. Ready to die. By now she was probably back at her desk WRITING TO PRISONERS!

But Myrtie, too, had known the hell this world can be. She had known loneliness, pain, being unloved, loss of home and family, drudgery of menial tasks to survive.

The difference was that Myrtie had recognised the vanity and purposelessness of life without God; the emptiness of life lived for self. She understood the futility of being unable to answer the questions: why was I born? why have I lived? where am I going? So she had cried out to God to lead her out of that hell in the only way anyone has ever escaped – by giving up her life to gain His life. Yes, Myrtie long ago had learned life's central paradox.

I turned away from that dreary lobby and passed through the doors into the warm June day. The air was fresh, clean, and I took several deep breaths to clear my head. But I could not clear away the memories of that day – nor would the passage of time. For in that Georgia nursing home God gave me an unforgettable vision of heaven and hell. The heaven of life with God. The hell of life without Him.

And God gave me the final link in my search to learn what loving God really means: Myrtie Howell. To believe, to repent, to obey, to be holy, to bind up the brokenhearted, and to serve.

Myrtie Howell knew all about *loving God*.

In the Arena: An Allegory

Late one spring evening I was in my library thumbing through the final draft of this manuscript. After months of work I was at last satisfied with the flow of logic and principles in the book; and I was especially happy with the concluding chapter. Myrtie Howell surely exemplified what *Loving God* is all about, a fitting end to a well-ordered book.

Occupied with my thoughts, I leaned back in my worn leather desk chair, hands clasped behind my head, and thought about the people whose stories I'd told. Scenes from my own life passed through my mind as well as I reflected on my spiritual pilgrimage, my beginnings, my journey thus far.

I don't know how long my thoughts drifted, but my reverie was suddenly interrupted by the shrill ring of the desk telephone. The caller was Dave Chapman, an old friend living in another state. Dave brushed aside my greetings and announced he was in town, at the airport, with several hours to spare before he had to catch a late flight out to the West Coast. He insisted he had to see me.

Within twenty minutes I heard a car pull into the driveway, then the slam of a door and the jab of the doorbell.

Dave looked the same as ever – sandy-haired, deeply tanned, with the kind of boyish good looks that can see a man from thirty to sixty without much change. He was dressed in his usual style, too – light oatmeal suit, oxford-cloth shirt, silk tie, and tasselled loafers.

I escorted Dave into my library and gave him the straight-backed, maple chair across the desk from me. He said he'd only stay for a few minutes, but that chair would help him keep his word.

'Okay, Dave, what's going on?' I asked, fighting the urge to yawn. I didn't bother clearing away the mound of paper between us, the cleanly typed final chapters of *Loving God*.

Dave started like a fighter coming out of his corner at the sound of the bell. He was so excited his sentences collided into one another; and he kept thrusting his index finger down on my desktop as he made his points, as a skilled lawyer might do on the mahogany rail of the jury box.

The Dave Chapman I'd known casually was a calm, successful businessman, not the kind of person to get so worked up. Conservative, perhaps a bit uptight, but certainly not a dynamo. What could have happened to change him so? He was animated, alive, with a self-assurance that was remarkable – despite the personal dilemma he was telling me about that now threatened his business, the political power he'd recently acquired, his friends, and everything he had considered important. His voice was strong, his eyes determined. I was mesmerised.

'Wait a minute. Slow down.' I exclaimed, coming straight up in my chair. 'I want the whole story, beginning to end. Take your time but tell it all.'

And for the next two hours I listened, enthralled, as Dave Chapman related the remarkable events of his life over the last few years. When he finished explaining his dilemma, Dave leaned as far back as the straight-backed chair would allow and waited for my response. But all I could do was stare at the mounds of paper on my desk.

'Well, what do you think?' he finally asked.

'What do I think? You want to know what I think?' I exclaimed. 'I think you've just rewritten the ending of my book!'

For, of course, he had. As much as I wanted to leave my book with its orderly flow of logic and theological soundness, concluding with the poignant but triumphant story of Myrtie Howell, life isn't like a book. Life isn't logical or sensible or orderly. Life is a mess most of the time. And theology must be lived in the midst of that mess.

Authors can write books about God and man, but for all

their illustrations and interpretations, it is no more than opinion from the bleachers unless it is lived. And life is not lived in the bleachers, but on the muddy fields by human beings who get bloody and bruised and who contend for the score to their last gasp.

So I decided to end this book with Dave Chapman.

Dave is nobody special. Well, actually that's not true. He's me; he's you; he's dozens of people you and I know – no hero or saint in the world's terms, no spiritual expert. Dave Chapman's story is our story; his struggles and decisions confront each of us every day. So I tell you his story – as I remember it – as he told it to me as the hours passed and that spring twilight darkened into night. I don't know whether Dave ever caught his plane that night. As a matter of fact, I haven't seen him since.

Dave's story began on a warm summer evening in 1979 . . .

He was late coming home. Though Dave owned his own accounting firm representing several of the largest businesses in the state, it really didn't require his working day and night any longer. But these gatherings of his wife's were getting harder to take, so he took refuge in working late.

Dave's wife, Kay, had become a Christian several years before. After that she had been out to evangelise her entire social circle, and had hit upon the scheme of bringing leading Christian speakers to address small dinner parties once every three months. These evenings had proved so successful that her pastor had asked whether Kay's parties might be integrated into the outreach programme of Calvary Church. Since Kay was running out of people to invite anyway – all of her social contacts had 'been won or run' as Dave expressed it – she agreed, and now gave quarterly Thursday evening punch-and-cookie receptions for a revolving guest list provided by the church. The speaker then remained as the Chapmans' house guest for the weekend while giving seminars at the church.

As Dave came in late this particular Thursday evening, the speaker, a Dr Jack Newman, well-known theologian, had already held the fifty guests spellbound for an hour talking about the historical background of the writing of the Gospels. The group was well into refreshments and conversation.

Dave greeted people superficially as he wended his way from kitchen to dining room, grabbed a tumbler of iced tea, and retreated to a hassock at the far end of the living room. Between sips, he watched the star of the evening surrounded by a semi-circle of admirers.

Jack Newman was tall and lean with a long, dark-complexioned face and black hair greying at the temples. His eyes were large and deeply set and his Roman nose gave an edge to his profile that suggested intelligence and wit. Somehow, his comfortable posture threw the gestures and mannerisms of those around him into high relief.

Dave became aware of how wide Lucy opened her mouth when she let out her whooping laugh; how craven Stan appeared, unable to stand still and meet the man's eyes; how uneasy others seemed as they posed and waited to impress with their questions. Every craning neck and twisted body tightened Dave's own shoulder muscles; he wished they would all clear out of his house.

Much later, when the guests were gone, Kay had shown Dr Newman his room and then gone on to the master bedroom to collapse; Dave, too restless to sleep, sat comfortably on a chaise-longue out on the screened-in back porch, a plate of left-over cookies at hand.

To his surprise, he heard footsteps and Dr Newman stepped onto the slate paving stones from the wide open doorway of the family room.

'Need a break of fresh air after all that, Doctor?' Dave asked.

'Yes, it's a beautiful night and I spotted this porch earlier this evening,' Newman replied. 'I've always felt a bit deprived that our place doesn't have one.' Newman had taken off his coat and tie, as Dave had, and his white shirt, with sleeves rolled back against his forearms, stood out sharply in the darkness.

'Have a seat, Doctor. After a long day, I always feel like I

can finally breathe out here.' Dave gestured to the wicker
chair separated from his by a small glass-topped table. Newman hiked his grey slacks at the knees and sank gratefully
into the comfortable cushions. The two men sat for a few
moments listening to the loud green whine of the crickets.

'You don't find the church people easy to take, do you?'
Newman asked.

'No,' Dave said, drawing the word out. 'Not always. But
that's not why I wasn't here for your lecture tonight. A client
had me hung up at the office. I really am sorry. Everyone said
you were great.'

'I was watching you with your guests tonight after you
came in,' Newman said, ignoring Dave's excuse. 'You looked
off in the distance, as if you were listening to music somewhere in the background. And you were at the same time
really looking everyone over. What was going through your
mind?'

'I guess I was just watching them in relationship to you.
They're such a bunch of turkeys sometimes.'

'You looked like something was wrong. I told myself that if
I got the chance, I'd try to talk to you. Care to tell me about
it?'

'Well, I didn't know it was so obvious,' Dave chuckled
rather forcedly. 'Sure, I'll tell you about it. With your
experience in the church and all, maybe you'll understand.
Which would be a good thing, because I sure don't. I just
know that every time I'm around those people it puts me in a
bad mood.'

'What kind of bad mood?' Newman asked.

'I don't know if I can describe it. It's sort of what you said –
about listening to background music. I have a hard time
feeling involved with what's going on around me. I mean I
feel that way all the time.'

'I've felt like that, Dave,' said Newman.

'You have?'

'Sure. Everyone has. We don't all go through it the same
way, but sooner or later most people feel that sense of
meaninglessness at some point in their life.'

'Well, it always gets worse when I'm around church people,' Dave said. 'It even makes me wonder about the whole business. Christianity, I mean. Maybe it doesn't work. For me.'

'You say that as if I might be offended.'

'Why not. You've given your life to it. And here I'm telling you I think it might be a dry run.'

'If it were, do you think I would prefer you not to try and tell me?'

That struck Dave. He thought of religious people as those not quite willing or able to look at life realistically. Newman seemed different – unintimidated – a quality Dave always looked for in business associates. He liked a man who didn't panic.

'How did you become a Christian, Dave?' Newman asked. 'Your wife said you both came into the church a few years ago.'

'Yeah, Kay's in the church all right. She wakes up in the morning, sings the doxology in the shower, then runs off to a Bible study, to some save-the-savages guild, to choir practice, to something that ought to be called Protestants for Prudery, and even attends a Christian exercise class called Praise-R-Cize, if you can believe! And seminars! I'm sure your talks are worthwhile, but after "life together", "family life", and "body life", Kay doesn't have time for our life.'

'But what about you, Dave,' Newman pressed. 'You must have thought Christianity was true at one time.'

'I don't know any more. I guess I did. If you want my testimony – well, it's nothing real spectacular. Remember, about the time Carter was elected president, when being born-again was the big thing? Well, Kay got caught up in it – was off every night to a revival service or a prayer meeting. She started talking about the devil and hell or she'd write little sayings on the kitchen blackboard. I'd even find the Bible on my desk opened at a certain page. I'll be honest, for a while she was driving me right up the wall.

'Then I met this fellow at the club. Like me, he had worked his way to the top. He gambled and belted his booze with the best of them. But one day I noticed he wasn't at the card tables any more. And soon his whole attitude changed. He had been a bundle of nerves; now he seemed calm, peaceful. And he started drinking ginger ale, for heaven's sake.

'So I asked him what had happened and he said, "I've accepted Jesus Christ and committed my life to Him." I felt like I'd been hit with a brick – that was the type of jargon Kay used all the time.

'I didn't want any of that God talk, not at the country club, too. But I did respect his decision and thought he seemed sincere. Months went by. Kay eased up a little, and I didn't mind so much when she shoved an occasional book my way. I'm not much of a reader, but I got so hooked on one that I stayed up two nights running to finish it. I went and saw my friend from the club and we talked until two in the morning. He talked about Christ in terms I could understand. He told me about his own relationship with a God who could be known. We prayed together, and then I went home.

'But I couldn't sleep, even after a couple quick nightcaps. It was a night like this – warm, but with a fresh breeze, so I came out here to the porch and stared out into the darkness, up at the stars. And that moment I knew, as I never had before, that there is a God. And I prayed the prayer my friend had given me.

'I guess I expected to hear the angels kicking up a ruckus, the divine cannons going off, but nothing much happened – except gradually over the next few weeks I began to feel different. I found it easy to lay off the martinis at lunch. And I completely lost my desire to gamble. You preachers would say I was "delivered" from those things, I guess.

'When I told my friend what had happened, he had me in a weekly prayer group meeting at the bank before I knew what had happened. Of course Kay was overjoyed when I told her. We both joined Calvary Church and started getting involved. In fact, they asked me to head a couple committees the moment I was baptised.

'But it's like a love affair that ran its course. Now I don't know if I ever really felt the love of God. I don't mean I'm drinking again or anything. I just don't feel anything. I wonder if it's possible to know God at all.'

Dave had been staring out through the screen as he talked. Now he turned slowly and looked at his guest. 'I'm not even sure I know what it means to have faith, if I ever did.'

'Faith is believing and acting – acting in obedience to the commands of Christ – even though you can't see what's going to happen,' Newman replied.

'That's the kind of simplistic answer you guys give that really stymies me. I'm not breaking any commandments. So what's wrong with me?'

'Are you sure?'

'Well, all right. I don't mean that I've stopped sinning totally, but God knows we can't be perfect in this life. I mean I've honestly tried to do everything the church asks. What more should I do?'

'I don't mean to be simple with you, Dave, but Jesus spelled that out pretty clearly: "Love the Lord with all your heart, mind, and soul, and your neighbour as yourself."'

'Well,' Dave said slowly, 'I try to do that. I mean I go to church and all that stuff – don't we do that because we love God? And nobody really knows how to carry out that "neighbour" stuff – we've talked about that in church discussions quite a bit. You know, the Good Samaritan bit and all. So where does that leave me?'

Newman sat quietly for a few moments, elbows on knees, hands clasped. 'Dave, the fact that you're struggling with all that is actually a good sign. It means you really do want to love God.'

'Come off it. You don't have to say that. I hate this business where Christians always feel obliged to be encouraging.'

'Let me ask you this, then. Do you love your wife?'

'Yes, very much. You don't stay married these days if you don't.'

'There ever come a time after you'd been married a while when you wondered whether you loved her at all?'

'Oh, sure. That's normal.'

'What changed things?'

'I don't know – just time mostly.'

'But you stayed faithful to your vows and to her, despite how you felt, right?'

'Yes. I've been lucky – never been tempted much.'

'I mean more than that,' Newman said. 'I mean you tried to love Kay as much as you could, despite your feelings.'

'Well, sure. It wasn't always easy though.'

'Right,' said Newman. 'Now what you need to learn is how to do the same thing with Christ. You promised Him something – to commit your life to Him and love and obey Him. So you do that no matter how you feel. And the longer and more you do that – obey Him – then you'll begin to feel your love for Him and His love in return. Just like you did with Kay.'

'But where do I start, when I'm not even sure I believe it will work?'

'The apostle John says "This is the love of God, that we keep His commandments." Straightforward, isn't it? But you can't obey them if you don't know them. So the place to start is in His book, the Bible, by studying.'

'Bible study is hard for me,' Dave said. 'Things always seem to crowd it out.'

'You can make the time if you really want to,' Newman said firmly. 'You will never know what God wants unless you seriously study His Word. But when you begin to do what He tells you there, you'll feel His love.'

Dave Chapman had no idea where that simple thought would lead him, but Newman's words were so direct that Dave felt a glint of hope, and he determined to get back to Bible study. For several weeks he got up thirty minutes early every morning to do it. He automatically felt virtuous, even though he rarely could concentrate on the text. His mind turned involuntarily to the work day ahead. Also, most of the study plans Newman had recommended seemed too strenuous – after all, he was new at this. So he chose what he liked to think of as his 'target method'. He read a favourite passage, such as the Sermon on the Mount and 1 Corinthians

13, and then made forays backward and forward, hoping eventually to hit the whole Bible in sort of overlapping circles of reading.

But he didn't seem to get anywhere. Sleeping in seemed more and more attractive. So he began studying after work. But his powers of concentration were even worse then. He would start to read, and the quiet of his office would entice his tired mind into reveries.

He tried attending the church men's study group that met every Friday morning for breakfast. But when there wasn't a genius like Newman around, Dave's natural inclination to resist instruction took over. He knew his attitude was rotten, but he couldn't keep himself from wondering just where Stan or Bill got off in their pseudo-exposition of the apostle Paul. Besides, they were always dragging in some guest to give his testimony, like the one who told about his sordid life of wine and women and the subsequent collapse of his successful business. Then one day he read a book by some born-again football jock, turned his life over to Jesus, and presto, praise the Lord, he stopped drinking and chasing around. And presto, his business was booming like never before. Instant pudding religion, Dave called it. All alike, all blah.

Then came one of those days. First he spilled egg on his shirt at breakfast, had words with Kay about the laundry's uneven use of starch, discovered that Kay's car which he had to use was almost out of gas, had words with her about that – the woman avoided gas stations like the plague – and got to work a half hour late. When he walked in, his secretary greeted him with the news that the controller of his biggest account, Fairway, had just called and *demanded* that Dave return his call the moment he walked in. Dave would have yelled at his secretary about putting the man off, but he saw the call had upset her already, and she wasn't the kind to be easily ruffled.

Dave went in and sat behind his oval rosewood desk and did a deep breathing exercise he had read about – supposed to calm you down. Then he placed the call. He was put directly through to Fairway's president, rather than the controller. Dave had never heard anyone so angry in his life.

One of Dave's brightest young associates, Brad Pelouze, had without telling anyone disallowed certain assets of a company Fairway had acquired. On the final audit, inventory was adjusted down by $100,000 – on the surface not that big a deal. But the net effect had been to reduce the earnings per share of Fairway just below the magic $10 needed for Fairway's underwriters to issue a new stock offering. Fairway would have to wait another year to raise the $7,000,000 it wanted for new acquisitions.

Fairway's president was in an unforgiving frame of mind. 'Don't worry about making it up to me,' he said in reply to Dave's entreaties. 'You're not going to be able to make it up to me. You're not going to be in business that long.'

Pelouze had made a dumb mistake, no doubt about that. He had been overly conservative and then had failed to tell the company's controller what he had done. Management didn't discover the adjustment until papers were filed with the Securities Commission for the stock offering, too late to change it. Worst of all, Pelouze had neglected to consult the accountant's bible, the 'generally accepted accounting principles' published by the American Institute of CPAs. If he had, he would have discovered he didn't have to make the adjustment.

A short time later Pelouze, a slightly built young man, sat before Dave. His face ashen, he glanced up once or twice at Dave, then gazed out the open window as though realising that his next place of employment lay somewhere out there.

Dave did not spare him. After the introductory lashings, he became bitterly vindictive. He flipped open his desk copy of the AICPA Professional Standards of Accounting. 'See this,' Dave said. 'Do you see this? You don't have to go to Duke for eight years, Mr Pelouze, to read this. Any schoolboy can read it. But you seem to be one of those educated beyond your intelligence.'

Much later, driving home after work, Dave's neck and

shoulders played back every tense moment of that day. Worse, his mind accompanied it with vivid instant replays of his scene with Brad Pelouze. He wished he could go back and do the scene again. Then, suddenly, his vindictive words became a different script: 'You call yourself a Christian, Chapman, and you don't even know the Bible?' He remembered the effort he had expended absorbing and digesting AICPA. His 'target method' wouldn't have worked with that. He wouldn't have had a chance of passing his CPA exams if he had studied with that approach. He realised he was treating the Bible like some magazine just flipping through, reading here and there as impulse moved him. He wanted spectacular results in his Christian life, but put in thoroughly mediocre effort. He would have to change or give it up.

The Pelouze incident prompted Dave to begin studying the Scriptures with dedication. Morning was the logical and best time for him to do this, so he arose one hour early and spent time carefully going over and thinking through the chapter each day. He devoted two nights a week to Design for Discipleship, a systematic Bible study course from the Navigators that Newman had recommended.

As part of his regimen, Dave also read three psalms each morning. But he began to discover that he only liked parts of the psalms; there were huge areas he had totally neglected – never even read. When he began to delve into those portions he got his first big shock: whoever had written these nice 'praise songs' had been a shrewd and intelligent man; they appealed to the mind as much as the heart. When he came across his first command in the psalms, he got his second shock: a commandment in the psalms? But there it was, as plain as day, and he could not think of a single thing he had ever done in his life to obey it: 'How long will you defend the unjust . . . ? Defend the cause of the weak and fatherless; maintain the rights of the poor and oppressed. Rescue the weak and needy; deliver them from the hand of the wicked' (Psalm 82:2–4).

Those were sentiments Dave identified with bleeding-heart liberals, those he had always characterised as standing 'with both feet planted firmly in the air.' But he couldn't escape the fact that this Scripture said that God condemns those who did not do this.

Though uncomfortable, Dave could not see how he was supposed to obey this commandment. It did not fit into the modern scheme of things. No 'poor' asked for an accountant's help. He didn't even know any poor people. And how could he defend anyone's cause? He wasn't a judge or a lawyer.

Then he began to notice that the psalms were full of comments about the rich and the poor. In fact, according to the psalms, how one treated the poor determined, at least in part, whether one was a righteous person or a wicked one.

Dave already gave quite generously to the church and to Christian causes. Having served as church treasurer, he knew he probably gave more than anyone at the church. But this did not seem quite the point of the psalms. Genuinely perplexed, Dave found himself sometimes annoyed with the message he got from his Bible studies.

Though the message upset him, he now understood it was true. He had read a little pamphlet Newman had written several years earlier, and the theologian's argument had convinced him. He realised the Bible was from God – His Word – and was absolutely true. It made him all the more uncomfortable.

At about this same time, Dave noticed that a man in his company was performing poorly. Jim Rutledge had spent most of his working life with Dave's company, punching adding machines and calculators, recording figures in a ledger sheet. Jim had always seemed content to plod along, even while co-workers started under his trainership eventually were promoted past him. But in recent months Jim had missed many days of work, and when he did show, his work was slow and full of errors.

So Dave made some discreet inquiries, then set an

appointment with Rutledge. In past years, finding what he had, he might have simply fired the man, but the psalms and Rutledge's long history with the company prompted Dave to think of ways to help.

Jim Rutledge entered Dave's office like a man coming to his execution. His eyes were glazed and veined, his colour pasty.

'Have a seat, Jim,' Dave gestured, and his employee sank into one of the wingbacked armchairs facing Dave's large desk. Rutledge took off his glasses and pocketed them, as if the action would make him invisible.

'Jim, I've called you in because, very honestly, I have been disappointed with your work lately – and we go back a long way together.' Dave then went on to enumerate some of his findings, as Jim sat quietly, not refuting him nor meeting his eyes.

Finally, 'Look, Jim,' Dave said, 'I know you have a drinking problem. I've had my own suspicions. I've confirmed it with others, including your family.'

Rutledge looked up, startled, his eyes showing a spark of denial, but Dave continued before he had a chance to speak. 'I'm not giving you an option on this, Jim. You're going to enter a rehabilitation programme. You need help.'

'I'll hand in my resignation right now, then, Dave,' Rutledge said. 'You don't know what that costs. Four thousand a month, minimum – my wife looked into it once. I don't have that kind of money.'

'I'll take care of the bill,' Dave said. 'It would be far more costly for me to waste your experience here.'

Rutledge gasped, tried to speak, but Dave cut him short, his tone more personal. 'I know something of what you're going through, Jim. I had a little battle with it myself. It will be tough, but you can lick it. I know you can. The place I've picked comes highly recommended.'

'How long?' Jim's hands trembled as he lit a cigarette.

'A month. Two, if necessary.' Dave paused a moment. 'Will your wife and family be okay?'

'They'll be fine. You don't know . . . Jean will be so

relieved. How she's held on this year . . . I kept waiting for her to leave me.'

'Well, the arrangements are made, and my secretary has all the information. See her and then go home and tell your family. You're due at the clinic by tomorrow at 5:00 P.M.'

Rutledge switched his cigarette to his left hand, stood, and grasped Dave's outstretched hand. Tears started to his eyes, and he turned and left the office quickly.

Dave basked in the glow of that conversation on his way home that night. Then, he began having second thoughts about the money. The company's medical insurance didn't cover a dry-out farm. He had half planned to take it out of his own pocket, but now he wondered if that was a wise plan.

Then he hit upon a solution. He personally owned the building his accounting firm occupied; the firm paid him rent. It had been a good tax device over the years. So he'd just increase the rent again, and he'd pay Rutledge's bill; in effect, the company would foot the bill. The rent was already high, and each time he increased it he was cutting into the company's profit-sharing plan, but he's managed okay with moves like this in the past.

How many times? a voice asked. *You've used this gambit so often that your profit-sharing plan is more theory than practice.* A few of the more senior associates already knew enough to grumble out loud about it – and they didn't know the half. In the past he would have brushed his conscience aside, but this time he could not.

He had planned to tell Kay what he had done for Rutledge, but found that the glow of his good deeds had died. So he sat through dinner in a moody silence. All evening he tried to rationalise his way out of the predicament. After all, what he had done to the profit-sharing was nothing extraordinary; as an accountant he knew enough to justify it to the IRS and all that. But the thoughts would not go away: in a perfectly legal way, he had stolen from his employees.

The next morning Dave skipped his psalms' reading, thinking he wasn't up to any references to the poor for a while, and went straight to where he was studying the Gospel of Luke in the nineteenth chapter. His reading began with the story of Zacchaeus, a wealthy tax collector. He remembered the story from Sunday school days because they had sung a song about Zacchaeus climbing into a tree in order to see Jesus. Today he read how Jesus invited Himself home with Zacchaeus and how people began to mutter about His associating with such a sinner.

But Sunday school had not prepared Dave for what he read next. 'Zacchaeus stood up and said to the Lord, "Look, Lord! Here and now I give half of my possessions to the poor, and if I have cheated anybody out of anything, I will pay back four times the amount."

'Jesus said to him, "Today salvation has come to this house."'

Dave slammed the Bible shut as though it had bitten him. He sat for a moment with his hands in his lap, looking straight ahead. Then, reluctantly, he opened the Bible, found his place, and read the passage again.

The meaning was perfectly clear: he should not merely pay Rutledge's expenses; he should make restitution for the money he had, in a sense, stolen from his associates. He immediately began calculating what this would cost him. He had a Mercedes on order; he could not possibly afford it if he did this. Just last week he had given Kay the go-ahead on looking for a Florida condo; he would have to tell her to hold off and he would have to explain why. He had never explained much about their finances to Kay, period. He hated to have to begin with a confession.

Dave had not known what hysteria lay just under his calm surface. He had not realised how much security he found in a comfortable bank balance, how profoundly superstitious he was about money. Giving the money back went against every fiscal bone in his body. He saw himself becoming easy pickings for every cause in the world. He saw himself dying penniless, with no legacy for his children. Rack and ruin, soup lines, and people jumping from tall buildings flashed before him.

The next day he went back to his normal reading of the

psalms, although a bit grimly, beginning to feel the Bible was not such a friendly book after all. In Psalm 37:25 he found a sly dig at his hysteria: 'I was young and now I am old, yet I have never seen the righteous forsaken or their children begging bread. They are always generous and lend freely; their children will be blessed.'

This was true, of course. Neither he nor Kay nor the children were likely to become beggars because he boosted the profit-sharing plan back up where it was meant to be. But the thought turned a crucial screw in Dave's mind. He began to see the religious dimension in the talk about the poor. For the rich depended on their wealth for security; the righteous were free to be generous, because their security was in God. As long as he hung onto his bank account as an insurance policy, he could never trust God wholly and would never fully experience God's blessings.

He had to do what was right in the Lord's eyes, no matter what the results might be for him or his family.

Dave made restitution, not only putting a healthy dent in his personal fortune, but causing him embarrassment and humiliation as well. He wondered sometimes whether he was losing his grip and knew some of his old friends thought so. But there was an end to what he had to do, and it had not thrust him into poverty. He felt a new sense of freedom and knew he had changed in a way he would have once thought impossible.

Kay was happy, too, and he had not expected that. He felt guilty punishing her for his own personal moral crusades. But when he hesitantly explained what he had done and his thinking about it all, she had looked at him with her wide, dark eyes and said, 'Oh, Dave, I'm so proud of you.'

They had been like honeymooners since.

In the months that followed, Dave noticed another change in his perspective. He found himself getting angry at the physical and psychological violence in the world. In fact, he became angrier each day.

When he discussed his feelings with Kay, she suggested he

call Dr Newman. Over the phone, Dave brought Newman up to date on what had happened in his life.

'So things seemed to be shaping up a bit in my life, and now I find myself unsettled again – and about things I am helpless to control. I mean before I always read the *Wall Street Journal* and avoided all that sob-sister stuff and sensationalism that makes headlines in the dailies. Who needs it! But lately I can't help myself. I seem compelled to know what's going on in the world, and then I read about drunk drivers, and abortion clinics doing a landslide business, and unemployed men and women committing suicide, and street crimes, and drug busts, and I can't say "Thank God, it has never touched me or mine" anymore. I am disturbed about it all – and angry. But it seems so futile to stew over it.'

Newman didn't really comment much except to say, 'Just think about all you have told me, Dave, and all you are becoming aware of. Something very special is coming your way. It usually does at this stage in one's spiritual growth. Keep your eyes open. And check out Luke 19.'

'You mean about Zacchaeus. I didn't mention it, but that's what triggered –'

'No, I mean the passage where Jesus comments on Jerusalem.'

When he got off the phone, Dave found the passage. It was after Jesus' Palm Sunday entry into the city. 'As he approached Jerusalem and saw the city, he wept over it and said, "If you, even you, had only known on this day what would bring you peace – but now it is hidden from your eyes."'

Tears filled Dave's eyes, and he recalled the many Old Testament passages he had read about Jehovah's anger. The God of the Old Testament and Jesus Christ were one, of course – the Father's anger and the Son's tears were one.

Suddenly Dave understood. He was angry at the world because he was beginning to see the world from God's perspective. He had always looked at it solely through the eyes of self-interest, self-preservation. But God's point of view demanded justice for everyone, for society. Dave had feared God's justice, His judgment on his own life, and still did. But that fear seemed insignificant before the vista of a world so rebellious against God.

Dave thought back to the first command he had read in the psalms and the one he had still not, despite his restitution, begun to obey: 'Defend the cause of the weak and fatherless; maintain the rights of the poor and oppressed.' *Sometime*, he thought, *a chance will come to do that. Don't let me miss it.*

Six months later an unusual speaker turned up at Dave's morning Bible group at the bank. Keith Marks was still in his twenties, with a leather jacket and thick reddish hair curling over his collar, a former convict and presently the state director of Prison Fellowship. Dave, of course, was familiar with Prison Fellowship and had been a heavy donor for several years – but he had never really thought much about prisons. Marks quoted familiar statistics about increasing crime in America and said that the expense of building enough prisons for all these criminals would require an impossible amount of money. Marks said the alternative was to take 'nonviolent' criminals out of the prisons and into halfway houses where they would participate in rehabilitation programmes and be required to make restitution to their victims.

While the subject was of interest to Dave, Marks' suggestion seemed utterly fanciful. Someone who could break into another man's home was not a Boy Scout; he was a criminal. How could you count on such a person to make restitution?

After the presentation, Dave asked Keith Marks this very question. Keith knew enough to turn away such wrath with a gentle reply; he suggested that Dave accompany him to the Tuesday night Bible study that Prison Fellowship conducted at the state penitentiary. It was only a twenty-minute drive from Dave's office.

Dave started to put him off, then thought. *Why not?*

The prison was a surreal and hostile world. Dave was unnerved by the clanging double bars, the stench of urine, cigarettes, and disinfectant, the suspicious, hardened faces of the guards, the burning lights from the tower. Later, back at home, he could still hear the echoing clicks of his own heels on those bare corridors.

But something beyond the prison itself got to Dave Chapman that night – nearly made him lose control. It was something in the Bible study itself that triggered his emotions. Dave and Keith had sat in a circle with the men in an ancient classroom, and each of the grey-uniformed prisoners had introduced themselves to Dave. *They each had a name.* Someone, some mother or father full of pride had called one 'Richard', another 'Julio', another . . . *They each had a name.* Dave sat with them, thinking about that simple fact for the rest of the evening.

Dave went back the next Tuesday night and the next and . . . Marks did not ask him to lead the Bible study, so he merely went, watched, and studied and listened to the men. Most of them looked like the kind of fellows he had parted company with back in high school when he had started college prep course; they were like the rough, coarse, ready-to-fight guys who ended up in auto shop until they quit school.

But these men soon became individuals with names and personalities. Dino looked as though he had been strung out on heroin for seven years, which he had, but he was one of the funniest people Dave had ever met. An older man with a quiet voice, almost an undifferentiated hum, became quite special to Dave. Though quiet, Fitzgerald was not shy and took to hanging around Dave for the few minutes they had after the meeting, gradually revealing his story. He had been an inventor, a rock climber, and a top engineer with Boeing. Dave checked him out and found Fitzgerald was telling the truth. He was in prison for tax evasion to the tune of $2,000, an unbelievably paltry sum to Dave, who had miscalculated by that margin dozens of times on his clients' returns.

Fitzgerald was the victim of a crazy system. Dino, on the other hand, had victimised himself; he was a confirmed needle freak and shot up anything he could get his hands on, even in prison.

Dave also met men who had been incredibly transformed by their conversions to Christ. One, Louis Lincoln, a giant black man with a mohawk haircut, was in for murder, but Dave honestly wouldn't have hesitated to recommend him as a babysitter. Louis was a lifer without parole, yet enjoyed life in a way that made Dave want to weep for his own lack of gratitude to God.

One big, gangly kid with pumpkin-coloured freckles caught Dave's attention because he was so defenceless and woebegone. Dave learned that Rick's grandparents had raised him after his mother decided he cluttered up her life. After dropping out of high school, he had worked at a gas station for a year and was now in prison for breaking and entering homes to steal television sets and stereos.

Dave's heart went out to Rick and as he talked with him every week, he gradually succeeded in inspiring the young man to get his high school equivalency certificate while in prison and learn as much about carpentry as possible in the prison's woodworking shop.

Rick did make progress, though at an agonisingly slow rate. At least, it seemed slow to Dave. Actually in nine months Rick was remarkably transformed. As the time of release approached, however, Rick seemed to retreat, worried about the world he would face.

Dave thought Rick might be all right if he could get a stable job and have a few people to turn to for help in the first months after prison, so he talked with Keith Marks. Keith suggested that Dave ask his pastor whether Calvary Church might 'adopt' Rick – help him find a job, a place to stay, and provide a circle of Christian friends.

The pastor sold the idea to the church board and most of the members took it up with surprising excitement. With their help, Rick struggled through the crisis of release and began to stabilise his life.

On the first anniversary of his release, Rick choked out his testimony at the Sunday evening service. The elder who had expressed the most doubts about the programme came to Dave and asked whether he could come along on the next visit to prison.

Dave was flying high, emotionally and spiritually. Unknown to him, however, events were shaping that would put his faith to its greatest test.

The first of these events began in the form of a public honour the next spring which gave Dave as much satisfaction as seeing Rick's success. After receiving the news on the telephone, he did an impromptu jig before rushing to tell Kay. The public announcement was made in one of the smaller meeting rooms of the downtown Holiday Inn. Kay, their son Doug and Christine, who had come home from college for the occasion, were there. So were a dozen members of the press along with camera crew from the local TV station.

The governor, a Republican running for his second term, stood at the podium and announced that Dave Chapman would be the chairman of his re-election campaign's finance committee. Dave had known the governor for years, had audited the books for his textile firm.

In his acknowledgment speech Dave said they expected to raise two million dollars and that the governor should be re-elected because he was restoring fiscal responsibility in the state capitol.

At home later, watching the news, Dave saw why he was the finance man and the governor was the governor. 'I tried so hard to sound responsible that I come off like some dull dim-wit,' he grumbled to Kay. She teased him that he was already getting ambitious, trying to outshine the governor. They laughed and hugged and Kay said how proud she was of him. All things considered, Dave could have died that night a most happy man.

The governor beat back minor primary opposition, and they began to gear up for the election. The battle with his Democratic challenger promised to be tough, but he led in the polls and had good organisation. The money was coming in; Dave was doing his job well. So much so that he wondered whether the governor might offer him an appointment in his administration. Anyway, he was certain all this would be good for his business.

Dave kept up his prison visits throughout the campaign. However, the penitentiary was not the same institution he had first visited two years before. The prison population had been growing at 12 percent a year and the facility had become crowded to the breaking point. The gymnasium had been pressed into service as a dormitory and certain hallways were cordoned off and used in the same manner. At last even the prison chapel was converted to a dormitory.

Places in training programmes and workshops were at a premium. Only the best-behaved got them. The most alienated and violent prisoners sat in their cells all day, brooding and becoming more and more angry.

Dave could feel the tension each time he entered the prison doors. And he saw it in the eyes of the prisoners. In the Bible study the men lacked concentration; they wanted to talk about prison conditions. But such talk, if allowed to continue, would lead the prison authorities to stop the study because it was getting 'too political'.

He could not blame the men for feeling as they did, so Dave spoke to the warden one day about the conditions. The warden politely pointed out that he had no control over overcrowding; the courts sentenced them and he had to imprison them. 'And a firm hand is the only way to deal with tensions like this,' he said.

Despite that firm hand, trouble began to brew. Each week it seemed the men had a new protest to tell Dave about. One day it was a sit-down in the prison compound; another time ten prisoners had begun a hunger strike, producing a list of demands.

As Dave talked to Fitzgerald after one of the Bible studies, the man slipped him a piece of paper.

'What's this?' Dave asked.

'Those are the demands,' Fitzgerald said softly. 'I thought

maybe you could telephone a newspaper and give them the dope.'

'Well, I'll have to think about it,' Dave said. Later, he decided that bringing in the media would do more harm than good. Dave had never approved of strikes. On the other hand, he understood the prisoners' frustration. The warden's only response to their demands was to lock up those who led the protests; he put them in segregated cells until they learned to 'behave' themselves. The segregation unit, where prisoners paced like caged animals and were allowed out only three times a week to shower, could break anyone down.

What can be done? Dave could not see an answer short of massive interest on the part of the legislature – and that seemed unimaginable. Prison reformers didn't usually get re-elected.

Then one Sunday night Keith Marks called Dave to tell him the Tuesday study had been cancelled by the warden. 'He said the protests have reached a serious stage,' Keith told Dave. 'The whole segregation unit is on a hunger strike, throwing their food into the corridor.'

'And they've got Louis locked up now,' Marks added.

'What did Louis do?' Dave was shocked.

'I'm not sure what he did, if anything. They're putting anybody who breathes loudly in segregation right now. The warden is determined to stamp this thing out. So there'll be no more Bible studies for a while. The warden thinks they got too political.'

'Can I still visit the men?' Dave asked.

'Yeah, visiting is okay. Just no meetings of any kind.'

The more Dave thought about Louis in the segregation unit, the more it bothered him. The unit was meant for violent, dangerous offenders. By locking up such prisoners, the rest of the men were protected. Or so the original justification went. But, in fact, the segregation unit was used as punishment for anyone the guards thought out of line. Some of the guards, Dave knew, would rather herd docile half-numbed sheep from one pen to the next rather than cope with human beings with emotions. *They mean to break Louis's spirit*, he thought. *To break his spirit* – what horrifying language about a human being.

Dave brought his troubled thoughts up to Kay as they lay in bed and again at the breakfast table. He grew so frustrated and angry as he talked that she suggested he call Dr Newman.

'You want me to get into more trouble?' he asked her.

'Why do you say that?'

'Every time I talk to that guy he thinks up some new scheme for messing up my life.'

'Dave, you know that's not true,' Kay smiled. 'He never tells you what to do.'

'No, but I always seem to end up doing what he wants anyway.'

Nevertheless, he called Dr Newman and discussed the situation. As it happened, the theologian was planning to be in town the coming weekend and said he'd like Dave to give him a tour of the prison if possible. Dave was fairly sure that as a long-time, trusted volunteer he could get Newman inside. In fact, he looked forward to being Newman's tour guide and teacher for once.

Dave watched Newman carefully, remembering his own shocked reaction to his first visit. Newman listened to what Dave said but gave few clues to what he was thinking or feeling. He asked few questions.

Dave himself felt the tension as they walked along the maze of concrete corridors in the main prison facility. When they passed the cells, men who knew Dave eagerly came to the bars to shake hands. Several men asked whether he knew that Louis was in the segregation unit.

After they had toured the workshops, the schoolrooms, the chapel-cum-dorm, Dave told Newman that he wanted to see Louis. 'Besides, I want you to see the centre of this tension.'

The segregation unit was a prison within a prison, with its own small, walled-in exercise compound. A guard accompanied them. When they reached the barred gate, it slid open and they walked inside and stopped. The gate slammed into place behind them; when it was fastened shut, the door ahead of them clicked open and they walked into the unit.

The stench struck them like a wall. Solid, putrid, it was the stench of human excrement, urine, choking cigarette smoke, and sweat. Prison always smelled, and the segregation was the worst because the prisoners couldn't get outside. But this was the worst Dave had ever encountered.

When they turned the corner, he saw why. The dimly lit corridor was blocked with refuse.

On their left was a high wall with thick glazed glass windows at the top. The brilliant lights flooding the exercise yard shone through, creating an eerie matrix of light and shadow. On their right was a wall of steel bars enclosing cement cellblocks. In between, on the corridor floor, lay a stinking mess covered with flies. Some of it was recognisable as food. Some of it was faeces. Some had been thrown up against the windows, still clinging there. A motion on the floor caught Dave's eye. It was a rat, gobbling into the awful stuff. His stomach flip-flopped.

'Why don't you clean this up?' he asked the guard.

'They threw it out there,' the guard answered. 'Let them clean it up.'

'But they can't clean it up. You only let them for showers a couple times a week, right?'

The guard shrugged. 'Warden says when they act like human beings, we'll treat them like human beings.'

Dave and Newman picked their way down the line of cells, gingerly avoiding the most obvious piles of filth. Most of the men lay on their bunks, smoking, staring up at the ceiling or at some invisible point in space. When they spotted Dave and Newman, they got up as if in a daze, came over to the bars and stretched their hands through for a shake. 'Hey, man, thanks for coming.' 'Hey what you doin' in here? Don't you know this is for animals?'

The light from the compound was too bright to permit restful sleep at night, while during the day the cells were too dim to read. Dave wondered how anyone could stand it. And coupled with the stench – so rancid and strong it hurt his sinuses.

They stopped at the cell of a young man with long, straight black hair with a sharp, protruding nose. Dave introduced him to Newman as 'Ray'.

'Ray is an Apache,' Dave said, 'and proud of it, right Ray?'

Ray merely nodded. His eyes were two seeds possessed by distant thoughts.

'Hey, Ray, where's your brother?' Dave asked. 'I didn't see him.'

A line of hurt glimmered over the prisoner's features, then after a silent moment he said, 'Man, I know you mean well. Didn't they tell you about Hubert?'

'No, they didn't.'

'Man, I thought that was why you came. You know, Hubert's gone. He hung himself. Right down here, man, just down there in the fourth cell.' Ray leaned out and pointed down the corridor in the direction from which they had come.

Dave stood in stunned silence as Ray continued. 'Dave, did you say this man is a doctor? I mean, can he get some sleeping pills? I just can't sleep. If I could sleep I think I would be okay. But I can't even close my eyes. I asked the guards for pills, but they say I have to wait until the doctor comes next week.'

Dave told him that Newman was not a medical doctor, but promised to see whether he could help get some sleeping pills for Ray. He said some words he hoped were encouraging, they offered to pray for Ray. He and Newman both put a hand through the bars to hold one of Ray's arms while Dave prayed briefly.

Ray stood with head lowered, like an animal waiting for a blow to the head. He stayed that way even after the prayer ended. Dave shook his arm slightly to get his attention.

'We'll be back soon, Ray. I'll pray for you.'

They went on in silence, placing their feet carefully, until they found Louis. Newman shook Louis's hand, then stepped back while Dave talked with him. Louis seemed his normal, hearty self as they talked, then – 'Dave, I think we better put this rap on hold. The professor . . . you'd better get him out of here.'

Dave turned to look at Newman. His complexion was grey, his eyes unfocused, and his head was tilted toward the floor. Dave grabbed his arm, and as they turned back the way they had come, Louis let out a hearty laugh. 'Hey, Dave, see if you can get one of the maids to come down and clean up a little. They try, you know, but they're nearsighted and they miss things, man!' His booming laughter echoed off the high concrete ceiling.

Newman made it out just in time to avoid being sick, but bent over clutching his knees for several minutes and gulping in air. 'I'm sorry, Dave,' he said when he stood upright. 'That smell –'

The guard had let them out into the central compound so Newman could get some fresh air. Gigantic walls surrounded them and from above them powerful lights beamed down on every inch of cracked concrete. The only hint of life was a scum of grass trying to push through those cracks. At one end of the concrete stood a basketball standard without a net.

'So this is where they exercise?' Newman asked, looking around.

'Well, yes, they get to come out once a day. Not the guys in segregation, you understand. But the others. They don't exercise much, though. There are over two thousand prisoners here – makes for rather large teams.' Dave gestured toward the bare basketball standard.

'What do they do, then?'

Dave shrugged. 'Most of them just stroll around. Some are physical fitness fanatics and work out as best they can. This is also where they do their drug deals. Let me show you something.' Dave led Newman to a corner of the compound and into a shadow created by the angle at which two buildings in the quadrant intercepted each other.

'They can't be seen here. The men tell me there's always some place like this in every prison – a dark spot the guards can't see from the walls . . . look!' Dave knelt down and pointed at the concrete. 'Blood stains. This is also where they beat each other, and this is where the rapes often occur.' Newman knelt beside Dave and stared at the spot as Dave said, 'You can't wash the blood out of the concrete.'

Newman put out his finger and gingerly touched the spot, then jerked his hand back. 'That's fresh blood,' he said. 'Look.'

It was just a dark spot, for in the artificial spotlight that reflected into the shadowed area there was no colour, only greys and blacks.

'Maybe from a rape,' Dave said under his breath. Looking around he saw other spots like it. It did look like fresh blood.

As Dave watched, Newman stood and walked away quickly, reached the wall of the compound and touched it with one outstretched palm, then slowly turned and walked back. Dave's already knotted stomach twisted tighter with premonition.

'What are you going to do about this?' he finally asked.

'About what?' Dave asked. 'About the rape? I can't do anything. I don't know what happened here, or to whom. And the guards don't care. They figure the prisoners have to take out their aggression somewhere so it might as well be on each other. Better that than on them.'

'No, I don't mean that,' Newman said quietly. 'I mean the conditions here. We wouldn't treat a dog the way these men are being treated.'

Dave shrugged. 'I agree. But what can I do? I've talked to the warden and he brushed me off.'

'You're getting pretty high up in the governor's campaign. You must have some influence with him.'

Dave shrugged again. 'Not too much influence, really. I did talk to him about it, though. It's hard to get even ten minutes, but I finally did. He says he had in mind a blue-ribbon committee after the election. He says we can't really do anything until after the election.'

'That's not going to accomplish anything,' Newman said. It was the only time Dave had seen disgust on his face.

'No, it probably won't. I told him I'd like to be on the committee, but I don't expect it to do great things. The public just doesn't care. They don't care and so the politicians don't care. What's in it for them? In fact, any politician who focuses on such an unpopular subject usually washes out his chances for re-election.'

'What if you made it a public issue?' asked Newman. 'Now, I mean. Wouldn't the governor have to do something if you put him on the spot? His own finance man? Before the election?'

Dave was suddenly at a complete loss for words. Across his mind flashed the memory of his television appearance when the governor named him to his position; he saw himself as dull, stodgy, painfully straight. He could not imagine himself in the role of public advocate.

'I'm doing my part already, Doctor Newman,' he said at last, feeling panic creep up his neck. 'I'm not a politician. I'm an accountant. I can't go on TV and put the governor on the spot. I'm an accountant.'

'But you're also someone who knows this prison. You know it as well as any other single individual. And you know something is wrong here.'

'Look, not only would the governor drop me. So would my clients. No one wants Ralph Nader to handle their books.'

'So you just forget about these men? You save your own skin and let them rot and die in there.' Newman's voice was no longer calm.

'Come on,' Dave said shortly. 'We've got to go.' The theologian's disapproval was too much for him. 'Talking won't do any good. We've got to leave here. The guard's going to get nasty.'

'Just give me a couple more minutes, Dave,' Newman said. 'I want to tell you something, and I want to tell you here under these lights, surrounded by these walls, standing by this blood. Then we'll go and I'll shut up.'

Dave hesitated, looking around nervously as Newman began his story . . .

'In the fourth century there lived an Asiatic monk who had spent most of his life in a remote community of prayer, raising vegetables for the cloister kitchen. When he was not tending his garden spot, he was fulfilling his vocation of study and prayer.

'Then one day this monk named Telemachus felt that the Lord wanted him to go to Rome, the capital of the world – the busiest, wealthiest, biggest city in the world. Telemachus had no idea why he should go there, and he was terrified at the thought. But as he prayed, God's directive became clear.

'How bewildered the little monk must have been as he set out on the long journey, on foot, over dusty roads westward, everything he owned on his back. Why was he going? He didn't know. What would he find there? He had no idea. But obediently, he went.

'Telemachus arrived in Rome during the holiday festival. You may know that the Roman rulers kept the ghettos quiet in those days by providing free bread and special entertainment called circuses. At the time Telemachus arrived the city was also bustling with excitement over the recent Roman victory over the Goths. In the midst of this jubilant commotion, the monk looked for clues as to why God had brought him there, for he had no other guidance, not even a superior in a religious order to contact.

'*Perhaps*, he thought, *it is not sheer coincidence that I have arrived at this festival time. Perhaps God has some special role for me to play.*

'So Telemachus let the crowds guide him, and the stream of humanity soon led him into the Coliseum where the gladiator contests were to be staged. He could hear the cries of the animals in their cages beneath the floor of the great arena and the clamour of the contestants preparing to do battle.

'The gladiators marched into the arena, saluted the emperor, and shouted, "We who are about to die salute thee." Telemachus shuddered. He had never heard of gladiator games before, but had a premonition of awful violence.

'The crowd had come to cheer men who, for no reason

other than amusement, would murder each other. Human lives were offered for entertainment. As the monk realised what was going to happen, he realised he could not sit still and watch such savagery. Neither could he leave and forget. He jumped to the top of the perimeter wall and cried, "In the name of Christ, forbear!"

'The fighting began, of course. No one paid the slightest heed to the puny voice. So Telemachus pattered down the stone steps and leapt onto the sandy floor of the arena. He made a comic figure – a scrawny man in a monk's habit dashing back and forth between muscular, armed athletes. One gladiator sent him sprawling with a blow from his shield, directing him back to his seat. It was a rough gesture, though almost a kind one. The crowd roared.

'But Telemachus refused to stop. He rushed into the way of those trying to fight, shouting again, "In the name of Christ, forbear!" The crowd began to laugh and cheer him on, perhaps thinking him part of the entertainment.

'Then his movement blocked the vision of one of the contestants; the gladiator saw a blow coming just in time. Furious now, the crowd began to cry for the interloper's blood.

'Run him through,' they screamed.

'The gladiator he had blocked raised his sword and with a flash of steel struck Telemachus, slashing down across his chest and into his stomach. The little monk gasped once more, "In the name of Christ, forbear."

'Then a strange thing occurred. As the two gladiators and the crowd focused on the still form on the suddenly crimson sand, the arena grew deathly quiet. In the silence, someone in the top tier got up and walked out. Another followed. All over the arena, spectators began to leave, until the huge stadium was emptied.

'There were other forces at work, of course, but that innocent figure lying in the pool of blood crystallised the opposition, and that was the last gladiatorial contest in the Roman Coliseum. Never again did men kill each other for the crowds' entertainment in the Roman arena.'

Dave leaned against the compound wall and stared at the cracked concrete floor as Newman finished his story. *The Romans killed men for fun*, he thought. *We destroy them . . . for what? . . . punishment? . . . under the guise of rehabilitation? . . . our own ambitions? . . . our fear? . . . our obscene unconcern?* He thought of Ray, locked in there beneath the shadow of his brother's noose; what was served by such suffering? He thought of Louis, of Fitzgerald, of Rick – they all had faces, they all had names. They were human beings.

Dave looked up at the row after row of windows. He watched the searchlights play on them. They were like an amphitheatre of eyes – eyes that chose not to see the circus here in the centre of the prison.

'All right,' he said quietly to Newman. 'I don't know where this will lead me, but I'll do what you want me to do.'

Newman shook his head. 'No, Dave, I'm not telling you what to do. I don't have the answers.'

That made him angry. 'Come off it! If you haven't been telling me what to do, what have you been doing? You want me to get on TV, make speeches, holler, jump on the wall and yell, "In the name of Christ, stop!"'

'No, Dave. I want you to do what God tells you to do. I pushed you only because I don't want you to shrug it off – but knowing you, you can't.'

Dave Chapman looked around again. The concrete underfoot held no answers, only the pool of blood. The sky beyond the floodlights was as black as a cavern. He would hear no voices. He had never heard voices. The prompting he had got as Newman spoke terrified him. It ran against every cautious, conservative fibre in his accountant's body. It threatened to destroy everything he had built in his business and in his position with the governor. But Newman was right. He could not shrug it off. He had come too far.

He had to get out of here and read the Bible and pray and look for direction. At that moment, oddly, he thought of that psalm David had written out of his years of experience: 'I was young, and now I am old, yet I have never seen the righteous forsaken or their children begging bread.' And that triggered thoughts of all that had brought him to this spot: of the summer evening on the porch when he had first met Newman, of his firing Pelouze for his mistakes on the Fairway account, of the restitution he had made to his employees, of his growing involvement with Rick and the other men here . . . and finally, he remembered the first command he had found in the psalms, the one he was still not sure he could claim to have obeyed:

> Defend the cause of the weak and fatherless;
> Maintain the rights of the poor and oppressed.
> Rescue the weak and needy;
> Deliver them from the hand of the wicked.

Newman had turned and was walking toward the doorway, and Dave Chapman stared at his back as he walked away.

What am I going to do? he groaned.

He did not know.

With Gratitude

The point is made in the section on the church that the Christian life cannot be lived alone. To follow Christ is to become part of a new community. The same may be said about writing a book on the Christian life. It can never be written in a vacuum; the author is inevitably influenced by the lives and writings of others. A book, therefore, is a synthesis of shared experiences – and that is certainly so in this case. *Loving God* draws on the teaching and lives of so many, past and present. Its preparation was very much a team effort.

My dear friend R. C. Sproul opened for me a whole new vision of the majesty of the God we serve, awakening in me a continuing desire for deeper knowledge. So I'm deeply grateful to R.C., not only for that inspiration, for his magnificent books and tapes, but for his encouragement – and his critique of this manuscript as well.

I've been privileged, too, to learn from some of the great scholars of our time. Richard Lovelace of Gordon Conwell Seminary patiently tutored me in the early days of my faith. My times of fellowship with Carl Henry, who has the rare combination of genius and humility, Francis Schaeffer, Jim Houston, John Stott, Vernon Grounds, Dick Halverson, and others have enriched me immeasurably. And I have been blessed to study and worship under two excellent pastors: Neal Jones of my own church, Columbia Baptist in Falls Church, Virginia, and Dr Charles Webster of Moorings Presbyterian Church in Naples, Florida.

In writing the manuscript, I have been assisted from the beginning by Ellen Santilli, a gifted young writer on the

Prison Fellowship staff. Ellen did much of the research, and with a skilled reporter's nose dug out the material for the chapters on Agape House and Judge Bontrager. Ellen's assistance was invaluable both in drafting some material herself and editing much of mine.

Two other writers helped with portions of the book. One was Harold Fickett, whose gift for storytelling first attracted me when I read his marvellously entertaining collection of short stories, *Mrs Sunday's Problem*. Harold helped with research and drafts of several stories. He and his research assistant, David Voth, were responsible for the powerful story of the church in the Hanoi Hilton.

The second was Tim Stafford. Early in 1983, as the publisher's deadline loomed ominously near and ministry responsibilities were heavily upon me, Tim stepped in to help with the final writing phases. His work, particularly in the crucifixion chapter, was truly inspired.

But the premier member of the team was Zondervan editor, Judith Markham. Judith shepherded this book from the raw and rough outline through the rigours of four drafts to the final product. Her editing was inspired. She never once lost her patience (no small feat for anyone who has to cope with authors), humoured me until she got what she knew all along was right, and was not content with less than our best effort. But it was an absolute delight to work with her; I've never met anyone who could be so demanding in such a nice way.

As with my first two books, I complete this task with a renewed appreciation of family and friends. Patty was typist, proofreader, critic, and silent sufferer during the long hours I spent locked away in my library. Patty's partnership in my books, ministry, and life is one of God's choicest gifts to me.

So, too, my co-workers at Prison Fellowship have given me wonderful support. Gordon Loux, who manages the ministry, has over the years become not only a beloved friend but a partner for me in every sense. Senior vice-presidents Ralph Veerman and John O'Grady shouldered part of my burdens as well as their own to give me time to write. I'm especially grateful to my secretary, Nancy Niemeyer, for keeping day-to-day matters under control while I was writing, as well as for typing large parts of the manuscript along with Gordon's secretary, Janie Perdew. And special thanks as well to Jeanne Moody for her careful research and fact checking, and to Anita Moreland for reading the manuscript.

I am most grateful to the several friends who read and critiqued the manuscript: first, an author I enormously respect, Philip Yancey, who gave tremendous guidance; Mary Babcock, a close friend in Miami; Charlotte Cauwels, a Prison Fellowship instructor and wife of board member Dave Cauwels; Len LeSourd, my dear friend and editor of my prior two books; Carl Henry; David McKenna, president of Asbury Theological Seminary; Elizabeth Sherrill, the gifted author who not only critiqued but also blue-pencilled a few chapters as she did for *Born Again* and *Life Sentence*; and Art Lindsley, who not only critiqued the book from a theological perspective but prepared the companion study guide as well.

As I write this, it is exactly ten years since I visited my dear friend, Tom Phillips, as the Watergate scandal exploded across the nation's press. Though I felt an awful deadness inside, I didn't think I was searching spiritually. But while Tom's explanation that he had 'accepted Jesus Christ' shocked and baffled me, it also made me curious. He was at peace with himself, something I surely wasn't.

Tom explained it all to me that sultry August night. I couldn't show too much interest, of course – I was senior partner of a powerful Washington law firm, friend of the President. But as I left Tom's house, I discovered I couldn't get my keys into the car ignition. I couldn't see them – the White House 'hatchet man', as the newspapers called me, the ex-Marine infantry captain was crying too hard. That night I was confronted with my own sin – not just Watergate's dirty tricks, but the sin deep within me, the hidden evil that lives in every human heart. It was painful, and I could not escape. I cried out to God and found myself driven irresistibly into His waiting arms. That was the night I gave my life to Jesus Christ and began the greatest adventure of my life.

A lot of sceptics thought it wouldn't last, that it was just a ploy for sympathy, a foxhole conversion. I don't blame them. If the tables were turned, I'd have thought the same thing.

But not once in these ten years have I doubted that Jesus Christ lives. There is nothing of which I am more certain. And not once would I have turned the clock back. My lowest days as a Christian (and there were low ones – seven months' worth of them in prison, to be exact) have been more fulfilling and rewarding than all the days of glory in the White House.

The years before conversion were death; the years since have been life and the adventure of loving God, the purpose of that life.

And so with each passing day, my gratitude to God for what He did for me – at Calvary and that night in my friend's driveway – grows deeper and deeper.

So, too, does my gratitude for those who have helped me along the way. To Tom Phillips who introduced me to the love of God; to Doug Coe, Al Quie, Harold Hughes, Graham Purcell, and Fred Rhodes who demonstrated that love; to those whose writing and teaching have challenged me; to a loving, supportive family, to Gordon Loux and my colleagues at Prison Fellowship who live it out with me in the dark holes of prison; and to the thousands of others who have prayed for me and written to me, I am deeply and eternally grateful.

CHARLES W. COLSON
June 1, 1983
PO Box 17500
Washington, DC, 20041

Special Acknowledgments

I am grateful for these materials and interviews extensively relied upon in certain chapters of the book.

Chapters 2–3: Alexander Solzhenitsyn, *Gulag Archipelago*, Harper and Row, 1975. See Part IV, Chapter 1, The Ascent.

Chapter 4: *Confessions of St Augustine*, Translation by John K. Ryan, Doubleday, 1960.

Chapter 5: John W. Montgomery, ed., *God's Inerrant Word: An International Symposium on the Trustworthiness of Scripture*, Bethany House, 1974. See essay by R. C. Sproul.

James Montgomery Boice, ed., *Does Inerrancy Matter?* publication of ICBI, 1979.

R. C. Sproul, *Knowing Scripture*, IVP, 1977.

Chapter 8: Curtis Mitchell, *Billy Graham: Saint or Sinner*, Revell, 1979.

Mickey Cohen, In My Own Words: The Underworld Autobiography of Michael Mickey Cohen, as told to John Peer Nugent, Englewood Cliffs, NJ: Prentice-Hall, 1975.

We are grateful for the interviews provided by Jim Vaus, J. Edwin Orr. George Wilson, Suzy Hamblen, and Charette Kvernstoen of *Decision Magazine*.

Chapters 9–10: Foy Valentine, *What Do You Do After You Say Amen*, Word, 1980.

Theodore Plantinga, *Learning to Live With Evil*, Eerdmans, 1982 (For one of the few books dealing with the nature and origins of sin and evil – and an excellent one at that – I'm especially grateful to Professor Plantinga.)

Chapter 14: Jerry Bridges, *Pursuit of Holiness*, NAV Press, 1982 (I am deeply indebted to Jerry Bridges; his very readable book on holiness was not only an invaluable reference for this book, but greatly helped my own under-standing.)

William Wilberforce, *Real Christianity*, modern edition edited by Professor James Houston, Multnomah Press, 1982.

I am grateful to Senator William Armstrong for his will-ingness to allow me to tell the story of his bedside vigil with a dying friend. With customary modesty, Bill said he saw nothing special in what he did; he had not even told his own staff about his experience. I am also grateful to Orv Krieger, Ken Hooker, Donald Adcox, Joyce Page, and Patti Awan for sharing their stories.

Chapter 16: Special thanks are in order for Bill Bontrager who opened his files and unselfishly gave many hours to interviews. Various movie producers have expressed an interest in purchasing the Bontrager story; in spite of the fact that its telling here might hurt Bill's chances to sell rights to others, he graciously agreed to our using it. We are grateful to Harry Fred Palmer as well for his cooperation.

Chapter 17: Francis Schaeffer, *Christian Manifesto*, Cross-way, 1981.

The story about Alexander Solzhenitsyn and the old man who made the sign of the cross was first told by Solzhenitsyn to a small group of Christian leaders and later recounted by Billy Graham in his New Year's telecast, 1977. It has been retold subsequently, most publicly by Senator Jesse Helms (R-NC).

Chapter 18: Special thanks to Paul Cho and his books.

Chapter 21: We are especially grateful to ex-POWs Norman McDaniel and James Ray for extensive interviews; in addition Howard Rutledge's book, *In the Presence of Mine Enemies*, Revell, 1973, was extremely helpful.

Epilogue: The story of Telemachus is found in Leslie D. Weatherhead's *It Happened in Palestine*, London: Hodder & Stoughton, 1936.

Notes

How It All Began

1. Shirley MacLaine, *Washington Post* Interview, 1977.
2. *Daily Word* (October 1982), 19.
3. Matthew 22:37–38; Mark 12:28–31; Luke 10:25–28.

Chapter 3

1. Alexander Solzhenitsyn, *Gulag Archipelago II* (New York: Harper and Row, 1974), 613–15.
2. Ibid., 613.
3. See Hebrews 11, the chapter often called the Hall of Fame of the Faithful, especially verse 39.
4. Matthew 8; Luke 7.
5. Job 13:15 KJV.
6. Acts 1:6 NIV.
7. Acts 1:7 NIV.
8. Matthew 22:36 NIV.
9. John 14:15 NIV.
10. 1 John 5:3 KJV.

Chapter 4

1. Italicised portions of this chapter are slightly paraphrased from *The Confessions of St Augustine*, translated by John K. Ryan (New York: Doubleday, 1960).

Chapter 5

1. 'Luke and the Iron Man' (American Bible Society, December 1976).
2. From an interview with Gonzalo Ba'ez Carrago, *Christianity Today* (5 March 1982).
3. Richard C. Halverson, *The Timelessness of Jesus Christ* (Ventura, Calif.: Regal Books, 1982), 46–7.
4. Luke 4:18–19 NIV.
5. John 5:39.
6. Matthew 4; Luke 4: Luke 24:25–27; Deuteronomy 8:3; 6:16; 6:13; John 17:17 KJV.
7. Matthew 28:18 NIV.
8. 1 John 1:3 NIV; Luke 1:1–4.
9. 1 Corinthians 15:17 NIV.

Chapter 6

1. John Dean, *Blind Ambition* (New York: Simon and Schuster, 1976), 233.
2. Acts 1:3 NIV.
3. 1 Corinthians 15.
4. Blaise Pascal, *Pensées*, translated by A. J. Krailsheimer (New York: Penguin Classics, 1966), 125.
5. Matthew 5:18; John 17:17.

Chapter 7

1. 2 Timothy 3:16; 4:2–3.
2. John Walvoord, *Inspiration and Interpretation* (Grand Rapids: Eerdmans, 1957), 18.
3. Letter to Jerome, quoted in James Boice, *Does Inerrancy Matter* (ICBF Foundation Series).
4. Martin Luther, *Table Talk*, quoted in above work.
5. Ibid.
6. 'Divino Afflante Spiritu,' September 30, 1943, from *The Papal Encyclicals* 1939–1958 (McGrath Publishing Co., 1981).
7. In the sixteenth century at the fourth session of the Council of Trent, the Roman Catholic church adopted the view that

'These truths and rules are contained in written book and unwritten traditions, which received by the apostles from the mouth of Christ himself or from the apostles themselves, the Holy Ghost dictating, having come down to us.' In 1950, Pope Pius XII reaffirmed the total inspiration of Scripture and criticised those who would pervert the belief that God is the author of holy Scripture. This was Humani Generis 1950, and in that critique of liberal exegesis the pope embraced three of the encyclicals: Providentissimus Deus issued by Leo XIII in 1893 in which it was stated: 'There is no error whatsoever in reference to Scripture'; Spiritus Paraclitus 1920; and Divino Afflante Spiritu 1943.

8. *Emerging Trends* (Princeton Religious Research Centre, December 1982), 4:10.
9. 2 Timothy 3:16.
10. John 17:17 KJV.
11. Genesis 3:3 NIV.
12. Luke 4:3–4 NIV.
13. Luke 4:8; Deuteronomy 6:13 NIV.
14. Luke 4:9–12 NIV.

Chapter 9

1. Richard Trench, Archbishop of Dublin.
2. Leviticus 26:40–41.
3. Psalm 51.
4. See Ezekiel 18:19–22, 30–32 and the entire prophetic literature from Isaiah to Malachi.
5. Matthew 3:3 NIV.
6. Mark 1:14 NIV.
7. Mark 24:47 NIV.
8. 1 Corinthians 11:27.
9. Acts 26:20 NIV.
10. J. Edwin Orr, 'The First Word of the Gospel' (an unpublished essay), 1980.
11. Dietrich Bonhoeffer, *Cost of Discipleship* (New York: Macmillan, 1963), 45–6.
12. 2 Samuel 11–12:13.
13. David Myers, *The Inflated Self* (New York: Seabury Press, 1980).

14. Ramsey Clark, *Crime in America* (New York: Simon and Schuster, 1970).
15. Jimmy Carter, 'Interview with the National Black Network', *Weekly Compilation of Presidential Documents*, July, 1977.
16. National Conference of Christians and Jews, New York City, 23 March 1982.
17. Jeremiah 17:9 NIV.

Chapter 10

1. *The Confessions of St Augustine*, translated by John K. Ryan (New York: Doubleday, 1960), 69–72.
2. Alexander Solzhenitsyn, *The Gulag Archipelago 1918–1956*, translated from the Russian by Thomas P. Whitney (New York: Harper and Row, 1975), 612.
3. Ibid.
4. Romans 3:23; 3:10.
5. Matthew 15:18–20; Mark 7:20–23.
6. *Confessions*, 144.
7. Ibid., 68.
8. J. Glen Gray, *The Warriors: Reflections on Men in Battle* (New York: Harper and Row, 1973).
9. Theodore Plantinga, *Learning to Live with Evil* (Grand Rapids: Eerdmans, 1982), see ch. 11.
10. From the shooting script of 'Patton' (Los Angeles: American Film Institute Library).
11. Acts 11:18.

Chapter 12

1. Luke 23:41 NIV.
2. 1 Kings 16:31 NASB.
3. John 16:8.
4. Romans 7:24 NIV.
5. Romans 7:7–8 NIV.
6. Romans 8:1–3 NIV.

Chapter 13

1. Phyllis Theroux, 'Amazing Grace', *Washington Post Magazine*, October 18, 1981, 38.
2. James 1:27 NIV.
3. Kathryn Spink, *The Miracle of Love* (New York: Harper and Row, 1981), 66.
4. Ibid., 157.
5. Luke 18:9–14.
6. Jerry Bridges, *Pursuit of Holiness* (Colorado Springs: NAV Press, 1982), 72.
7. Exodus 20–23.
8. Exodus 24:3,7 NIV.
9. Exodus 29:44–45 NIV.
10. Leviticus 12:44. The Greek word in Scripture is *Hagios* meaning 'set apart, unique, different, above the ordinary'.
11. John 1:14 NASB.
12. Revelation 21:3 NASB.
13. William Wilberforce, *Real Christianity*, edited by James H. Houston (Portland, Or.: Multnomah, 1982), 87. Also, see ch. 15, note 1.

Chapter 14

1. Ephesians 4:24–32; Colossians 3:12–13; Ephesians 5:1–21; 1 Thessalonians 4:3–7; 1 Corinthians 6:9–10; Galatians 6:2; 1 Corinthians 6:12; 8:9–13; 10:31.
2. Galatians 6:9,7 NIV.
3. John Brown, *Expository Discourses on 1 Peter* (1848) reprint edition (Edinburgh: Banner of Truth Trust), 1:106.
4. John 14:26; 17:17; Romans 8:9–11; 1 Corinthians 2:12–13; 6:11; 1 Thessalonians 4:7–8.
5. Malcolm Muggeridge, *Something Beautiful for God* (New York: Harper and Row, 1971), 66.
6. Romans 6:2, 11–12.
7. Bridges, *Pursuit of Holiness*.
8. Ibid., 84.
9. John 14.21 NIV.

Chapter 15

1. Wilberforce later wrote a biting and prophetic book challenging the church on the issue. It was first published in the early nineteenth century and entitled *A Practical View of the Prevailing Religious Systems of Professed Christians, in the Higher and Middle Classes in This Country, Contracted with Real Christianity*. It is now available in a modern edition as edited by James Houston (See ch. 13, note 13). This is highly recommended reading, for Wilberforce wrote the prophetic insight not only for the England of his time, but for today, especially for the church in America.
2. Exodus 19:6 NIV.
3. Deuteronomy 16:20.
4. 2 Samuel 8:15.
5. 1 Kings 3:9 NIV.
6. Isaiah foretold the One who would ultimately bring 'justice in the earth', the Messiah, the perfect image of holiness and justice. See Isaiah 42:3–7.
7. Jeremiah 22:13, 16 KJV.
8. Amos 2:7–8.
9. Amos 8:5–6.
10. Amos 5:14.
11. Amos 5:24 NASB.
12. *Freedom and Faith*, edited by Lynn Buzzard (Westchester, Ill.: Crossway Books, 1982), 161.
13. Matthew 5:17.
14. Luke 4:18–19 NIV; see also, Isaiah 61:1–2.
15. Luke 4:20–21 NIV.
16. Matthew 25:42–43 NW.
17. Matthew 5:13–16.
18. Matthew 6:33 KJV.
19. *Freedom and Faith*, 73.

Chapter 17

1. Garth Lean, *Strangely Warmed* (Wheaton: Tyndale, 1979), 62.
2. Howard Snyder, *The Radical Wesley* (Downers Grove, Ill.: Inter-Varsity Press, 1980), 86–7.

3. *The Letters of the Rev. John Wesley, AM*, edited by John Telford (London: The Epworth Press, 1931).

4. Romans 13:1–2; 1 Peter 2:13–14.

5. Francis Schaeffer, *Christian Manifesto* (Westchester, Ill.: Crossway Books, 1981), 91.

6. 'A godly warning or admonition to the faithful in London, Newcastle and Berwick,' *Works of John Knox*, collected and edited by David Laing. Edinburgh: Woodrow Society 1836 –1848. (Reprinted in New York: AMS Press, 1966), 6 vols.

7. Hebrews 11:23; Daniel 3; Acts 4:18–20.

8. Revelation 11:15 NIV.

9. Schaeffer, *Manifesto*, 121.

10. Jon Johnston, *Will Evangelicalism Survive Its Own Popularity?* (Grand Rapids: Zondervan, 1980).

11. Schaeffer, *Manifesto*, 28.

12. Malcolm Muggeridge, *The End of Christendom* (Grand Rapids: Eerdmans, 1980), 23.

Chapter 18

1. Mark 1:15.

2. Jim Wallis, *Call to Conversion* (New York: Harper and Row, 1981).

3. Ibid.

4. 1 Peter 2.:9.

5. Exodus 19:6.

6. Inspired by the New Testament example of the early church.

7. Paul Yonggi Cho with Harold Hostetter, *Successful Home Cell Groups* (Plainfield, NJ: Logos International, 1981), 16.

8. Halverson, *Timelessness of Jesus Christ*, 104.

9. 1 Corinthians 12:26 NIV.

10. In Philippians 3:10 Paul wrote that he longed for the 'fellowship of suffering,' for then in a real sense he was sharing in the suffering of Christ.

Chapter 20

1. Jacques Ellul, *The Political Illusion*, tr. from the French by Konrad Keller (New York: Vintage Books, 1972).

Chapter 21

1. This chapter is a composite drawn both from documentation of
   events that happened to American POWs in Vietnam and from
   interviews with James Ray and Norman McDaniel. While
   some names are fictitious, the incidents are not.